The Healing Of Bad Memories

Do you have chronic, unexplained physical illnesses?

Childhood memory gaps?

Vague, recurring guilt feelings?

Unexplained anger?

Frightening flashbacks?

These are just a few of many symptoms that might indicate possible hidden trauma from your childhood — trauma that, without recognition and resolution, can lead to an adult life of insecurity, fear and frustrating relationships.

FREEING YOUR MIND FROM MEMORIES THAT BIND will gently guide you through a process for uncovering and resolving those hurts from your past. Join Fred and Florence Littauer on a journey toward freedom and wholeness! You are about to discover the genuine inner peace of God that comes with His healing of bad memories.

Freeing Your Mind

FROM
Memories
That Bind

FRED & FLORENCE LITTAUER

29 Oct 88

Here's Life Publishers

P.O. Box 1576, San Bernardino, CA 92402

Eighth Printing, April 1992

Published by
HERE'S LIFE PUBLISHERS, INC.
P. O. Box 1576
San Bernardino, CA 92402

Library of Congress Cataloging-in-Publication Data
Littauer, Fred.
    Freeing your mind from memories that bind: how to heal the hurts
of the past / Fred and Florence Littauer.
    p.   cm.
    ISBN 0-89840-232-8 (pbk.)
    1. Adult child abuse victims — Pastoral counseling of.
I. Littauer, Florence, 1928-   . II. Title.
BV4463.5.L57   1988   88-22816
248.8'6 — dc19   CIP

Scripture quotations designated KJV are from the *King James Version*.

Scripture quotations designated NIV are from *The Holy Bible, New International Version,* © 1978 by the New York International Bible Society, pub ished by the Zondervan Corporation, Grand Rapids, Michigan.

Scripture quotations designated TEV are from *Today's English Version,* © 1966, 1971, 1976 by the American Bible Society, published by Thomas Nelson Inc., Nashville, Tennessee.

Scripture quotations designated NASB are from *The New American Standard Bible,* © The Lockman Foundation 1960, 1962, 1963, 1968, 1971, 1972, 1975, 1977.

For More Information, Write:
L.I.F.E. — P.O. Box A399, Sydney South 2000, Australia
Campus Crusade for Christ of Canada — Box 300, Vancouver, B.C., V6C 2X3, Canada
Campus Crusade for Christ — Pearl Assurance House, 4 Temple Row, Birmingham, B2 5HG, England
Lay Institute for Evangelism — P.O. Box 8786, Auckland 3, New Zealand
Campus Crusade for Christ — P.O. Box 240, Raffles City Post Office, Singapore 9117
Great Commission Movement of Nigeria — P.O. Box 500, Jos, Plateau State Nigeria, West Africa
Campus Crusade for Christ International — 100 Sunport Lane, Orlando, FL 32809, U.S.A.

Contents

PART III: EXPLANATION

To the people who
know they are victims,
think they might be victims,
have memory gaps,
have unexplained physical or emotional problems

and

To the counselors
who want a tool to aid them
in working with victims—

This book is for you.

FOREWORD

I am anxious and worried, you comfort me and
make me glad (Psalm 94:19, TEV*).*

In the last few years the number of incest and abuse
cases that surface during the time of one weekend retreat
have increased so overwhelmingly that we have suggested
to the committee in charge to offer a training period for lay
counselors before the start of the retreat. As we have taken
Christians with little or no counseling experience and gone
over the basics of abuse, the symptoms of the victim as an
adult, the profile of the offender, and some immediate steps
toward restoration, we have been amazed at how they can
comfort other hurting women.

We teach them to avoid using guilt-producing phrases
such as: "If only you'd pray more," "If you were really
spiritual . . . ," "If only you'd forgive, forget the past and
move on," "It's not as bad as you think," "It's no big deal,"
"Let's just cheer up and smile." If we can stay away from
such sentences and agree with the person that their
problem is a big deal, that we love them unconditionally,
that we don't judge them or think less of them because we
know their past, and that there is hope, these lay comforters can be the catalyst for healing.

So many adult victims have never had anyone believe
them since the abuse started at an early age. They have felt
alone and powerless and when they've tried to fight, the
abuser and other family members have told them it's all in
their heads or it's no big deal.

One of the women from a training session we did in
Brandon, Manitoba, wrote to us of how she feared sitting

9

in the prayer room during an Alliance Women's Retreat and being available to counsel. When her assigned time was over she "breathed a sigh of relief. That is when the Lord decided that Jean and Evie needed someone and although I felt so inadequate, He gave me words and strength that I didn't know were there. Your teaching and insights this weekend will influence me forever and I praise the Lord for you both."

Although we have no intention of producing counselors, we do want to equip those who are helpers already with some understanding of victimization and at least keep them from doing more harm than good. We estimate that 90 percent of the people we speak to in conferences will never seek professional counsel for a variety of reasons. There isn't one where they live, they can't afford the fee, their husbands wouldn't let them go, their churches don't believe in counseling, the last counselor gave bad advice or, as we hear all too often, tried to seduce them. Because so many have nowhere to turn and feel doomed to a lifetime of emotional pain, we have tried to minimize the damage and give some steps toward restoration by encouraging those who feel called to provide comfort and hope to others.

Another woman wrote us from the same retreat in Canada:

> This has been three days full of information. Sorting it out and applying it will take time (but it will be well worth it) . . . especially as a young mom.
>
> Thank you for your obedience to come and minister to us (and the thousands of others in the days ahead). You have really poured yourselves out like a "drink offering." I'm glad for Paul's picture in you both.
>
> You have encouraged me to keep counseling those God leads my way. I learn so much with these people. Your books have been a great help.
>
> Thanks for helping us to shine a little brighter as stars holding out the word of life. That's what it's all about.
>
> I thank the Lord for you and am praying God's best in all your schedule to come.

It was after this particular retreat as we drove off

across the barren fields toward Minot, North Dakota that we knew we had to write this book. We had to have a clear and simple tool to put into the hands of hurting people that would give them hope. If they could find a competent Christian counselor, the work done in this book would give them a basis for their healing process. If they have to take the steps alone or with a friend, this book will show them how to free their minds from the memories that bind.

All of the illustrations, letters and lives that are shared in these pages are real. They are real-life tragedies and victories that have happened to people just like you and us who have given permission to use their hurts to bring hope and healing to others. All but one of the names and locations have been changed, primarily to protect the privacy of those others involved in these dramas of life.

The name Marilyn Murray is her real name. We eagerly await the as yet untitled and soon to be released work of her own unbelievable experiences from victimization to identification to restoration. Watch for it.

Florence and Fred Littauer
San Bernardino, California

How to Read This Book

This book is designed to be a resource, a workbook, a tool for you to use in learning and understanding things about yourself that you may never have thought of before. It is a book you will want not only to read, but to "work through." Make it personal; keep it generally private. Mark it up liberally with a highlighter and an underliner. Make it work for you. Make note anytime you feel emotions welling up inside in response to something you are reading. It may be very significant, for *our emotions remember what our mind has forgotten.*

If at any point you recognize yourself in these pages — if our experiences or observations touch off disturbing memories from your own life — we *strongly encourage* you to seek the help of a professional Christian counselor who understands and is experienced in helping people with the healing of memories.

PART I

PRESENTATION

(Florence)

*Becoming Willing to Root Out
the Problem*

NOTE

This book suggests a series of adult symptoms which, in the authors' view based on research and extensive interaction with audiences, might indicate some form of repressed childhood trauma such as emotional deprivation or physical, emotional or sexual abuse. The authors also suggest a course of action which in their experience has proven effective in helping people begin the process of restoration from such trauma. The authors are not professional counselors, and strongly recommend that the reader who identifies with the symptoms and situations in this book seek the help of a qualified Christian counselor who specializes in the gentle recollection and resolution of childhood traumas. For those readers who do not have access to such a counselor, this book is intended only as a starting point to aid in recognizing the possible need for help as well as the potential for emotional healing from a traumatic past.

It should also be emphasized that most states have laws requiring the reporting of any ongoing cases of child abuse. Readers are urged to become familiar and act in accordance with such laws.

1

"NOT IN *OUR* CHURCH!"

Listen to what the Spirit says to the churches!
(Revelation 2:7, TEV).

It was 5 o'clock on a Saturday afternoon in a stately southern church. Fred and I had concluded our Personality Plus seminar at 3:00. The response had been exciting as we'd told stories of our thirty-five years together and showed how an understanding of the personalities could be used to heal many marriage, family and relationship problems.

In the afternoon I'd mentioned that some people put on a mask over their real personality because of child abuse, a controlling parent, or an alcoholic home. I showed that Fred's family members were so domineering that each generation of strong-willed Cholerics forced the next group to put on a phlegmatic mask of peace. This message on masking and manipulation took only thirty minutes of the whole day's program, but it had a breath-taking effect.

As the people filed out, they gave me the usual positive comments, but a few added thoughts such as these:

An elder smiled and said, "You didn't need the part about abuse in *this* church. We're all Christians."

An elegant lady with a patronizing tone added, "You're from California, honey, where you have all those problems. You don't realize we are different here. This is the South."

The associate pastor let me know, "You're a little ahead of your time here. Our people haven't even heard of incest and no one in our church drinks."

An elderly matriarch of the wealthiest family in the church summed up the local opinion. "We're just one big happy family made up of lots of little happy families."

Had I not known better, I might have felt I'd mentioned a dead issue, but soon those who had held back until the rush was over came up one by one.

A young girl with hurting eyes whispered, "My father's abused me since I was four years old. I've never told anyone before because I knew they wouldn't believe me. You're the first person I thought I could trust."

A heavy-set lady with a puffy face grabbed onto me and began to cry. "I've been a misfit all my life. Nobody loves me. Nobody cares. My father left me when I was three and my mother married this awful man . . . " She couldn't go on as she sobbed and heaved for breath.

A professional woman in her thirties shook hands and stated, "Everyone thinks I've got it all together, but I was molested as a child and it's turned me against men. I've been married twice and I just broke my engagement to *him*." She pointed to a pleasant-looking man leaning in the doorway. "He's weak just like the rest of them. Why do I choose these losers?"

By five o'clock I realized I'd been standing since 8:30 that morning and yet there were four women still in line. The church staff had left, Fred was counseling a lady at the book table, and the janitor was setting the flowers in place for Sunday morning. I dropped onto the front pew wondering why I hadn't thought to sit an hour before. I called the faithful four who had waited an hour to talk with me and asked them to sit around me. "Since it's late, why don't you each tell me the nature of your problem and we'll see if there's any similarity."

A Common Thread

The common thread among these four women was that they all had gaps in their memories. There were parts of their past which they couldn't remember at all. A few years ago I might have been amazed at the coincidence of finding four women in one church with such poor memories, but today I can take a calculated guess that all of these women are victims of some kind of childhood trauma. We've all heard stories of someone in the heat of battle or in an accident who lost a limb and didn't feel the pain until much later when the shock subsided.

As God gives us the ability to shut down our physical senses when we are in the midst of excruciating circumstances, so He provides an emotional escape when the situation is more than we can bear. When a little child is violated beyond her ability to emotionally handle the abuse, God gives relief by drawing a curtain of reprieve over the mind. The facts are still there, stored in the file drawers of the brain along with one hundred trillion other possible items, but they are covered up for the moment waiting for the damaged child to grow up and mature enough to be able to take the abusive evidence out, put it on the table, look at it, feel the pain again, and begin a program of restoration.

The natural emotions that were put to death in the child need to be brought to life and allowed to grow. Even though the person has an adult body and mind, the emotions have been shut down and left behind in the devastation of childhood trauma or abuse. The woman can be left there, forever reacting out of childish emotions; having no normal feelings; unable to establish meaningful relationships; sitting under a black cloud of unexplained depression; suffering physical pain, stomach problems, allergies and headaches; and never living up to her potential. Or, she can be encouraged to go back prayerfully to the little lost child, bring her out in the open, and help her to grow up.

As I faced these four women sitting at my feet at the front of "the church that had no problems," I wondered where to start. What can you do in a group in a limited amount of time with the chairman pacing nervously in the back of the church waiting to take you to your hotel and be done with the day's responsibilities?

I asked each woman to share what she did remember of her childhood.

Joan

Joan told of happy times with her family in Chicago but when she mentioned her summers on her grandfather's farm in Canada her expression changed. "I never got car sick but each time we'd head for Canada, I'd get a nervous stomach. I'd beg my mother to take me home, but she'd tell me I'd get over it. When she'd go to leave me for the summer I'd cry and scream but she'd push me away and say 'You've got to learn to grow up and get along without me.' I can still picture the car turning the corner at the end of the street and knowing I wouldn't see her again until September."

When I asked who took care of her on the farm and what happened, she could recall only that she was terrified when her grandfather came toward her and he made her stay out in the barn with him instead of in the house with her grandmother. Joan has chronic stomach problems, a fear of men, and on her few visits to the farm as an adult she got carsick.

Missy

Missy remembered the day her father walked out on her mother. She was five and recalls her mother turning in tears and saying, "It's all your fault. If I hadn't had you, he wouldn't have left me." Missy has no memories from that point to age sixteen, when she left home to marry a sailor who abandoned her as soon as he found out she was pregnant. She never married again, but she had been through many affairs which all ended traumatically. Her only daughter married an abusive man at age sixteen and is now back living with Missy. They are both miserable and feel like failures.

When I asked if her mother had remarried, she said no, but she had a vague recollection of different men living with her mother from time to time. Missy hated men, was angry at her mother, and resented her daughter's failures. She was extremely overweight and even though she attended church she didn't think God could ever love her.

Missy was obviously suffering from repeated rejections, but her memory blanks probably indicated some sexual mistreatment from her mother's male friends. With her mother and daughter living similar lives she could see that a negative pattern had been established and she didn't know how to break it.

Heather

Heather was the church secretary and was a high achiever. She remembered little before her high school years when she determined to become a winner. She had been a compulsive student, made the high honor roll and had won a scholarship to the state university. She'd married a pastor who was just like her father whom she doted on. They had always been "very close," and now that her husband had left her and her mother had died, she was back living with her saintly father, a church elder.

Heather had migraine headaches that would cripple her productivity for days. She also had occasional asthma attacks, and she was allergic "to just about everything." She had just turned forty and was terrified that she might be losing her grip. When I questioned her relationship with her idolized father, she could only recall that her mother worked as a nurse at night and "for a treat" her father would let her sleep with him.

If "nothing happened," why was Heather at forty a nervous wreck? Why did she have extreme headaches and attacks where she thought she'd gag to death? What had her husband done to her and why had he left? Why did she feel waves of guilt over living back with her father again? Why was her childhood a long blur? Is there something strange about this father-daughter relationship?

Lauri

Lauri had bleak memories of her childhood and knew

she couldn't have been molested because there were never any men around. She had been raised by her mother and grandmother who were both legalistic Christians and were opposed to any type of fun or entertainment. Life was colorless and uneventful except for routine trips to church. When Lauri would ask about her father, her mother would snap back, "He was a rat and we're better off without him." The grandmother would nod in agreement. These two women obviously had no use for whoever the father was and seemed to hate men in general.

Lauri had never dated and had a love-hate relationship with her mother. She was uncomfortable with her, yet lonely without her. Her emotions were those of a child who needed her mother yet who knew she was supposed to grow up and get along without her. Lauri was thirty-five, had no ambition and little self-esteem, and worked four hours a day in the church nursery. "I'll never have any children of my own, so I might as well play with the babies," Lauri sighed as she spoke. There was no sparkle in her eyes; she had given up on life.

Unresolved Pain, Unexplained Guilt

Once I had heard these four biographies, I asked if they would be willing to pair up and work with each other to help discover the source of their problems. They had waited more than an hour to talk with me and they wanted some tangible advice. Joan had been to several doctors about her stomach problems and took medication with each meal. Missy had been on repeated diets, had never lost more than ten pounds at a time, and always had gained the weight back. Heather had gone to the church counselor who had told her she was the strongest person he'd ever met and she didn't need any help. "Everyone has a headache now and then so don't worry about it," he had said. Lauri had never sought any counsel as she didn't know what to say. "I'm amazed I stayed to talk with you," she whispered.

Joan and Missy volunteered to work together and Heather took little Lauri under her wing. I suggested they plan to spend the following Saturday in pairs. Before that time they should start each day in prayer asking the Lord to restore their memories. Knowing that the Holy Spirit gives recall, they should write down whatever came to their minds: childhood incidents, feelings, upsets; people, family members, their real opinions about them; homes and rooms that bothered them.

They should then study a Psalm each day and carefully note how David called out in his need to a God who cared. They should fashion their prayer time after his: the call to their Father God, the pouring out of their true feelings, the thanksgiving to the God who answers prayer, and the praise for an Almighty Counselor.

They agreed excitedly to the simple guidelines, to get together the next week, and to keep the personal information confidential. I suggested as they met in pairs for one to question the other about their childhood for several hours and then to reverse the procedure in an effort to find the source of their individual hurts.

As we prayed, I asked the Lord to reveal truth to them. Were Joan's stomach problems really physical? Was Missy's weight a symptom of something else? Were Heather's headaches rooted in some past situations? Was Lauri's indifference more than inertia? How could we help these women?

As Fred and I returned to the hotel and sat down to review our day, we realized we had both been surrounded by hurting women at every break. Many had limited memories similar to my last four; many started by saying, "I've never told this to anyone before"; and all of them were weighted down by unresolved pain and unexplained guilt. What could we do?

From our twenty years of ministry and our constant study of God's Word, we know that the Bible contains all truth and that Jesus is our healer. But why are so many Christians who also know the Scriptures suffering so intensely?

We agreed. We had to write a book giving the steps to

freedom. We had to have something we could place in the arms of the emotionally crippled. We did pray with them and give them hope, but we so often felt as we left a group of hurting women to go on to our next assignment that we were deserting a sinking ship. Even though women and children go first, where would they go? Who would help them? Would they drown in a sea of troubles? How could we throw a life-saver to so many? We had to put what we'd found to work into a book that could be used as a hands-on tool to rescue those in distress.

We've tried not to take sides in the Christian counseling debate or espouse new theories or doctrines, but to put in writing the facts we find from our personal experience and the procedures we've discovered to be effective in

Freeing Your Mind from Memories That Bind.

2

SEARCHING OURSELVES

*I, the Lord, search the minds and test
the hearts of men (Jeremiah 17:10, TEV).*

Before we analyze our symptoms and start our journey of uncovering our hurts of the past, let's look at our basic God-given personalities and see what the Lord had in mind for us before we ran into the trials and traumas of life.

We know that God created each one of us with a special personality, that He knit us together in our mother's womb, that our frame was not hidden from God when He made us in that secret place, that His eyes saw our unformed body and that all our days were written in His book before one of them came to be (Psalm 139:13-16, paraphrased NIV).

At the end of Psalm 139, David calls to God as we should: "Search me, O God, and know my heart; test me and know my anxious thoughts. See if there is any offensive way in me, and lead me in the way everlasting" (verses 23,24, NIV).

Throughout the Bible we find admonitions that tell us to examine ourselves, judge ourselves, put ourselves to the test and search ourselves. Even though we have a gift for giving advice to others, the Scriptures don't recommend that pursuit. Instead, we are to focus our attention on evaluating our strengths: "If there be any virtue, look on these things" (Philippians 4:8, KJV); and on bringing our weaknesses to the Lord: "If we confess our sins, he is faith-

ful and just to forgive our sins and cleanse us from all unrighteousness" (1 John 1:9, KJV).

In both cases the results are conditional upon our
making the first move. How do we do that? How do we
evaluate our strengths and weaknesses? When Fred and I
were baby Christians wanting desperately to obey God's
will, we looked for instruction that would help us grow.
Fred made an appointment with the pastor to go for lessons on the Christian life. The pastor was surprised and
said he wasn't quite sure what to teach as no one had ever
asked him to give any private lessons on spiritual growth.
After three hours of casual instruction, the pastor said,
"Well, that's about it. I've taught you all I can think of so
now you're on your own." And sure enough we were!

With no more formal instruction than Fred's three
hours, we became instant leaders. This transformation was
not dependent upon our brilliance but upon a special gift
God gave us to fill an obvious leadership vacuum in our
Christian community. At the same time that we heard
God's call to service, we became aware of the four basic
temperaments first taught by Hippocrates to his medical
students more than two thousand years ago.

Four Basic Temperaments

Immediately I identified myself as a *Sanguine*: optimistic, fun-loving, friendly, colorful, talkative and
humorous.

I had thought there was only one Fred in life, but in
my study I found one-fourth of the world was like him.
Melancholy: deep, thoughtful, introspective, analytical,
genius-prone, sensitive to the needs of others.

In looking further, I discovered both Fred and I were
part *Choleric*: strong-willed, impulsive, active, goal-
oriented, practical and quick. We couldn't believe that we'd
found ourselves in print.

The fourth type was the *Phlegmatic* (like my mother):
calm, cool, easy-going, objective, mediating, inoffensive,
loved by all.

As soon as we got a handle on ourselves and our family, we had a new understanding and acceptance of each other. Lauren was like Fred, Choleric and Melancholy. Marita was a duplicate of me, Sanguine and Choleric. Our adopted son was Melancholy. My mother was Phlegmatic and Fred's mother Choleric. Now we could see why, when the two mothers were together, Mother Littauer called the shots and Mother Chapman followed pleasantly behind.

With Fred and me, a little knowledge is a dangerous thing. We couldn't keep these concepts to ourselves, so we invited ten couples to our home and began to teach the temperaments. In spite of our limited background in the subject, we saw marriages transformed and individuals healed right there in our living room. People who were well-intentioned but clueless as to why they were having relationship problems suddenly saw themselves in a new light. "That's why I can't get along with him. If only I'd known this years ago."

With the success of our first venture we began to speak on the personalities for small groups, couples retreats, church meetings, assemblies and conventions. Fred made out charts and I gathered humorous examples. Later I wrote *Personality Plus, Your Personality Tree,* and *Personalities in Power,* all on this subject using this basic understanding as a tool to help us examine ourselves.

That is how we wish to use the personalities in this book—as a tool, not a theology—as a yardstick by which we may measure our strengths and weaknesses. As we have helped people to find themselves and learn to get along with others, we have been gratified by letters attesting to the value of the personalities as a tool for maturing in the Christian faith. One such letter came from a member of the Community of Christian Family Ministry (a religious order in the Episcopal Church Diocese of San Diego, California, which has single and married people as members):

> Thank you for the multiple blessings that your book *Personality Plus* has brought to our Community.
> About three years ago we were seeking the guidance of the

Holy Spirit in how to mature in Christ as individuals and learn to
love and serve each other and Jesus more fully. We had made formal commitments to each other in the body, we had lived together
and ministered together for many years but felt that God wanted
to break new ground in us. Since a great part of our purpose "is
to live out the gospel as an intentional family," anything which
furthered this would be welcome. The Lord literally knocked the
book off the rack and into the shopping cart of one of our Coor-
dinators, and we have never been the same again. We instantly
recognized each other by the descriptions and even laughed at ourselves. We not only recognized ourselves but we understood more
thoroughly how God had made us.

       We had lived together so long "walking in the light" that the
results of the test, with just a few exceptions, were no surprise.
However it made certain tendencies, strengths and weaknesses
more understandable and enabled us to be less critical of each
other. We also now had clearer insight into the ways to go about
assisting each other to grow in grace. Through the grace of God,
the power of His Holy Spirit, and the insights Jesus showed us
through your book we are being transformed. Of course the Lord
Jesus has used many other things to make us more His people but
we thought you would be interested and encouraged to hear our
story.

    As you begin a study of the four personalities with an
open mind and heart, God will use this tool as a framework
where you can evaluate yourself and learn to get along with
others. On the following pages are some charts for you to
study and a Personality Profile for you to take.

Personality Profile

DIRECTIONS — In each of the following rows of four words across, place an X in front of the one word that most often applies to you. Continue through all forty lines. Be sure each number is marked. If you are not sure of which word "most applies", ask a spouse or a friend.

STRENGTHS

#								
1	___ Adventurous	___ Adaptable	___ Animated	___ Analytical
2	___ Persistent	___ Playful	___ Persuasive	___ Peaceful
3	___ Submissive	___ Self-sacrificing	___ Sociable	___ Strong-willed
4	___ Considerate	___ Controlled	___ Competitive	___ Convincing
5	___ Refreshing	___ Respectful	___ Reserved	___ Resourceful
6	___ Satisfied	___ Sensitive	___ Self-reliant	___ Spirited
7	___ Planner	___ Patient	___ Positive	___ Promoter
8	___ Sure	___ Spontaneous	___ Scheduled	___ Shy
9	___ Orderly	___ Obliging	___ Outspoken	___ Optimistic
10	___ Friendly	___ Faithful	___ Funny	___ Forceful
11	___ Daring	___ Delightful	___ Diplomatic	___ Detailed
12	___ Cheerful	___ Consistent	___ Cultured	___ Confident
13	___ Idealistic	___ Independent	___ Inoffensive	___ Inspiring
14	___ Demonstrative	___ Decisive	___ Dry humor	___ Deep
15	___ Mediator	___ Musical	___ Mover	___ Mixes easily
16	___ Thoughtful	___ Tenacious	___ Talker	___ Tolerant
17	___ Listener	___ Loyal	___ Leader	___ Lively
18	___ Contented	___ Chief	___ Chartmaker	___ Cute
19	___ Perfectionist	___ Pleasant	___ Productive	___ Popular
20	___ Bouncy	___ Bold	___ Behaved	___ Balanced

Personality Profile

WEAKNESSES

#				
21	___ Blank	___ Bashful	___ Brassy	___ Bossy
22	___ Undisciplined	___ Unsympathetic	___ Unenthusiastic	___ Unforgiving
23	___ Reticent	___ Resentful	___ Resistant	___ Repetitious
24	___ Fussy	___ Fearful	___ Forgetful	___ Frank
25	___ Impatient	___ Insecure	___ Indecisive	___ Interrupts
26	___ Unpopular	___ Uninvolved	___ Unpredictable	___ Unaffectionate
27	___ Headstrong	___ Haphazard	___ Hard to please	___ Hesitant
28	___ Plain	___ Pessimistic	___ Proud	___ Permissive
29	___ Angered easily	___ Aimless	___ Argumentative	___ Alienated
30	___ Naive	___ Negative attitude	___ Nervy	___ Nonchalant
31	___ Worrier	___ Withdrawn	___ Workaholic	___ Wants credit
32	___ Too sensitive	___ Tactless	___ Timid	___ Talkative
33	___ Doubtful	___ Disorganized	___ Domineering	___ Depressed
34	___ Inconsistent	___ Introvert	___ Intolerant	___ Indifferent
35	___ Messy	___ Moody	___ Mumbles	___ Manipulative
36	___ Slow	___ Stubborn	___ Show-off	___ Skeptical
37	___ Loner	___ Lord over	___ Lazy	___ Loud
38	___ Sluggish	___ Suspicious	___ Short-tempered	___ Scatterbrained
39	___ Revengeful	___ Restless	___ Reluctant	___ Rash
40	___ Compromising	___ Critical	___ Crafty	___ Changeable

NOW TRANSFER ALL YOUR X's TO THE CORRESPONDING WORDS ON THE PERSONALITY SCORING SHEET AND ADD UP YOUR TOTALS.

Personality Scoring Sheet

STRENGTHS

	SANGUINE POPULAR	CHOLERIC POWERFUL	MELANCHOLY PERFECT	PHLEGMATIC PEACEFUL
1	Animated	Adventurous	Analytical	Adaptable
2	Playful	Persuasive	Persistent	Peaceful
3	Sociable	Strong-willed	Self-sacrificing	Submissive
4	Convincing	Competitive	Considerate	Controlled
5	Refreshing	Resourceful	Respectful	Reserved
6	Spirited	Self-reliant	Sensitive	Satisfied
7	Promoter	Positive	Planner	Patient
8	Spontaneous	Sure	Scheduled	Shy
9	Optimistic	Outspoken	Orderly	Obliging
10	Funny	Forceful	Faithful	Friendly
11	Delightful	Daring	Detailed	Diplomatic
12	Cheerful	Confident	Cultured	Consistent
13	Inspiring	Independent	Idealistic	Inoffensive
14	Demonstrative	Decisive	Deep	Dry humor
15	Mixes easily	Mover	Musical	Mediator
16	Talker	Tenacious	Thoughtful	Tolerant
17	Lively	Leader	Loyal	Listener
18	Cute	Chief	Chartmaker	Contented
19	Popular	Productive	Perfectionist	Pleasant
20	Bouncy	Bold	Behaved	Balanced

TOTALS _____

Personality Scoring Sheet

WEAKNESSES

#	SANGUINE POPULAR	CHOLERIC POWERFUL	MELANCHOLY PERFECT	PHLEGMATIC PEACEFUL
21	Brassy	Bossy	Bashful	Blank
22	Undisciplined	Unsympathetic	Unforgiving	Unenthusiastic
23	Repetitious	Resistant	Resentful	Reticent
24	Forgetful	Frank	Fussy	Fearful
25	Interrupts	Impatient	Insecure	Indecisive
26	Unpredictable	Unaffectionate	Unpopular	Uninvolved
27	Haphazard	Headstrong	Hard-to-please	Hesitant
28	Permissive	Proud	Pessimistic	Plain
29	Angered easily	Argumentative	Alienated	Aimless
30	Naive	Nervy	Negative attitude	Nonchalant
31	Wants credit	Workaholic	Withdrawn	Worrier
32	Talkative	Tactless	Too sensitive	Timid
33	Disorganized	Domineering	Depressed	Doubtful
34	Inconsistent	Intolerant	Introvert	Indifferent
35	Messy	Manipulative	Moody	Mumbles
36	Show-off	Stubborn	Skeptical	Slow
37	Loud	Lord-over-others	Loner	Lazy
38	Scatterbrained	Short tempered	Suspicious	Sluggish
39	Restless	Rash	Revengeful	Reluctant
40	Changeable	Crafty	Critical	Compromising
TOTALS				
COMBINED TOTALS				

POPULAR SANGUINE SUMMARY
"Let's do it the fun way."

Desire:	Have fun
Emotional Needs:	Attention, affection, approval, acceptance
Key Strengths:	Can talk about anything at any time at any place with or without information. Has a bubbling personality, optimism, sense of humor, storytelling ability, likes people
Key Weaknesses:	Disorganized, can't remember details or names, exaggerates, not serious about anything, trusts others to do the work, too gullible and naive
Gets Depressed When:	Life is no fun and no one seems to love him
Is Afraid Of:	Being unpopular or bored, having to live by the clock or keep a record of money spent
Likes People Who:	Listen and laugh, praise and approve
Dislikes People Who:	Criticize, don't respond to his humor, don't think he is cute
Is Valuable In Work:	For colorful creativity, optimism, light touch, cheering up others, entertaining
Could Improve If:	He got organized, didn't talk so much and learned to tell time
Tends to Marry:	Perfects who are sensitive and serious, but the Populars quickly tire of having to cheer them up all the time, and of being made to feel inadequate and stupid
Reaction to Stress:	Leave the scene, go shopping, find a fun group, create excuses, blame others
Recognize by:	Constant talking, loud volume, bright eyes, moving hands, colorful expressions, enthusiasm, ability to mix easily

(The four temperament summaries are reprinted from Florence's book, *Personalities in Power.*)

POWERFUL CHOLERIC SUMMARY
"Let's do it my way."

Desire:	Have control
Emotional Needs:	Sense of obedience, appreciation for accomplishments, credit for ability
Key Strengths:	Ability to take charge of anything instantly, make quick, correct judgments
Key Weaknesses:	Too bossy, domineering, autocratic, insensitive, impatient, unwilling to delegate or give credit to others
Gets Depressed When:	Life is out of control and people won't do things his way
Is Afraid Of:	Losing control of anything, such as losing job, not being promoted, becoming seriously ill, having rebellious child or unsupportive mate
Likes People Who:	Are supportive and submissive, see things his way, cooperate quickly and let them take credit
Dislikes People Who:	Are lazy and not interested in working constantly, who buck his authority, get independent or aren't loyal
Is Valuable in Work:	Because he can accomplish more than anyone else in a shorter time and is usually right, but may stir up trouble
Could Improve If:	He allowed others to make decisions, delegated authority, became more patient, didn't expect everyone to produce as he does
As A Leader He:	Has a natural feel for being in charge, a quick sense of what will work and a sincere belief in his ability to achieve, but may overwhelm less aggressive people
Tends To Marry:	Peacefuls who will quietly obey and not buck his authority, but who never accomplish enough or get excited over his projects
Reaction to Stress:	Tighten control, work harder, exercise more, get rid of offender
Recognize By:	Fast-moving approach, quick grab for control, self-confidence, restless and overpowering attitude

PERFECT MELANCHOLY SUMMARY
"Let's do it the right way."

Desire:	Have it right
Emotional Needs:	Sense of stability, space, silence, sensitivity and support
Key Strengths:	Ability to organize, set long-range goals, have high standards and ideals, analyze deeply
Key Weaknesses:	Easily depressed, too much time on preparation, too focused on details, remembers negatives, suspicious of others
Gets Depressed When:	Life is out of order, standards aren't met and no one seems to care
Is Afraid Of:	No one understanding how he really feels, making a mistake, having to compromise standards
Likes People Who:	Are serious, intellectual, deep, and will carry on a sensible conversation
Dislikes People Who:	Are lightweights, forgetful, late, disorganized, superficial, prevaricating and unpredictable
Is Valuable In Work:	For sense of details, love of analysis, follow-through, high standards of performance, compassion for the hurting
Could Improve If:	He didn't take life quite so seriously and didn't insist others be perfectionists
As A Leader He:	Organizes well, is sensitive to peoples' feelings, has deep creativity, wants quality performance
Tends to Marry:	Populars for their personalities and social skills, but soon tries to shut them up and get them on a schedule, becoming depressed when they don't respond
Reaction To Stress:	Withdraws, gets lost in a book, becomes depressed, gives up, recounts the problems
Recognize By:	Serious, sensitive nature, well-mannered approach, self-deprecating comments, meticulous and well-groomed looks (exceptions are hippy-type intellectuals, musicians, poets, who feel attention to clothes and looks is worldly and detracts from their inner strengths)

PEACEFUL PHLEGMATIC SUMMARY
"Let's do it the easy way."

Desire:	Have no conflict, keep peace
Emotional Needs:	Sense of respect, feeling of worth, understanding, emotional support, harmony
Key Strengths:	Balance, even disposition, dry sense of humor, pleasing personality
Key Weaknesses:	Lack of decisiveness, enthusiasm and energy, but has no obvious flaws, and has a hidden will of iron
Gets Depressed When:	Life is full of conflict, he has to face a personal confrontation, no one wants to help, the buck stops with him
Is Afraid Of:	Having to deal with a major personal problem, being left holding the bag, making major changes
Likes People Who:	Will make decisions for him, will recognize his strengths, will not ignore him
Dislikes People Who:	Are too pushy, expect too much of him
Is Valuable In Work:	Because he cooperates and is a calming influence, keeps peace, mediates between contentious people, objectively solves problems
Could Improve If:	He sets goals and becomes self-motivated, he were willing to do more and move faster than expected, and could face his own problems as well as he handles other people's
As A Leader He:	Keeps calm, cool and collected, doesn't make impulsive decisions, is well-liked and inoffensive, won't cause trouble, but doesn't come up with brilliant new ideas
Tends To Marry:	Powerfuls because they respect his strength and decisiveness, but later the Peacefuls get tired of being pushed around and looked down upon
Reaction To Stress:	Hide from it, watch TV, eat
Recognize By:	Calm approach, relaxed posture, sitting or leaning when possible

The Popular Sanguine wants to have fun.

The Powerful Choleric wants to have control.

The Perfect Melancholy wants everything right.

The Peaceful Phlegmatic wants to avoid conflict.

When you score your Personality Profile, you may be almost all one personality or a combination of two. Natural combinations are:

Popular-Powerful: "Do it my way and it will be fun."

Powerful-Perfect: "Do it my way and it will be perfect."

Perfect-Peaceful: "Do it right but not if it will cause trouble."

Popular-Peaceful: "Let's have fun but not if we have to go somewhere to do it."

You may be asking yourself what this analysis has to do with freeing your mind. If you are, you will be interested to know that the most frequent comment we get after a personality seminar is, "This has freed me up to be who God wants me to be." We know from experience that when a person begins a program of self-evaluation, God opens his or her mind to new revelations. God desires truth in our innermost parts and the personality analysis gives us a way to work ourselves into the truth.

Almost everyone is able to find a personality pattern that fits and feels natural, but some of you may have difficulty in deciding which word applies. In the back of *Your Personality Tree,* there is a section with the definitions of all the words. This gives the meanings that we had in mind when we created the profile. After you have checked one word on each line (forty marks) transfer the marks to the scoring sheet and add them up. Place the totals on the next page in the four squares:

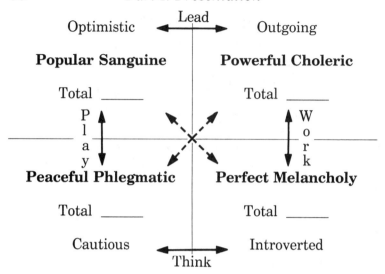

The most common combinations are the outgoing, optimistic Popular-Powerfuls (Sanguine-Cholerics) who make excellent leaders, and the cautious, introverted Perfect-Peacefuls (Melancholy-Phlegmatics) who like quiet, reflective thinking. You may be 50 percent of each in these two types.

Other normal combinations are strong, organized Perfect-Powerfuls (Melancholy-Cholerics) who accomplish much and really like to work. You will probably not be 50-50 of these two but more like 60-40. If the 60 is in the Powerful, the person will be more optimistic, directive, quick-moving and will do his organizing in his head. If the balance is 60 percent Perfect, the person will be somewhat pessimistic, quietly directive, slower moving and will do his organizing on paper. A high percentage of business executives are this Perfect-Powerful combination.

The Popular-Peaceful (Sanguine-Phlegmatic) will tip more in one direction than the other. If the person is mostly Popular, he will be a light-hearted, good-humored, easygoing, fun-loving optimist. If the Peaceful prevails, he will be slower-paced, laid-back, unconcerned, less noisy and have a dry sense of humor. This combination is always friendly, relaxed and appealing but these individuals are poor handlers of money and often can't quite pull life together at one time. They believe all work and no play make Jack a dull boy.

Now that we have seen the natural combinations, what does it mean if you are a little bit of everything? Many people seem to think they are spread evenly around and that this pattern is probably more spiritual. That conclusion is possible, but not likely.

1. Recheck the profile and the scoring sheet to make sure you did it according to the directions. Some people come out scattered because they didn't transfer the marks properly.

2. Reread the Peaceful strengths and weaknesses on the scoring sheet and see if you could fit most of them. Often Phlegmatics are more balanced than others and they have more trouble in deciding which word to choose.

3. Review the meanings of the words in the back of *Your Personality Tree* and ask a friend to go over the choices with you.

4. Realize that your childhood may have been a gray, dull existence, a dysfunctional home where you had no control, or a situation where you had to play different roles to get along with different people and have ended up being all things to all people to such a degree that you can't find the "real you" inside. Take some prayerful time to seek a possible answer to this all-purpose personality.

"Just What God Wanted Me to Be"

Carol had been confused about her personality. It seemed to be a little bit of everything, but after three days at our CLASS (Christian Leaders and Speakers Seminars) seminar she came into an understanding and acceptance of who she really was:

> Dear Florence,
> Last month I attended your CLASS in Fort Wayne, Indiana. Nearly every day since, I have wanted to write.

Last year I had taken the Personality Profile as a part of the counseling I was receiving. At that time I had a smattering of each of the temperament strengths, but nothing outstanding. However, fifteen of twenty weaknesses were in the Sanguine category! For a year I have wept over being a Sanguine. The tears would start every time Barbara (my counselor) would talk to me about accepting the person God had made me to be. She would encourage me to accept and thank God for being who I am. At the seminar I took the profile once again. I was astonished to discover that I am actually Sanguine-Phlegmatic in practically equal proportions. What a revelation this information was. It explains to me many things which have puzzled me for so long.

First of all, the tears over being a Sanguine came from the conflict created whenever I tried to have fun and/or to accept my scatter-brained, joyful self. I have been married for over twenty-five years to a Choleric-Melancholy man who sees having fun as frivolous and worthless. Whenever I would allow myself to be joyful or relaxed, strife would follow. I would then withdraw, think I had done something wrong, and become depressed.

One Phlegmatic characteristic I have is that I am frequently blank. That is, I don't always think about situations, ideas, etc., particularly those things that do not affect me personally. This way of being never bothered me. In fact, it was sometimes a very peaceful way to live. Since it was such a source of irritation to others, I attempted to eradicate this from my life. Then, I discovered that *how* I think about things isn't right! So I tried being all things to all people and became a nothing.

Daily, since the seminar, I am learning that I am a somebody, created to be just what God wanted me to be. There are years of bad habits to deal with, but it is easier having the assurance that God didn't mismatch me and that I have worth in His sight.

Knowing that I am strongly Phlegmatic has also enabled me to accept being Sanguine and I now have more joy and less internal conflict. Thank you for your willingness to serve God and share the knowledge He gives you. I appreciate you very much.

Survival Masks

If you come out one-half Popular Sanguine and one-half Perfect Melancholy, our experience shows that one of these two is a mask put on for survival at some point in life. What could have caused this? Usually some type of physical, emotional, sexual or verbal abuse was so severe or so repetitive that the child shut down his or her normal God-given personality and put on a mask to cover up the pain.

Kathy came to CLASS and thought she was Perfect Melancholy mixed with Peaceful Phlegmatic. She appeared low-key, intelligent, thoughtful; she was also troubled, remote and depressed. She had such pain in her eyes that it hurt to look at them. During her three days with us she met with our staff leader, Georgia Venard, who helped her peel away the extreme pains of her childhood. Behind the pain was a little Sanguine girl whose life had been no fun. Here is her story in her own words:

As I shared with you while I was there, it was the Personality Profile that did me in. When I got into my hotel room that first night of the seminar I tried to change it, but I could not erase the fear, insecurity, instability and depression that were my life.

In Georgia's small group I randomly selected a magazine ad of a lady wearing a mask with the caption that read, "Are you the lady who's wearing this mask?" or something like that. It was at this point that I became totally undone and couldn't properly function from there on.

Georgia allowed me to talk, cry and escape from our assignment. The group support was what I needed.

As the events of each day unfolded, I came to realize that I had been wearing a Melancholy mask of pain and a Phlegmatic mask of peace at any price. Only those who have been there can understand how it feels for the first time in one's life to have your eyes opened and be able to see. For me it was the first time in over forty years. I had no idea why my life was filled with the turmoil and depression that it was until my time at CLASS.

My traumatic childhood began when I was eighteen months old. Mother came home from the hospital with baby sister and that night my father shot my mother (she lived for two weeks) and my four-year-old brother. He also shot himself, but lived the rest of his twenty-one years in an institution. My sister and I were spared, but we were to learn from the grapevine. Because I knew little about it at the time, I grew up with the fear that he would come back for me.

When I was a senior in high school, my adoptive dad (my natural mother's brother) got sick (mentally) and hung himself in our cellar. We had lived with this wild man for four months in fear for our lives.

In 1970 I had a cancerous thyroid removed. I lost a seven-month baby—our first—a girl. My husband got leukemia and passed away twenty months later in 1984. I have two sons, one is a nineteen-year-old dyed-in-the-wool Sanguine. Both sons are married. That's my life in a nutshell so that you can see where I'm coming from.

It wasn't until CLASS that I understood for the first time that I had pushed a lifetime of pain out of my mind and that it held me in bondage throughout my childhood and a completed marriage. The understanding of this and the temperaments help me to see the problem and put my life back together again. It has been like a giant jigsaw puzzle coming together.

Though I have sensed for years that the Lord wants to use my experience with grief and loss to bring hope to others, I did not see the complete picture until now. I know now that I have a story to tell that began at CLASS and that there are people who need to hear.

Sometimes we put on a mask as an adult trying to please a mate, a pastor or the whole Christian community. Irma came to a weekend retreat as a deeply committed, serious, spiritual Christian. During our time of personality teaching, Irma's perception of herself changed drastically and she wrote to tell me:

Dear Florence,

I have discovered the real me and I have learned it's not just okay to be the real me, but that I *need* to be the real me. What a relief! I am a Choleric-Sanguine who has been trying to be a Melancholy-Phlegmatic.

Thirteen years ago when I became a Christian my fun stopped. As a new Christian I was "assigned" two different girls to disciple me. I was thankful for their personalized teaching but they were both Melancholy. So the message I was picking up was that to become mature as a Christian means to become a Melancholy. There were also Melancholy-Choleric women who were suggesting I was dressing not quite conservative enough. So I became a Melancholy — or tried very hard to. Now, especially in the past eighteen months, I have felt starved for fun. I would say to my friends, "Don't you crave some excitement in your life?" They would look at me with concern and I felt like they were thinking, "Uh oh, I think Irma is looking for an affair." (You see, in the past three years I have lost about twenty pounds and I am being noticed by men.) So I would begin to fight this desire for fun and yet all that was in me was crying out for fun. I wanted to enjoy myself but I also wanted to become spiritually mature as a Christian (which in my mind meant becoming a Melancholy).

I was completely discouraged when I concluded that I was a

Melancholy-Phlegmatic and my husband was a Phlegmatic-Melancholy. "Where Do We Get Fun From???" You know what I discovered? I can have fun and still be a mature Christian. I am free to be me. Free to have fun and also become mature. It is possible — I have seen it in you!

Thank you for assuring me that the teachings I had been receiving were not true. I do not have to feel guilty that I am a leader and my husband does not have to be ashamed and feel that he is less than a man because he is not a controller. I am invigorated — I feel I have run a marathon and won — a thousand pounds have been lifted. Praise God! I am free to become the woman God intended for me to be!

With much love and deep respect,
Irma

People who have been abused, controlled or manipulated often put on the Melancholy mask of pain and perfection or give up by putting on the Phlegmatic mask of peace at any price. This last mask is often worn by a Powerful Choleric who has been beaten down and who has wrapped himself or herself in a cloak of indifference. "Who cares anyway? What does it matter? I'll just let them have their way." Powerful persons want to control but if they sense they can't win, they refuse to play the game. They put on a mask of peace and tune out on at least part of life.

The Powerful Choleric mask of control is donned by any of the other personalities who don't want to be in charge but who are pushed into a parenting role at a young age. This can be caused by an alcoholic parent who is irresponsible, a set of working parents who put responsibility on one child to oversee the others, a home where drugs rob the children of consistent and loving discipline, or by parents who are extremely immature. Whenever the child says to himself or herself, "This family is not going to make it if I don't take charge," the child is assuming a demanding role and becoming a little controller. This mask of premature power becomes confusing to the child in charge and causes swings of passive-aggressive behavior as he grows up.

As an adult this person avoids responsibility until there is a vacuum of leadership; then he jumps in strongly, surprising those in observation. Frequently this person doesn't become consistently successful and often quits a job or project before the desired conclusion. When you are aware of the backgrounds that force masks on innocent children you can be more tolerant of their adult mistakes.

Suddenly in Charge at Age Five

Joyce's whole life was a series of ups and downs caused by a pair of parents who were forced into marriage, who didn't love each other and who shouldn't have had any children. Her father abused her mother and her. As a little child she tied a pet rabbit to her swing to give it a ride. When it died swinging, her mother accused her of purposely killing her pet.

After her parents fought and her father left her mother unconscious on the floor, her mother gave up on the whole scene and left home. Joyce was suddenly in charge of the household at five years old and became the mother to her little sister. Can you see that this child had to put on the mask of control and become responsible for a hopeless situation which, she was made to feel, was her fault? When she was six her father put her and her four-year-old sister on a train from Denver to Tennessee where her mother was living. After they had left he called their mother and said they were on their way. All across the country, Joyce had to watch over and control her little sister.

When her mother met them she was angry at them for coming, as if they'd had a choice. After a year the children were put on the train again and sent back to the father in Denver who had married an alcoholic. The father continued to abuse Joyce and in high school she ran away from home because she had been beaten with a dog leash.

Typical of the abuse victim, Joyce became promiscuous, deceptive and out of control. She took drugs and became hooked on cocaine. At nineteen she got pregnant and when she went crying home to her father he said, "If you keep this baby, don't ever come home again." Rejected and defeated, Joyce defied her father and kept the baby. She tried different ways to win her father's love and attention, but not until his deathbed did he give her credit for raising her son unmarried and alone. His last words were, "Take care of your brother," putting a burden on her even in his dying moments.

A friend sent her to hear Reuben Welch who stated, "You don't have to go up to God, He comes all the way down to where you are." She cried out to God to come down and He became real to her. As a Christian Joyce has made strides but she is still living a self-defeating lifestyle, quitting jobs when she sees success ahead. When Joyce came to me in tears she had no money and no insurance and her son needed knee surgery.

A Double-Masked Couple

The Sanguine mask of popularity is not so common as the mask of pain, the mask of peace at all costs, or the mask of control, but it is often found in Christian homes where the family must exude the joy of the Lord at all times no matter how they really feel. "Don't come out until you have a smile on your face. A real Christian is always happy. Be ye joyful!"

A child who is assigned to cheer up an ailing parent, who is expected to be adorable and witty like her sister or who is forced into an up-front role which does not fit her natural personality may put on the mask of attempted popularity to please a parent.

Fred and I met with Alan and Susie in a restaurant. They had been in our seminar, had taken their profiles and had come out confused. They both were Sanguine-Melancholy, two of the opposite blends and a combination which is indicative of masking. Since opposites usually marry each other, our job was to find out which one was the real Sanguine wearing a Melancholy mask and which was Melancholy with a Sanguine mask. As they entered, Susie was somewhat disheveled with her hair bouncing and her blouse half in and half out. This alone would be enough to cross her off the meticulous Melancholy list. She looked around the restaurant and said wide-eyed, "I've never been here before. Isn't this adorable! Look at the flowers on the wallpaper." As she bubbled on Alan murmured, "Sit down and shut your mouth." The joy left her face, she put on her Melancholy mask, and she sat down.

I had noticed that Alan dusted off his seat with his napkin before he sat down, the act of a perfectionist. By observation I guessed Susie was Sanguine and Alan was Melancholy. Why did their profiles indicate "split personalities"?

Every so often Susie would come into her own and be funny but then Alan, who appeared to have no sense of humor, would cut her down. They were both overweight and talked about how much the other one was eating. At this point Fred asked Alan if he'd given Susie a compliment lately. She said no as he said yes.

"What was it, Alan?" Fred asked again.

"Just the other day I told her she was really pretty for someone so fat."

By the time we heard their life stories we understood their antagonism toward each other. Susie had been abused as a child, had run away from home and married in her teens, and had found herself in an abusive marriage with a man who beat up both Susie and her baby. She divorced this man and raised her child alone. Susie met Alan in the church where she found the Lord and they both sang in the same group. Alan seemed fun when performing and Susie was so glad to find a "straight man" who was loving and not abusive.

When they got married Susie found that Alan wasn't much fun "off stage." He'd been a meticulous Melancholy bachelor and he didn't want her to touch anything. Nothing she did was right and although he didn't hit her, he nit-picked her to death and abused her verbally and emotionally. By the time we saw them, they were ready to separate. She was swinging in and out of her moods and he was depressed at her imperfections.

It was easy to see why Sanguine Susie had put on a mask of pain but I didn't know how Alan could possibly see himself as Sanguine. As I questioned him on his childhood, he told me how his family had been a traveling Christian singing group. The mother was a jolly, chubby, foot-tapping gospel singer and his father was the Melancholy arranger. His two Sanguine sisters got all the attention on stage and without knowing what he was doing, he put on the mask of popularity and tried to be the life of the party. As an adult he still wore the mask on stage in his singing groups but took it off as he headed into the wings.

This double-masked couple was headed for divorce because they had no tool to use in examining their problems. Once we showed them what they were doing to each other and why, they were able to reverse their destructive path.

As you start on your journey to free your mind from memories that bind, search your past for any masks you may have put on for self-preservation. Use the Personality Profile to give you a basis for your patterns of behavior and then walk through this book step by step to a freedom and peace that passes all understanding.

3

SEDUCTION, SUBJUGATION OR SATANISM?

You show no shame for the way you abuse me
(Job 19:3, TEV).

In the past twenty years Fred and I have loved teaching the concept of the four personalities to Christian groups, and we have seen amazing results. People have suddenly realized that just because their spouse is different doesn't mean he or she is necessarily wrong.

Among the positive responses were people who couldn't figure themselves out, ones with "split personalities," ones who vacillated between highs and lows, ones who no longer found joy in their Christian life. As we prayed, questioned, studied and thought about these conflicts and confusions, we began to uproot deep resentments toward parents and indications of abuse in fine Christian homes. At first we tried to look the other way, assumed we'd found exceptional cases, and hoped we wouldn't have to deal with these problems. But they didn't go away. In fact, everywhere we went desperate people poured out of the pews and begged for answers. Our office phones rang for help and Fred found himself counseling men and women from all over the country and Canada. Many had already sought counsel and had been told everything from "Just pray about it" to "You'd better check into the mental hospital immediately." There had to be a middle road—

Bible-based answers with practical steps to emotional and spiritual freedom.

Before any of us can help ourselves or comfort others we have to become aware of the validated fact that physical, sexual and emotional abuse does take place in good Christian homes.

> Being in a family that is "religious," even "evangelical" or "fundamental," does not guarantee a youngster protection from sexual abuse. . . . The problem exists. Because we want it to go away does not mean that it will go away. Our very silence allows it to grow to horrifying proportions. Abused children all too frequently become adults who abuse their own children. The sins of the father are being visited upon the children. Silence will not help survivors pick up the pieces of long-term sexual problems, wretched self-images, or severe personality disorders. Nor will silence confront the guilty with their need of confession, forgiveness, and redemption. Two things need to be broken—first our long, uneasy silence; then as a consequence, the cycle of sexual abuse.
>
> The church, empowered by the living Christ, is able to offer healing through supportive, loving community only when we lose our fear of walking into the hell of pain-filled lives so that the abused as well as the abuser can be set free.[1]

Physical Abuse

Physical abuse obviously entails any blows to the body, any curtailment of movement such as being tied up, even tickling if the child is held down and can't get away. Extreme punishments we have heard about include children being held upside down for long periods of time; being beaten and locked in a closet, tied to a tree, chair or bed post; being deprived of food and water. Once physically abused, the child will react negatively to even the threat of mistreatment and the sight of the weapon constantly hanging in view will produce a nervous and unbalanced child.

Emotional and Verbal Abuse

Emotional and verbal abuse comes from hostile, demeaning and threatening words. Sighs, shrugs and hopeless glances are often enough to put a child into despair.

The death, divorce, or other departure of a parent without positive emotional support can be the start of lifetime feelings of rejection. Being pointed out as "a mistake," "the one we didn't want," "the dumb one," or "the homely one" can cause a hopelessly low self-image. One friend I had who hated to go shopping for clothes finally explained that her mother would always say to the salesgirl, "If you can find anything that will look good on *this* one, it will be a miracle."

Constant yelling, nit-picking, and negative comments or any treatment that belittles children will cause some degree of emotional abuse. Making them wear clothing that sets them apart in a peculiar way is damaging and builds up a base of resentment and anger which will explode at some later time. Making religious practices so heavy and the rules so negative that God becomes an ogre often leads to repressed hostility and later rebellion. Any parental behavior or methods of discipline that stifle natural emotions and degrade the child's worth will often be as damaging as physical abuse.

Over the years Fred and I have observed one family who are considered to be pillars of the church. The father, Dan, had been beaten by his father and he often told of the hostility in his childhood home. He prided himself that he had not laid a hand on little Danny and yet as we visited in their home we saw Dan look down at Danny with anger in his eyes, insult him in front of us, and yell at him if he failed to follow demeaning instructions flawlessly. Both Fred and I wondered if physical abuse could have been much worse and when Fred tried to open up the subject for conversation, Dan scoffed at the possibility that he was not a loving father. Danny is now a teen and could accurately be called "a wimp." He is flunking every subject in school, he trembles at the sound of his father's voice and is unable to communicate with any adult for fear he'll say something wrong and be corrected. He has no drive or enthusiasm for life and he has turned away from God even though he's spent years in Christian school. He is a ripe candidate for drugs and rebellion.

When Dan speaks of Danny, it is with heart-broken disappointment; yet he sees no connection between Danny's failures and his behavior. When my husband tried to talk with him about the problem, Dan rejected even a suggestion. "Everything in my life is going great but Danny. I guess the Lord's given him to me as my thorn in the flesh. It's really no big deal."

But it is a big deal. God gave us these children for our intelligent instruction and spiritual guidance. God planned that our children would be not a thorn in our flesh but an arrow in our quiver.

> Sons are a heritage from the Lord,
> children a reward from him.
> Like arrows in the hands of a warrior
> are sons born in one's youth.
> Blessed is the man
> whose quiver is full of them (Psalm 127:3-5, NIV).

Sexual Abuse

Forms of sexual abuse include a parent fondling an infant's genitals, ogling the child in puberty, making the pre-teen take showers with the opposite-sex parent, forcing the child to masturbate, insisting on nude swimming together, having the child arouse the parent, exposing himself in a provocative way, or molesting the child by inserting objects in the vagina or rectum. Any violation of an individual's privacy in the sexual area can have life-long effects on emotional behavior and maturity. The aggressor often feels that if he doesn't actually rape the victim, he has caused no harm, but we have talked with women whose fathers did no more than stare at them in the bathtub who manifested severe symptoms of sexual abuse.

Rape is forced sexual intercourse (oral, anal, or vaginal penetration) and incest is sexual contact within the family structure. Until recently incest was narrowed to those related to each other but because of the increase in step-family living, the term has been broadened to include anyone the child accepts as part of the family. In *Betrayal of Innocence*, Susan Forward writes:

> I define incest as any overtly sexual contact between people who are either closely related or perceive themselves to be closely related (including step-parents, step-siblings, half-siblings, and even live-in lovers if they have assumed a parental role). If that special trust that exists between a child and a parent figure or sibling is violated by a sexual act, that act becomes incestuous. . . . Incest generally develops in a troubled family. Rather than causing a breakdown in the family, most incest is a result of such a breakdown. Family members are often emotionally isolated from one another and there is usually a good deal of loneliness and hostility before incest occurs.[2]

No matter what the degree of abuse, the victim always feels guilty. The aggressor puts the blame on the child who readily accepts it and starts a pattern of life-time guilt and blame, assuming responsibilities that are not rightfully hers and making apologies for everyone's mistakes.

A very depressed girl approached me after a Personality Plus seminar and asked if she should read my *Blow Away the Black Clouds.* I asked her how long she'd been depressed and her quick answer was, "Forever."

"Were you an incest victim as a child?"

She hesitated before saying, "Not really." When I asked her what "not really" meant, she replied, "My brother had sex with me for fifteen years and I've felt so guilty. I went to Adults Molested As Children and the counselor told me it wasn't incest because my brother was only two years older than I was. If it wasn't incest, what was it?"

This dear girl had been a victim for fifteen years and in her search for help was told the age of the abuser was a criterion for the label of incest. The counselor may have told her many positive things but her hearing cut off when she was told she wasn't an incest victim. She continued to feel guilty, dirty, worthless and depressed and she wondered why. There is no age limit on incest.

Because of the natural trust of a child for her parents and her love for her siblings,, the violation of her body by a family member is devastating and causes her to say to herself, "I'll never trust anyone again." She becomes suspicious of others and considers herself to be of no worth: "If I were a good girl, he wouldn't have done this." Abuse at home means there's nowhere to run for protection.

Seduction, Subjugation or Satanism

There are many types of sexual abuse, but we will look briefly at three general categories and call them *Seduction, Subjugation* and *Satanism*. Although the latter is what we see the least, there is an increasing use of little children in *Satanic* rituals. These acts are highly abusive and sexual and include tortures too brutal to mention here. Because cases are showing up all over the country with similar satanic patterns, law enforcement agencies are receiving training in how to spot these abuses. As Christians we like to feel these problems are not in our town and that Satan has no power, or we go to the other extreme and blame every misdeed on him.

Subjugation is where the violator takes pleasure in exerting power over the victim. The idea of sexual contact is not only for gratification but for control over another person who is smaller, weaker, and unable to fight back. The molester usually has an extremely low self-image and has often been abused as a child himself (or herself). The perpetrator is often a brother with his friends who want to conquer little sister or a step-father who feels he is owed some action in return for supplying a home for the child.

Excessive use of alcohol by any family member often lowers his sense of responsibility, eliminates his conscience, and puts a tiger in his tank causing him to perform abusive acts he would not do when sober. Drugs can transport the user into a world without inhibitions and drive him into experimentations he can't even remember later.

Mary told Fred about her abusive grandfather with whom she and her mother had lived for many years. When he drank he would come into her room with an axe in his hand and force himself upon her. He let her know if she ever told her mother what he'd done, he would cut her up in pieces with the axe and bury her under the front porch. She lived in terror as he kept the axe on the mantle in full view and she knew he meant business. She never told her mother and now as an adult she lives in that same house. Although her grandfather is dead, she still has physical reactions of fear each time she walks across that porch.

Seduction abuse is often the most difficult for us to comprehend as it combines loving treatment with sexual molestation. The child is told he or she is very special right from the beginning and receives gifts, favors, and extra treats after each sexual encounter. The child who has no frame of reference for parental love assumes this must be the way daddies or mommies behave and yet inside there is a feeling of guilt that belies the words of affection.

One man whose young daughter had told me of his seductive behavior with her was considered by his church to be a model father. "He's so loving with her." "He spends so much time with her." "He just dotes on his little girl." All those things were true but what no one knew at the time was that he had made her into a little wife and had a deeply incestuous relationship with this twelve-year-old girl. As we brought this to the mother's attention she didn't really want to do anything about it as she was content to let the daughter assume her responsibilities. The mother was emotionally immature and still had what she called "a lovey-dovey relationship with Daddy."

The pastor's reaction was, "He's a fine Christian man and I'm sure she was just making it all up." In trying to get some action on the child's need to be rescued from this incestuous lifestyle, I met denial from the father, indifference from the mother and disbelief from the pastor. No one wanted to rock their boat.

People often ask "If there's really incest in the church, why doesn't someone do something about it?" This simple case is an example. If we deny there is a problem we won't have to look at it or do anything about it. Apathy is the easy way out. Look the other way and hope the problem will go away.

If the apostle Paul were to step into such a situation, what would he say? Paul wrote to the church in Corinth, "It is actually reported that there is sexual immorality among you, and of a kind that does not occur even among pagans: A man has his father's wife. And you are proud! Shouldn't you rather have been filled with grief and have put out of your fellowship the man who did this?" (1 Corinthians 5:1-2, NIV) ". . . But now I am writing you that you must not associate with anyone who calls himself a brother but is sexually immoral . . . " (1 Corinthians 5:11, NIV).

In Leviticus 18 God speaks to Moses about unlawful sexual relations. He acknowledges that "everyone is doing it," as we say today, but that the believer must refrain from any immorality. "You must not do as they do in Egypt, where you used to live, you must not do as they do in the land of Canaan, where I am bringing you. Do not follow their practices" (Leviticus 18:1-3, NIV). God doesn't care how many people are doing what, that doesn't change the rules. Among the detailed prohibitions, incest is the first item: "No one is to approach any close relative to have sexual relations. I am the Lord" (Leviticus 18:6, NIV).

Is it time that the church stop accommodating worldly practices and letting them fester quietly, and begin to take a stand by teaching God's rules on sexual morality? Perhaps God is saying to Christians today, "I see you are moving your family from Egypt to Canaan. Those places are known for their immorality and impurities and they don't care about what I think. But you are a believer and you must live by My standards wherever you are. Don't let me hear you say that My morals are out of date, that I'm old-fashioned, that I've not kept up with the times, for my rules are for a reason, not a season."

4

"BUT HE'S A CHRISTIAN..."

I shall weep over many who sinned in the past and have not repented of the immoral things they have done, their sexual sins and lustful deeds (2 Corinthians 12:21).

One of the greatest hindrances to dealing with possible sexual molestation is the idealistic view we hold that a real Christian man, deacon, elder, teacher, pastor or evangelist would never have done "any such thing." Fred and I can understand this optimistic feeling, for only a few years ago we were of the same opinion. We didn't think we'd ever met a victim and surely we'd never find an abuser among the Christian leaders with whom we had frequent fellowship.

Had we given the whole subject a thought we might have pictured the victim in some slum home in New York City, the abuser as some sleazy drug addict hiding out in an alley, and the mother a lazy, apathetic, unkempt woman lolling on a couch in a seedy tenement watching soap operas. Surely these people would not show up in our churches and if they did, one trip to the altar would save their souls, redeem them, clean them up, change their lives, and make them acceptable to God and the rest of us. Oh, how we wanted to believe the happy-ever-after Christian life!

In January 1981 we sponsored the first of what has become our Christian Leaders and Speakers Seminars. During the first sharing time we learned that seven out of the thirty-five outstanding Christian speakers I had personally invited were sex abuse victims. As we continued in CLASS we frequently were faced with leaders who had been abused in some way.

I began to keep records by creating a "Troubles in River City" chart listing about fifty types of negative situations from rape and incest to alcohol and drugs to divorce and depression to bankruptcy and financial failures. On the second day of CLASS we have everyone fill out the chart by checking off any items that have been problems in their life or the life of a close family member. In adding these up we have found that at least 30 percent of the homes have alcoholic traumas and 50 percent of our Christian leadership women have been abused themselves or have a victim in their immediate family. These overwhelming statistics showed Fred and me that there were indeed troubles and someone had better bring the issue of abuse to the fore in the Christian community.

As Paul said to Timothy, "I didn't ask for this job; it was God who appointed me as an apostle-teacher."

Portrait of a Victimizer

Contrary to general opinion, an incest offender usually is not a violent person or an obvious ammoral misfit. Although to describe one abuser to fit all would be as impossible as recounting the life of Abraham Lincoln and assuming all presidents would be like him, there is value in constructing a profile of a possible offender to provide some basics and dispel some myths.

A majority of abusers are religious men who participate in church activities and leadership. Because they know their basic compulsions to family sexual abuse, they tend to build a good reputation in church and community as a cover. One case I know of at this writing is in court. The five-year-old victim gave her mother and grandmother a complete description of what her uncle allegedly did to her. She has the symptoms and a doctor verified the abuse. The uncle, in the tradition of a typical victimizer, has done so well to build his value to the church that the pastor and six church leaders showed up in court to attest to his virtue. Not one of them has any idea that a good Christian man like him could have done any such thing.

Another reason the abuser spends time in church, I assume, is in the hopes the Lord will do a great miracle on him one day without any great work on his part.

The victimizer is often a legalistic Christian holding others to the letter of the law and a moralist who looks down upon those who don't meet his standards. He often picks up current causes, especially if they are against something, and he is definitely opposed to any kind of counseling. He prides himself on being a family man, keeps his children bound quietly and closely to him and is against any family visitation program. He appears very protective of his flock and often doesn't allow them to go on church picnics, campouts, or overnights at a friend's house, "all for their own good." He carries a big Bible, has a ready supply of memorized verses, and says "Amen" loudly at any appropriate moment. When it's his word against a child's, he is programmed to win.

Underneath the religious facade is a lonely man, probably abused as a child, who has deep feelings of inadequacy and wants desperately to be in control of his life or at least someone else's. He is socially immature, unable to relate with others on a feeling level and incapable of discussing anything deeply meaningful with his wife. Their sexual relationship ranges from mechanical to non-existent and he usually feels inadequate and unfulfilled. If anyone really got to know him, they would find a pitiful self-destructive shell of a man.

The probable reason why incest is more prevalent in Christian homes is because this empty man is too religious to have an affair and in seeking some sexual outlet, he turns inward to a family member — usually the oldest, or most available, daughter.

The abuser is clever in covering his tracks, adept at excuses, and convincing in denial. He usually doesn't think he's hurt the child and in some cases even feels he's done her a favor by showing her she's special. If caught he is instantly ready to place the blame on his unresponsive wife and on the victim who seduced him. "If you hadn't been so adorable, appealing, etc., I wouldn't have loved you this much."

Shakespeare wrote in King Richard III:

> And thus I clothe my naked villainy with odd old ends stol'n forth of holy writ.
> And seem a saint when most I play the devil.[1]

5

"WHERE WAS THE MOTHER?"

But they have all turned away
(Psalm 53:3, TEV*).*

The most frequent questions asked when a male-perpetrated incest case comes to light are: "Where was the mother? Didn't she know? Why didn't she stop him?"

We all want answers to these questions and tend to place instant blame on the apparently neglectful mother. There are no accurate statistics because most of these incest cases are never reported, but therapists feel that a majority of these mothers did know at least some of the abuse being put upon their daughters.

One night at a CLASS banquet I went to different tables to ask what each woman remembered about her mother. I was writing *Raising the Curtain on Raising Children* and I wanted some examples of what people would instantly recall about their mothers. At one table, the first four women all said, "She didn't protect me as I thought she would." Each one volunteered that she had been sexually abused by her father and in each case the mother had turned away and done nothing.

The first thing to realize is that many of these mothers have been in some way victimized themselves. Therefore, the thought of sexual molestation is not so shocking as it would be to someone who has not been abused. The mother almost always comes out of a dysfunctional family where learning to deny reality was an essential part of life. To face the day-to-dreary-day existence of an alcoholic father, an

58

often-drugged mother, a brutal brother, a promiscuous sister, or any similar combination, the individuals involved have unwillingly become experts in denial. They've made excuses for why father couldn't go to work or why mother forgot to show up at school for an appointment. Life has become a tragic and deceptive game. When a woman from such a background gets married, she invariably marries a man with the capacity to molest. If she senses her daughter is being "played with" by her husband, she tends to look the other way, hope it's not happening, and deny the possibility.

Incest or Child Abuse

Symptoms

As a child:	Fear	Blame & guilt	Hiding away
	Helplessness	Bedwetting	Asthma
	Inferiority	Nightmares	
As a teen:	Early rebellion	Feeling worthless	Promiscuity
	Acute depression	Talk of suicide	Prostitution
	Looking downward	Running away	
As an adult:	Gaps in memory	Repeated victimization	Flashbacks
	Perfectionism		Migraines
	Sacrifical work	Overweight	Allergies
	Lack of faith in God	Nightmares	
As a wife:	Poor choice of mates	Abusive to children	Lack of trust
	Accepting of abuse	Controlling	Suspicious
	Frigidity	Lack of emotion	Promiscuity
	Extreme anger		

Profile of an Incest Offender (Usually a victim himself)
Rigid, religious, legalistic, high morals
Quiet, well-mannered, withdrawn
Believes in obedient children
Believes in subordination of women

Portrait of the "Unaware" Mother

The mother who consciously or subconsciously allows the damaging activity to proceed is typically a woman who has been victimized herself and who has little interest in sex in marriage. This doesn't mean she hasn't been promis-

cuous as a teen or between marriages, but at the point
where her daughter is being abused she is usually disinterested in sex and is frankly relieved if her husband, as one
woman put it, "lays off me."

She is frequently cold, aloof, and distant with her husband and other family members and she exhibits little
warm affection to her children. Since they are craving attention, the devious seduction by the father initially comes
as a pleasant change from mother's indifference. She is
usually disappointed in how life has turned out, disil-
lusioned because none of her dreams came true and
depressed over her current circumstances. She's given up
on feelings and often plods through life mechanically. The
only way she can handle what's going on around her is to
deny the negatives and hope for a better day tomorrow. The
mother is often resentful toward her own parents and hostile toward her husband and other men.

Frequently, the mother looks for avenues of escape
and according to her background, education and financial
situation, she may seek experiences of different types.
Some look for escape in alcohol and drugs, further widen-
ing their break with reality. Some become obsessively active in church work and trusting the children "to the Lord."
Some become sickly and take to their bed. Some have multiple affairs. Some take courses or go back to college, giving
themselves a positive excuse to get out of the house. Some
go into the work force, finding fulfillment in a job that
diverts their attention from home problems and puts some
cash in their hands. Some spend much of their time at the
country club, the golf course, tennis lessons, aerobics clas-
ses and beauty treatments.

Whatever the avenue of escape, this mother emotionally abandons her family, opening up an easy path for the
father to establish close and often abusive relationships
with the daughters. As the mother tunes out, whether it's
through sickness, work, play or religion, she usually hands
over the household responsibilities to the oldest daughter.
As the daughter becomes the "little mother" she often be-

comes the "little wife."

Although this profile of the co-dependent mother gives typical possibilities, there are obviously many fine Christian mothers who have done all the right things and still have a husband who is secretly seducing their daughters. In no way do we wish to place blame, but only explain some possibilities of why the mother often doesn't seem to know.

The Naive Mother

Another reason the mother may not be aware is if she is a very innocent, unsuspicious woman who never even imagines that her husband, or any man, could be doing any such thing. She has grown up sheltered and hides her eyes from anything that is not pure and virtuous. The husband of this saintly woman practices loving deception and hides his actions carefully. When the molestation comes to the surface, she is in a state of shock and disbelief.

One case like this was Amy Lou, a southern beauty queen. She radiated innocence as she told me about her little six-year-old girl who kept pulling down her panties and those of her friends to look and play with her "private parts." Amy Lou had taken her to three different counselors who, from the description Amy Lou gave, all said it sounded like normal curiosity. As we talked, I showed her the list of child abuse symptoms and she agreed the child had many of them. When she spotted "abnormal fears" and "asthma" she said, "My son has both of those. He is afraid of everything, he wakes up screaming in the night, and he gags with asthma as if he's going to die."

Both of these children had been guilty of molesting neighborhood children, they showed a very early preoccupation with sex, and they each were on medication—the boy for his asthma and the girl for severe headaches.

There was little doubt in my mind that both of these children had been abused—probably by their father whom Amy Lou admitted had a "roving eye" and many affairs over the years. But Amy Lou was shocked, overwhelmed, and about to faint at the thought that her "good Christian husband" could have done something like this.

When asked, the children told how daddy "plays games with us when you're not home." His games were group masturbation from the time they were little, keeping their focus on sex and making them feel it was a fun part of life and all right to teach their friends.

Amy Lou was fearful to confront her husband because "He gets angry when I infer he's done something wrong." He obviously has controlled her with threatened bursts of anger and she has avoided looking for trouble.

Whether the mother has had a history of victimization herself or is so naive and innocent she can't imagine such problems, it is possible for the children to be molested and the mother not be aware.

6

DEVASTATING THE INNOCENT

We were ashamed and disgraced, because we sinned when we were young (Leviticus 31:19).

The Seduction

No child is born with a desire to be abused. But each baby has a longing to be loved, and when this affection is not given naturally in a positive way the child will take whatever attention comes his way. When a little girl is left alone with a father who is a potential perpetrator she doesn't know at first that this stroking and caressing could possibly be wrong. He tells her she's special and she can sense that she is pleasing her daddy. As he becomes more daring, her pleasure may turn to pain and soon she develops a love-hate relationship with her father. She loves the pleasure and hates the pain.

The Shame

Even if a child has never been taught any morals, she still has an inner conscience telling her that what's going on is wrong. She begins to feel dirty, she's ashamed that she allows herself to be used over and over, and she absorbs a guilt that hangs over her for life. She's afraid her friends will find out. She thinks people can tell by looking at her that she's a bad girl. As these feelings of shame flood over her, she may begin to pull her hair toward her face to hide herself or she may actually cower in closets, corners, or under beds. She may gain weight as a barrier to her father's advances. She may try to become perfect in hopes that if she were a good girl he'd leave her alone.

The Silence

Because of her shame and guilt, the child decides to keep silent about her home situation. Sometimes she doesn't want to hurt her mother by letting her know and sometimes she's tried and been rebuffed, never to try again. The perpetrator often uses threats to keep the child quiet: "If you tell, I'll beat you, send you to live with old Uncle Harry, tear all your clothes up, give away your dog." And many other creative threats. He may try pity: "Your mother never loves me and you're all I have." "If you tell on me, they'll put me in jail and you'll have no daddy any more."

The child doesn't know where to turn and so she suffers in silence.

The Secrecy

With one or both parents coming out of homes where denial of problems was the norm, it is easy to see how incest becomes a big secret. "This is just between us." "No one else should ever know." "Your mother would be so upset with you if she knew I loved you most." "This is a secret just between us." "Don't tell your sisters about our special times; they'd be jealous."

As the victim is impressed with the need for secrecy and silence, she often withdraws into a lonely world of her own. What can she talk about with her friends or mother? Her overwhelming concern in life can't be discussed.

Soon her life becomes one of denial and cover-up and it is often in the heartbroken silence of her pain that she wills her mind to draw the curtain on her grief, causing her in later years to have gaps in her childhood memories.

The Stress

When seduction leads to shame, followed by silence and secrecy, stress is the result. How can a child be full of guilt and self-blame, have to keep quiet about the biggest hurt in her life, and secretly cover up for her father's actions and not be under tremendous stress? Such stress leads to being late or absent from school, falling asleep in class, withdrawing from her schoolmates, or becoming a social misfit.

What can she do about it? If she tells Mother, Daddy will be blamed and hurt her even worse. If she reports Daddy to someone he might be taken away to jail and the family would be left with no food or money. All the alternatives look so impossible to the child that she stands the stress for life, developing many psychosomatic symptoms along the way.

The first line I hear from women who were victimized as children is: "I've never told this to anyone in my whole life."

The Sequence in Real Life

Emilie is a teen-age girl who has been through these steps. Her father took a close interest in her from the time she was a baby. He had a double chaise lounge in the basement in front of the TV and he would relax there with her under a big blanket. When I asked the hysterical mother, Bette, if she had not thought it a little odd that her husband had spent sixteen years under a blanket with his daughter in the basement summer and winter alike, she just thought he'd been a loving father.

He had indeed been loving as he'd fondled little Emilie from such a young age that she thought playing with each other under a blanket was what daddies and daughters did. They became an inseparable team and often went on trips together. Bette was glad to be alone and get her work done and she never realized that Emilie had become the little wife. Having come out of an abusive home herself, Bette was relieved that her husband demanded little from her sexually. In her pre-teen years Emilie went from seduction to shame. As her father began to take her to motels to "teach you about life where we won't disturb Mommy," she began to feel that there was something wrong with this activity even though she liked the dedicated attention and fun places he took her to eat afterwards. She told him she'd learned enough and didn't want to do this any more.

He feigned hurt and self-pity and told her he needed her love because "Mommy's too busy all the time." He put guilt upon her by saying, "You're the only person I've ever loved," and so she continued their dates in silence. By her teen years she had few friends because she was "so close" with her father that there was little time for normal activities. People in the church praised him for the time he spent with Emilie and he even started a father-daughter club to promote better relationships.

No one knew their secret.

Finally the seduction, shame, silence and secrecy led to such stress that Emilie told a friend who was inquisitive about sex what she knew from experience. The friend was frightened and told her mother, who called Bette. Upon confrontation Emilie confessed and the father was removed from the home by the authorities. The church was aghast!

The unbelievable conclusion was that when given a choice of which parent to live with, Emilie chose her daddy and she was awarded to him. Even if she ultimately leaves him, her whole perspective on normal sexual relations has been so perverted that she has little chance of a happy marriage.

Bette is divorced, alone and still in a state of shock.

7

THE PRESENTING PROBLEM

Nothing is pure to those who are defiled and un-
believing, because their minds and consciences
have been defiled (Titus 1:15, TEV).

Anyone who has done any type of counseling knows that frequently the presenting problem is not the real problem. In the area of child abuse, the adult seeking help often doesn't consciously remember what happened or doesn't realize that her molestation as a child has any bearing on her current situation.

Many times she will begin with her marriage problems. In the past I would have tried to give her advice on how to be more loving to her husband, assuming that her difficulties were behavioral. Now, if I sense any symptoms of abuse, I move quickly into possible childhood problems to find the source of the pain. So much counseling time is wasted trying to modify people's behavior without taking into account the bleeding wound of childhood abuse. Many victims have already become perfectionists trying desperately to please everyone in hopes they can be relieved of their overwhelming feeling of unexplained guilt. When a counselor only gives them practical ways to improve their behavior it adds to their self-deprecation and low-worth.

Frequently an abuse victim has difficulty in accepting that God loves her unconditionally because her father who said he loved her violated her body. If her earthly father (step-father, uncle, etc.) professed love and at the same time hurt her, how can she believe in a loving God? Our image of God usually ties in with our feelings about our fathers.

"I Had a Normal Childhood..."

I find that a victim with gaps in her memory often uses the sentence, "I had a normal childhood." Also, for the victim, whatever his or her childhood was, it was "normal." One woman on a Sally Jessy Raphael show said, "My father and brother tickled me frequently on my genitals. It wasn't until I was an adult that I realized this wasn't normal."

It never ceases to amaze me how many victims, when they become believing Christians, affiliate with a church where a father-image leader decrees edicts of behavior from the pulpit that are far from "normal." While sounding spiritual, these men may actually be living a totally different lifestyle behind the scenes.

The combination of emotional death, sexual promiscuity, inability to look others in the eye and revulsion toward sex even without the previous symptoms would be strong enough evidence to point to childhood sexual abuse of some sort.

For the typically dysfunctional victim, sex becomes a way of looking for love with all the wrong people. Without some intensive searching of her childhood memories to come up with the cause of the distorted life, a dedicated prayer and study program, and a feeling of forgiveness from the Lord, a victim is patterned for repeating problems.

So many symptoms could not be coincidental. As victims face the possibility of childhood abuse, they can begin the steps that will ultimately free their minds from the memories that bind.

8

BECOMING WILLING

You were the first, not only to act, but also to
be willing to act. On with it then, and finish
the job! (2 Corinthians 8:10-11)

Our Lord is not willing that any should perish eternally or emotionally, but how many of us are willing to do what
it takes to become free? It seems logical that we would all
want to improve our circumstances and yet as I offer alternative possibilities for healing, many choose to do nothing.
The status quo, miserable though it may be, is often the
easiest path. Doing nothing takes no effort and demands
no change. In Philippians 2:13 Paul says, "God is always at
work in you to make you willing and able to obey his good
purpose" (TEV).
   Is it God's good purpose that we be freed of constrict-
ing emotional and physical pains? Of course it is. God is not
glorified by an army of cripples trying to find enough
strength to hoist His banner. He wants us whole and healthy. If it is His will that we be healed then we can know
that He is always at work in us to make us willing and able
to accomplish this feat. He is *at* work to get us *to* work.
   As Christians we often want to improve our situations
but without too much effort on our part. We want spiritual
victories the same way we want to lose weight without ex-
ercising or changing our lifestyle. But to free our minds
from memories that bind takes work on our part.
   Oswald Chambers wrote about people who stopped
short of a complete commitment to Christ, ones who didn't
want to go all the way and do sincere business with God:
"The inevitable process began to work and now you are in

prison, and you will only get out when you have paid the uttermost farthing." Does that sound familiar? Are you for some reason in the prison of your mind? Are you willing to pay the price to get free? The farthing for you will be time to journalize, pray, study and read; it will be time spent with relatives in searching through old closets and finding secret skeletons; it will be a determination to follow through on whatever the Holy Spirit brings to your recall.

Chambers goes on, "God is going to bring you out pure and spotless and undefiled. . . . the moment you are willing that God should alter your disposition, His recreating forces will begin to work. The moment you realize God's purpose, which is to get you rightly related to Himself and then to your fellow men, He will tax the last limit of the universe to help you take the right road. . . . Do now what you will have to do someday."[1]

What a guarantee we have in our Christian faith that God is always at work in us to make us willing and able to obey His purpose; to tax the last limit of the universe to help us take the right road. Yet He's not there to do our work but to equip us to do it. He's not a giant genie in the sky available to do magic tricks when we call on Him, but He will help us to take the right road.

"Why Bother?"

One day after a seminar a group of women waited to talk with me. As I explained that it was hard work to reach back into the past and deal with the powerful memories, one lady asked, "Then why should we bother to do it?" In other words, why not leave well enough alone? I explained that if a person is happy, well adjusted, and has no emotional or physical problems there is no necessity to dig into the past. This analytical search is only for those with unexplained headaches or illnesses, marriage problems, or gaps in their memories. I went on to list symptoms and then asked this woman if she had any. She said, "I might have some, but why should I do something about it now?"

I then shared how many women do not want to look

behind them for explanations of their emotional problems; then when they hit forty the past jumps out from behind a bush and tries to strangle them. By then their defenses are weak and their symptoms intensified.

"I'm forty," she said. "What else happens?"

"Often the headaches become migraines and wipe out your ability to cope."

"I have migraines that sometimes last three weeks. I can't lift my head and any noise about kills me." By now she was less defensive.

I added, "Frequent pain diminishes our ability as wives and mothers and often causes marriage problems."

She started to cry as she added, "My husband told me last week if I didn't shape up and get over my constant ailments he was going to leave me."

Suddenly she answered her own question of why she should bother to deal with her pains of the past. Her marriage and her life were at stake.

One of our CLASS staff is in the process of going back and rebuilding her life from the bottom up. In answer to my question, "Why do you need to do this?" she wrote me:

> I've had numerous emotional and physical symptoms for the past forty years. Prayer alone hasn't brought me healing.
>
> Although the repression of the memories of my molestation was a God-given protection for me as a child, as those memories have recently returned to me I've realized that God wants me to know truth — truth about myself and my feelings about what happened, and truth about Him. It is the truth that sets me free (John 8:32).
>
> In many ways emotionally I'm still that little girl who was molested. Accepting that little girl in her pain and learning to love her rather than hate her gives the Lord freedom to love and nurture her to health. He is helping me change thought and behavior patterns which I've had for many years.
>
> Dealing with the *symptoms* alone doesn't bring healing; dealing with the *root* of the problem does.
>
> "Going back" is a rebuilding process, starting from a new foundation of truth that the Lord gives me.

Here is the essence of a letter we received from Gina, in her very own words:

Dear Fred and Florence,

I have just returned home after the ladies retreat. I have never met anyone before who in less than an hour could understand my feelings of fear and anger without making me feel neurotic or that I was "dwelling in the past."

As the session concluded, I remembered very clearly an incident with my own father that left me feeling guilty and angry. My parents were as far apart as a couple could be and still live in the same house. They never shared a bedroom or any affection or showed much affection for us.

I always felt my father treated me like a wife and not a daughter. I never witnessed any affection toward my sisters from him. I felt I was getting all the attention because of my looks and I never meant much else to him except when he wanted to fool around. One day when I was at least fifteen, as I was home alone, the rough-housing began and I ran to my room thinking he would drop it. But he followed me and ended up on top of me, holding my hands on the bed and kissing my neck. He made it seem like innocent tickling and rough-housing, but it made me scared and uncomfortable.

I got away from him and began to keep my distance from him and not be alone with him. At first I thought I was exaggerating or making a big deal about it, but the more I thought about it then and now, the more uneasy I felt. Why didn't he ever tease any of my sisters? Why wasn't he ever affectionate with my mom? Was this what was making me feel angry, like running away, like crying, like I had done something wrong? I felt like crying a lot, but I didn't know why. I would cry myself to sleep.

I still can't remember anything from before I was seven years old. I show many of the "symptoms" of early sexual abuse such as fear, helplessness, inferiority and guilt as a child, feelings of worthlessness, thoughts of suicide, a feeling of running, and promiscuity as a teen. I have flashbacks to when I was home (and thoughts of being raped or hurt) and migraines.

I have been married ten years this year and have three children. I love them all dearly as well as my husband, but I feel more and more extreme feelings of anger (exploding at little things), a need to be in control of everything at home, lack of trust in everyone, suspicions of many people I know, lack of emotion, loss of interest in sex.

I have also had a problem with fainting and blacking out since I was twenty or so—but there have never been any medical reasons for it. I came home last night and shared your material with my husband. He wanted me to forget it and quit living in the past. He is willing to help me, but I know he doesn't understand.

He came from a broken, alcoholic home, but it doesn't seem to bother him.

Then why do I feel so bothered and angry about my past when people who have had worse pasts can forget theirs? I know my parents would die if I were ever attacked or hurt in an accident or suffered a terrible disease — but they don't know they have hurt me more than any one of those.

I am not a terrible, cranky old hag. I used to be a very pretty, good natured person who wanted to enjoy life. You gave me the courage this weekend to find the reason for the hurts and pain I feel so often.

Gina

Another example of the tragic pain and lifetime distortion from the promised abundant life is the letter we received from Cindy. At the time she wrote the letter, she still had not uncovered the real cause, the source of her "pit of depression."

Dear Florence,

I'm a thirty-nine-year-old mother of three children. My husband and I have been married for nineteen years, and they have not been years of marital bliss. About four years ago I fell into an unimaginable pit of depression. I've never experienced anything so devastating before in my life. During this time I spent a total of ten and one-half months in the psychiatric ward of the hospital, had a total of twenty-two shock treatments and tried to end my life on three separate occasions. At one time while I was in intensive care, after a suicide attempt, the doctors told my husband there was no hope for me and that I should be committed to a long-term facility.

My husband really loves me and stuck by me through it all. So did God, even though many, many times I questioned His presence.

For the first sixteen years of our marriage my husband abused me sexually. He admits that now.

Two years ago I was forcefully raped by two men I worked with. My doctor refuses to talk to me about it; but my pastor, through spiritual guidance, has been able to very carefully help me learn to deal with it. I am now shutting down my emotions completely. It's hard for me to cry, to laugh, to enjoy life. I still desperately need counseling to deal with the depression and the rape. God has been with me through it all even though I questioned His presence so much.

I grew up in a home with four sisters and no brothers. My

father verbally abused all of us while my mother innocently stood by. He's a very negative man. Three of the five of us are seeing psychiatrists. So far I'm the only one who's been hospitalized, but my parents are ashamed that their daughter has psychiatric problems so they avoid talking about it. I've experienced an awful lot of damage from my childhood, especially toward my self-esteem. Most of my childhood is erased from my memory for some unexplainable reason. I'm hoping that someday I'll be able to remember bits and pieces of it.

The Christian world desperately needs people to let them know that there is hope despite all the onslaught of Satan's evil forces.

I feel the need to tell others there is hope, that God really does care, but I don't know where to begin. There's so much to talk about. There is a light at the end of the tunnel for me — my depression has eased up quite a bit as I am now planning for the future. I'm still having trouble getting in touch with my feelings, but I know there is hope for me.

Cindy

If you have had a trouble-free life, if you've been crowned Queen of the May and married Prince Charming, if you've never been depressed for more than an hour at a time and if you have positive loving relationships with all of your family members, you may not need to spend time in introspection and prayer. You may dedicate your spiritual life to intercession and praise — intercession for those less fortunate and praise to God for His bountiful blessings.

But if you have uneasy feelings about yourself, have not lived up to your potential, have limited childhood memories and undiagnosed symptoms, you will want to follow Oswald Chambers' advice: "Do now what you will have to do someday."

9

THE SAVIOR HEALS
(Fred's Story)

*Ye shall know the truth, and the truth shall
make you free (John 8:32).*

"Daddy, we love you too much to let you sink by yourself." Those words, in a five-page letter from one of my daughters, caught my attention. Not fully favorable attention, but I surely had to try to understand what she meant. I loved her, adored her as a near-perfect daughter. But I was confused. What did she mean by "sink by yourself?"

I was a Christian, in fact, very committed to the Lord. I studied frequently, if not daily. Not just casual readings to tell myself I had read the Bible, but in-depth studying with the aid of references. I knew the Word, I loved the Word, and felt God had often spoken to me through His Word. At the age of thirty-seven, after attending a small evangelical church for one year in North Haven, Connecticut, I found life. I had previously spent more than twenty-five years in a cult where I had been taught that they had all truth and the only truth.

When my two sons were not healed of genetic brain defects, Florence and I left "church" altogether for a couple of years. Separately, and under different circumstances, we each received Jesus Christ as Lord and Savior. We began to grow and soon were active and effective bodies serving our Lord. Even though I experienced ups and downs in my new life in the Lord, the "trend line" was always "up." As I continued to grow in knowledge, my faith grew. The Lord changed me. I was, and I felt like, a new person. I had found purpose and peace in my life. But despite my own feelings, there was apparently something in my emotions that I was not seeing.

As I digested the content of my daughter's letter it became clear that my family saw anger in me. How could they see anger in me? I wasn't angry! I was a happy person. I whistled frequently, often without even being aware of it. On some occasions when I would go into a bank or supermarket where I was known, I would be asked, "How come you're not whistling today?" Whistling was just natural for me, a natural sign of a happy person.

But my family didn't see me as a happy person. They saw me as angry. That didn't make sense to me. I was confused, and frankly, I was hurt that they couldn't see the real me!

It was true, if anyone cared to ask, that there were some things deep inside me that frustrated me at times. Mainly, I didn't feel loved. I felt accepted, but I didn't feel supported. I didn't feel that I was really appreciated. I didn't feel that anyone really understood or cared to understand the real me, what it was that made me tick. I did, however, find solace and strength in the knowledge that God did love me, and that Jesus did die for me, and would have died for me alone. His love was the "counter-balance" for the other love I didn't feel I was receiving.

Disappointment → Frustration → Anger

All this added up to disappointment. Continuing disappointment led to frustration. It could also have led to depression, but by God's grace I was spared that. However, I learned later that frustration is at the threshold that crosses over to anger. It was anger that my family saw in me. They saw something in me when I couldn't see it. They had been living for years and years with a father and husband whose hurts and frustrations had become anger, who was a facade of joy and peace that masked the pain underneath. So well was it hidden that even I was unaware of its existence.

When those who loved me tried to reach me with what they saw, I disagreed. I wasn't angry; I had the joy and peace of Jesus in my heart. They weren't seeing the real me.

Who was right? Naturally, for years I thought I was right! The truth was, we were both right. I did have the peace of God and the joy of Jesus much of the time. But there was a deeply repressed anger inside me of which I was seldom aware. My family told me I was "in denial." I denied I was in denial! They insisted. That made me angry! It also proved again to me that no one really cared about how I felt. No one cared enough to try to understand me.

Two Significant Steps

Then two very significant things happened in my life. First, I began to write out (journalize) my prayers to God. It turned out to be such an enriching experience that I have been writing out my prayers daily ever since, missing only a day here and there. I found I did not have to be too busy to put God in first place in my life and in my day. I found I could make the time for Him. Writing out my prayers to the Lord soon became so important to me that I made sure my other activities were scheduled to accommodate my prayer journalizing. Without my being aware of it, God began a work in me, a healing of that hidden anger. It was gradual, a process.

I don't know just when it began or when it became complete. After six months the healing had made substantial progress. Only sporadic traces remained of those feelings of frustration. Proof of this came in a most pleasing way when a young woman spoke to me at the annual Southern California Women's Retreat and said, "I see such a change in you since last year." I was grateful that there was a discernible difference, but it did also make me wonder what she had seen in me the previous year.

The second significant factor happened when, at the suggestion of my family, I entered a two-week period of intensive counseling to uncover the source of that repressed anger whose existence I now recognized. I was surprised to find how much my childhood experiences and feelings were the cause of my feelings of frustration.

I was also shocked to find that some of those experiences were actually a form of sexual abuse, albeit the most minor — but nevertheless devastating to me emotionally. To another person, similar experiences might have had little residual affect, but not so to me with my emotional make-up. I also found that I was a victim of emotional deprivation resulting in deep feelings of rejection which permeated every aspect of my teen, adult, family and business life. After being exposed to victimization in women the preceding few years through our ministry, I suddenly found that I was a victim!

Feelings of Rejection

As the middle of five children, I generally felt left out of the privileges accorded the older two and out of the attention the younger two received. As a child I frequently cried; family movies often show me crying. I remember my brothers and sister called me "La-La." No one told them not to. That didn't do much for my bruised, sensitive nature. I had been an unhappy child, with generally poor peer relationships. Why? Why did I develop these early feelings of rejection, of being unloved, of thinking no one cared about me?

As I explored my childhood experiences and feelings, I couldn't remember being physically loved, nurtured, and cuddled, which is food and nourishment to any child. I have a picture of myself at about the age of three. As I look into the eyes of that little boy, I see no life, no sparkle. There is no joy in his countenance. I can remember only two times in my childhood when I felt love and support from my mother. Both occasions followed a "blow-up" when she got upset with me and I had to apologize and promise that "one day she would be proud of me." In that pledge to my mother I can see that the little boy in me was really crying out for the affirmation he never received. Instead, it should have been the parent telling that to the child. I recognize now that all my life, in my strivings to achieve, I had been trying to fulfill that pledge to her and to make myself feel good about me.

I recalled that my mother frequently "got upset" and often at me. I was always required to apologize because she was upset. My mother was the dominant figure in the home, and though there rarely was a financial crisis that I can remember, it seems we were always involved in the management of an emotional crisis.

I remembered my maternal grandparents who both lived to ninety-seven! I came to realize that they were both master manipulators. Ever since my mother was a child they had so controlled her strong personality that she lost forever a sense of her own true identity. She came to one of our conferences several years ago and in taking the Personality Profile, identified herself as mainly Phlegmatic with some Sanguine. When we asked the conference to break up for discussion into four groups by personality, Mother went in with the Phlegmatics. When Florence (who knew without any question that Mother was very Choleric, with a little Melancholy) dared to suggest she was in the wrong group, Mother banged her fist on the table and vehemently said, "I am a Phlegmatic, and this is where I'm going to stay!" All her reactions, "banging," vehemence and words were Choleric. She didn't have an ounce of Phlegmatic in her! She did not know herself—her personality had been obliterated by her parents. To their last days on this earth, Mother always jumped to their demands.

I later learned that my mother, because of her own mother's interference, married a man (my father) she didn't really love and had five children she never really wanted by him. Although she became a Christian later in her life, she was never able to experience the inner peace and joy that was available to her.

Why My Parents Couldn't Express Love

As children and teenagers, my brothers and I were always involved in athletics. I was competent at all sports but never excelled in any. The one event in my entire life that my father came to see was a mile race when I was in the tenth grade, and he arrived after the race was over. I was hurt but didn't allow myself to think about it.

My father had graduated from Yonkers Central High School in Yonkers, New York, a large suburb just outside the city. I was proud that he had played football and in his senior year was "all county," one of only eleven young men to receive that honor. That meant he was not only an athlete, but a "star"! As I thought about it, I saw that he had four sons, all athletic, but he rarely spent time with any of them developing or encouraging their athletic skills. Why? He was an athlete himself. It dawned on me that this was not natural.

Then I realized I never saw my father upset. I never saw any real physical affection between him and my mother. Why? He either had no emotions or never showed them. I can now see that his emotions must have been totally suppressed as a child by his parents. He was one of six children, and they all seemed to just "miss" in life.

I was able to understand why I never felt loved as a child. Neither of my parents loved themselves or had any idea of how to express love to their children. They were deeply scarred by their childhood. My father had literally no adult emotions at all. Mother's emotions were explosive. She was filled with repressed anger, which periodically erupted.

Little Fred was also deeply scarred. It is no wonder that I carried unmatured emotions of rejection into adulthood. I began to understand why Florence could never fill the craving I had for love, encouragement and support. It wasn't even fair to expect her to fulfill in marriage what my parents had been unable, and had failed, to provide for me as a child. Nevertheless, I still craved that affirmation. Florence tried but eventually gave up trying to satisfy the bottomless pit of my emotional needs. This, in turn, reinforced my feelings of rejection which ultimately only the

Lord could, and did, heal.

During the period of introspection I tried to recall my childhood feelings. I could only remember generalizations. I was unhappy, I was often lonely, I cried, felt unloved, and did things to attract the attention I so wanted. I could remember almost no incidents that gave rise to those feelings. In contrast, I could remember every detail of my childhood home. Rooms, furniture, pictures on the wall, colors, all the specifics are still clear in my mind. But feelings? I couldn't bring them up. I realized why. My feelings had been totally suppressed. I even remember building an emotional wall around me so I could never be hurt again.

Sexual Suppression

Childhood rejection and suppressed emotions were the first areas uncovered. Next I began to examine the sexual aspect of my childhood. Anything that had a sexual connotation had never been discussed or brought into the open in a healthy manner. Normal sexual inquiry would either be passed over, or I would be made to feel I had done or said something terrible. More suppression. This was abuse in its mildest form. It served me poorly in my teen and formative years, and into adult life when things sexual sometimes become compulsive.

When my father died just before my eighteenth birthday, I came home from college for the funeral. Instead of letting me return afterwards, Mother kept me home and moved me into her bedroom, somewhat as a surrogate husband. To this day, I don't fully understand why. My younger brother in high school was at home, had a driver's license, and could do everything I could do for her.

I recalled that during those several years my mother and I were roommates she would often get into bed with me, or I with her, in the evening. We would talk and she would hug me in her arms. It didn't seem strange to me at the time. Finally, Fred was getting the love and attention he had craved and missed so much as a child. But there was one other dynamic of which I was completely unaware.

What must a young man in his late teens or early twenties be careful of if he is in bed with his mother? Though there was no sexual touching, no molesting, no fondling what-soever, I had to be very careful to not allow very normal and natural sexual drives to be activated. I could not allow myself to become aroused while in bed with my mother! Suppression again. Suppression of very real and ap-propriate feelings in an inappropriate situation. This was sexual abuse—not of my body, but of my emotions.

I came to see that I, too, was a victim. Everything sexual had been suppressed throughout my childhood and formative years. Couple that with my somewhat traumatic feelings of rejection and no wonder Florence married an emotional mess when she thought she was getting an at-tractive young man with promise.

The Healing Power of God's Love

I now was able to comprehend why I had such tender compassion in the depths of my soul for women who had been sexually abused in childhood. I could identify with them. I had been there. Now I can understand why God has allowed me to have the knowledge and insight on this sub-ject of sexual abuse that He has given to me. He has now healed me of rejection. I understand fully His acceptance of me, and I no longer crave continuing proof of it from my family. He has healed me of my sexual abuse. I no longer have that periodic compulsion to fixate on things sexual or turn to some extra-marital form of fulfillment of sexual drives as I did when I felt rejected. The actual form of my sexual abuse was relatively minor, but its effect on my emo-tions and behavior was extremely major. But God has healed me and I know that if you are a victim also, He can and will heal you.

He has healed me of my anger, a direct and usually in-evitable result of childhood rejection and sexual abuse. The major part of that healing process was my total commit-ment to the Lord and my deep desire to align my life com-pletely with His. This was accomplished through written prayer and Bible study. Of significant help in speeding the process was my recognition that my parents did the best they could for me. I was not unloved; I didn't *feel loved.* Their shortcomings were not intentional, but circumstantial. I also recognized that they were both victims of emotional deprivation themselves. The unrecognized and repressed anger that I had subconsciously directed toward them was graciously being converted into compassion by the loving Lord who resided in me. Jesus came to set the captive free (Luke 4:18). I was one of those captives, but now, praise God, I am free.

PART II

IDENTIFICATION

*An Inventory to Help You
Discover the Source(s)
of Your Feelings*

READY, AIM, WRITE

Write down in a book everything that I have told you (Jeremiah 30:2, TEV).

As we start our search for freedom, we must first put our feelings on paper exactly as they come to us without editing them for group consumption. We must express our raw inner emotions without running them through our mental purifier that says, "a real Christian wouldn't feel this way."

The idea of expressing our true thoughts on paper is not new. The psalmists cried out their deepest feelings to God. C. S. Lewis in *Reflections on the Psalms* tells about the free, open way in which the psalmists wrote:

> For here one saw a feeling we all know only too well, Resentment, expressing itself with perfect freedom, without disguise, without self-consciousness, without shame—as few but children would express it today . . . Hatred did not need to be disguised for the sake of social decorum or for fear any one would accuse you of neurosis. We therefore see it in its "wild" or natural condition.[1]

In order for our journalizing to have the desired therapeutic effect and not be just a diary of events, we must "let ourselves go" on paper. The inventory of questions that follows will help you to take a candid, thorough look into your past.

As you work through the questions in this inventory, keep a journal and write down what feelings come to you as you answer the questions. We have already found that a combination of these questions and prayerful writing in response to the emotions that arise, will give you a solid start as you begin the healing process. A therapist friend of ours feels that journalizing is so important in counseling victims that she will not talk to them on the phone until they have written down their feelings and crystalized their thoughts. When they call her back they may read what they have written. Frequently, she says, they come up with the answer to their own emotional problems while writing.

Keep your journal private and hidden so that you will be able to express yourself freely. Begin with some positive reflections on "Important People in Your Life" and proceed from there through each section of the inventory. When you have completed Part II, we will discuss the possible significance of your discoveries in Part III.

CAUTION

Some of us have had very hurtful experiences as children. Some of us have suffered vicious acts to our bodies or emotions. Some of us had our spirits broken in pieces by adults who didn't realize what they were doing. Sometimes they did know — sometimes we were knowingly hurt.

Some of us remember quite well what happened, but for others the memories are hazy. Some can remember very little. And some of the exercises you will do on these pages may bring back very hurtful and painful memories. If you find yourself starting to sob or cry uncontrollably, if your body starts to quiver, if you feel intense anger,

DO NOT CONTINUE

without the help of a qualified Christian therapist who is trained in the gentle recollection and resolution of childhood traumas.

We also suggest that you have another trusted person — a spouse, family member or friend — who will encourage you, listen to you, pray for you, and comfort you. Unless your support person is a spouse or adult child, he or she must be of the same sex as you.

A. IMPORTANT PEOPLE IN YOUR LIFE

As you have walked down the pathway of your life there have been people who inspired you, people who encouraged you, people who believed in you, people whom you wanted to be like. These people have had a positive impact on your life. They made you feel good about yourself. Try to think of at least five such people. They might have been a father or mother, a brother or sister, a Sunday school teacher or grade school teacher, a camp counselor or scout leader, a neighbor, relative or friend. Who were these people? Describe them below.

1. Name _____

Relationship to you _____

What they did for you or told you: _____

_____

_____

2. Name _____

Relationship to you _____

What they did for you or told you: _____

_____

_____

3. Name _____

Relationship to you _____

What they did for you or told you: _____

_____

_____

4. Name _____

Relationship to you _____

What they did for you or told you: _____

_____

_____

5. Name _____

Relationship to you _____

What they did for you or told you: _____

_____

_____

B. IMPORTANT EVENTS IN YOUR LIFE

Certain events or things that happened in your life had a significant positive effect on you — perhaps even changed the whole course of your life. What good things have happened in your life? Describe four of them below.

1. Year_____ Where_____

What _____

_____

_____

2. Year_____ Where _____

What _____

_____

_____

3. Year_____ Where _____

What _____

_____

_____

4. Year_____ Where _____

What _____

_____

_____

C. DISAPPOINTMENTS IN YOUR LIFE

While most of us have experienced some important and wonderful events in our lives, we've also had some hurts or disappointments. That's part of the life process. Oftentimes God allows these to happen to help us see our need for Him. What were the three most disappointing or hurting things that happened to you? Describe them below.

1. Year_____ My age_____ What happened? _____

_____

_____

How I felt about it then: _____

_____

What effect I think it has had on me:_____

_____

_____

_____

2. Year_____ My age_____ What happened? _____

_____

_____

How I felt about it then: _____

_____

What effect I think it has had on me:_____

_____

_____

3. Year_____ My age_____ What happened? _____

_____

_____

How I felt about it then: _____

_____

What effect I think it has had on me:_____

_____

_____

1. EARLIEST MEMORIES

How far back into your childhood can you remember? These questions will help you return to your earliest experiences, bringing them back into focus. Knowledge of these will lead to understanding of how they may be affecting your adult emotions and behavior.

1. Think for a moment. What is the earliest scene or memory that comes to you from your childhood? _____

_____

_____

Where does it take place? _____

_____

What are you doing?_____

_____

Who is in the scene with you? _____

_____

Is it a clear scene or a fuzzy scene?_____

Is it a happy scene?_____ How old are you? _____

2. What is the next memory that comes to your mind?

_____

_____

Where does this one take place? _____

_____

What are you doing?_____

_____

What are you wearing? _____

_____

Who is in the scene with you? _____

_____

Is this one a happy memory?_____ Does this scene actually happen before____ or after____ the one you described in #1 (or not sure____)? How old are you in this scene?_____

3. Do you think the earliest age that you have been able to focus on in numbers 1 and 2 above would be normal___ or unusual___ for most people? Do you think your early memories are clearer___ or fuzzier___ than most people would have? Why do you think so?

4. Would you describe your early childhood as happy or as unhappy_____? If you feel it was unhappy, why do you think you felt unhappy?_____

_____

Do you have similar feelings today? Yes___ No___ If so, why do you think you do? _____

_____

If your earliest memories in questions #1 and 2 are later in your childhood than two and one-half or three years, place an X in this box.   ☐

2. MEMORY GAP

By a memory gap, we refer to any portion of your childhood that you can remember little or almost nothing about. Such a period may be between certain ages, for example from five to eight, or it may be from birth to a certain age, perhaps, six. Some adults have very clear memories of almost all of their childhood, with no "missing pieces." Others, especially women, often have very specific "gaps" or no memory at all.

Do you have periods in your childhood where your memory is blank?_____ If your answer is "Yes," or "Not sure," answer each succeeding question carefully. If you have clear memories of your childhood, proceed to the next section.

As you reflect on your childhood, of what years of age do you have little or no memory? _____ to _____ years.

Starting at the eighth grade and going back, list each teacher in school that you can remember. If you can, identify each house or place you lived in for each grade. Write in the street name or some other characteristic of the house or apartment. In the third column, mark an "H" in the space if that was a happy year of your life, a "U" if it was not. Leave blank any spaces you don't know.

	Teacher	House	Happy/ Unhappy
8th Grade:			
7th Grade:			
6th Grade:			
5th Grade:			
4th Grade:			
3rd Grade:			
2nd Grade:			
1st Grade:			
Kindergarten:			
Age Four:			
Age Three:			
Age Two:			

Look back at any blank spaces for teachers. Even if you can't remember their names, but can remember what they looked like, write in a descriptive word. Do the same with houses or places.

Now look back to how you remember each year. Were there any you marked "happy" that you're not sure about now? If so, put a circle around that "H."

It is amazing, but some people have flashes of memory as early as one year old. Where does yours start?_____

Are there "gaps" in your memory record above? If so, place an X in this box.   ☐

3. BAD ROOMS – BAD HOUSES

You have probably had some happy experiences as a child. You likely also have had some unhappy or hurtful experiences. These hurtful experiences may be associated with some particular house you lived in, a certain room in that house, or with the house of a relative or neighbor. If you have difficulty in remembering some of the houses you lived in as a child, stop now for a moment. Pray that the Holy Spirit who guides you into all truth and searches your memory would help you as you answer these questions. If you ask, He will answer.

To assist you in recounting your houses, turn back to Section 2 on page 94 and copy the names or description of your houses or homes in each of your grade school years. Then in the spaces provided, write in the word "good" if you have good *feelings* about that house. If you have negative, confused, unhappy, or bad *feelings* about that house, or about that year of your life, write in the word "bad." If you cannot remember, or simply do not know, put a "?" in the space.

	HOUSE	GOOD – BAD – ?
8th Grade	_____	_____
7th Grade	_____	_____
6th Grade	_____	_____
5th Grade	_____	_____
4th Grade	_____	_____
3rd Grade	_____	_____

2nd Grade   _____   _____

1st Grade   _____   _____

Kindergarten _____   _____

Age Four   _____   _____

Age Three   _____   _____

Age Two   _____   _____

    Look back at your childhood homes and put a circle around every word "bad" that you have written in. Note: If you have no "bad" memory houses, and no "?" houses, skip the rest of this section and go on to the next. If you have only "?" houses, you may want to do this section now, or perhaps, come back to it later.

    A. Starting with the first "bad" house you have circled, where was that house?_____ _____

Check off everything on the list below that you can remember about it that applies:

___ One-story   ___ Apartment   ___ Barn

___ Front porch   ___ Elevator   ___ Brick

___ Fields in back   ___ Basement   ___ Painted

___ Detached garage ___ Fence in front   ___ Attic

___ Two-story   ___ Tool shed   ___ Wood

___ Back porch   ___ Inside garage   ___ Color

___ Woods in back   ___ Fence in back

Your age when you lived there?_____

B. Adults who lived there:

___Mother   ___Uncle/name_____   Age___

___Father   ___Friend/name_____   Age___

____Stepfather   ____Aunt/name_____   Age____

____Stepmother   ____Cousin/name_____   Age____

____Grandmother ____Other/name_____   Age____

____Grandfather

Other children who lived there:

____Brother/name_____ Age____

____Brother/name_____ Age____

____Brother/name_____ Age____

____Sister/name_____ Age____

____Sister/name_____ Age____

____Sister/name_____ Age____

Adults who sometimes visited:

Name_____ Describe_____ Age____

Name_____ Describe_____ Age____

Name_____ Describe_____ Age____

Look back at all the people you remember from that house. Are there any whom you have bad feelings about, any you hate or resent? Any whom you don't ever want to see again because of childhood feelings? If so, put a circle around that name.

Think of any babysitters you might have had in that house. Did any of those "bad" names babysit you?____

Which ones? _____

_____

Were there any babysitters you were afraid of?_____

Why? What do you remember? _____

_____

Who was that person? _____

_____

Try to describe that person: _____

_____

C. The "Bad" House

Do you know why this is a bad house?_____

If your answer is "Yes," describe why you feel that way:

_____

_____

Did someone do something to you that was sexual, that was wrong, that was inappropriate? _____

Do you remember who it was?_____

What happened to you? What was done to you? _____

_____

_____

If your answer is "No," try to remember that house.

Note: That "bad" house may not have been your house. It might have been someone else's house — Grandma's, an aunt or uncle's house, a friend's house, a neighbor's house, perhaps a house where you vacationed in the summer. To help you remember it, if you need to, you might want to draw a simple layout of the house on a separate piece of paper, showing the rooms, stairs, front and back doors, etc.

Now, in your memory, go back to that house. Start walking into the house, walk into each room, into the bathrooms, upstairs, into the basement, into the garage. Try to picture the furniture in each room, the carpet or rug, where the door was, where the window was. Did it have a closet?_____

Is there one room in particular that you can't remember?_____ What room, or whose room is it?_____

_____

Is there one room you don't want to remember?_____

Is there a room that you are afraid to go into?_____

Is it a "bad" room? What room, or whose room is it?

_____

What do you think happened to you in that room?____

_____

_____

As you think of this "bad" room, are you:

___Crying?   ___Shaking?   ___Angry?

___Curious?   ___Tense?   ___Breathing hard?

Do you feel like quitting this memory exercise? _____

Did someone do something to you that was sexual?____
That was wrong?_____ That was inappropriate?_____

What happened to you and who did it? _____

_____

_____

_____

Was there another, or even more, "bad" houses in your earlier childhood? _____ If so, on a separate piece of paper, answer these same questions regarding that other house, or houses.

If you had a "bad" house, or one of your childhood houses had a "bad" room, place an X in this box. ☐

4. MENTAL FLASHES

Mental flashes have some similarity to dreams. They differ in two significant areas—we are awake, and the flashes usually do not tell a story. They are simply a brief mental picture of someone or something. They are sometimes described as visions. They become significant, as with dreams, when they recur over and over. They may be an insight to a long forgotten feeling, event or experience.

Before starting this exercise, relax, sit back, and think. Try to remember any mental pictures that have flashed into your mind at any time of your life. Take your time. Do not rush it. Allow your mind to wander through your past— into your childhood, grade school, summer times, junior high, and even high school

Note: If after ten minutes or so, nothing comes to your mind, you may want to go on to the next section. If at some later time the memory of a mental flash comes to you, return to this page and complete the questions.

Is there a recurring mental picture coming to your mind?_____ How many times would you guess you have seen it?_____ How often do you think you have seen it?

_____

What is it? _____

Describe it: _____

_____

Is it a person?_____ Who is it? _____

Who does it remind you of? _____

How do you feel *now* about that picture?

Angry?____	Happy?____	Disinterested?____
Upset?____	Content?____	Curious?____
Aroused?____	Excited?____	No Feelings?____

If you have answered this section, place an X in this box.   ☐

5. CHILDHOOD PHOTOS

One of the most revealing things you can do to recall your childhood feelings is to look at pictures of yourself. You may be amazed at how much these photos will cause you to remember. If you do have "memory gaps" of your childhood, they will help you fill in the missing pieces of your life.

Get as many pictures together as you can. If you only have a few, ask parents or brothers and sisters. They may have pictures you don't have, especially group pictures of which you are a part. Line them up in chronological order, starting with the earliest. Look at them carefully to see if you are "happy" or "unhappy." Focus particularly on your eyes. The eyes often reveal the inner emotions or hurts that are masked by a "smile for the camera."

1. As you look at your pictures, do you see a child who is often unhappy?_____

2. Are you often crying or sad in the pictures?_____

3. Are you generally happy in the earlier pictures and then later sad?_____ If so, about what age does the change seem to take place? _____ years.

4. Can you "read" anything about your feelings by look-

ing at your eyes?_____ What do you think your little self is feeling? _____

5. Do you think there is any sign of pain or hurt in your eyes?_____

6. As you have looked at these pictures of yourself, do you feel an emotional reaction, a lump in your throat or tears? Anger, a tense feeling, perhaps pains or a headache?_____

If you answered "Yes" to any two of these questions, place an X in this box.   ☐

6. EYES

Eyes are often described as the mirror of the soul. They do frequently reveal how we feel. If we feel good, joyful, and everything is going well, our eyes are likely to be sparkling. If we feel weighted down and depressed, tense or under stress, our eyes may well reveal that. Our eyes also can be clues to our feelings about ourselves as children.

1. Think of your mother; look at her eyes. What do you remember about her from her eyes? Check each word that you think applies. Add any others that come to your mind.

___ Anger	___ Sadness
___ Deadness	___ Sparkling
___ Fear	___ Tenderness
___ Fun	___ Tension
___ Hate	___ Tired
___ Joy	___ _____
___ Life	___ _____
___ Pain	___ _____

____ Intense   ____ _____

____ Lifeless   ____ _____

2. Now think of your father's eyes. Put a circle around each of the words above that you think apply to him.

3. Can you remember anyone in your adult life saying something to you about your eyes looking painful, hurt or sad?_____

4. Look carefully at your eyes in a mirror. What are the first six words that come to your mind describing what you see in your own eyes. Write those words down quickly in the spaces below:

_____   _____   _____

_____   _____   _____

5. If you don't see much of anything in your own eyes, ask someone else to do the same thing, to look into your eyes and tell you the first six words that come to mind describing what they see. Write them down and later enter them in the spaces below.

_____   _____   _____

_____   _____   _____

What do your eyes reveal? Are the words negative such as: sad, hurting, dead, frightened? If so, place an X in this box.   ☐

7. PERSONALITY SPLITS

By personality splits we refer only to your own scored results on the Personality Profile found earlier in this book. In no manner do we refer to the term in the clinical psychology sense. How you evaluate yourself often reveals how your childhood has affected your adult personality. Look at your score on your own personality profile:

1. Did you score fairly evenly in three columns?_____

2. Did you score fairly evenly in four columns?_____

3. Did you score predominantly in the Sanguine and Melancholy columns?_____

4. Did you score predominantly in the Choleric and Phlegmatic columns?_____

If you answered "Yes" to any one of these questions, put an X in this box.   ☐

8. DREAMS

1. Can you think of some dream that you have enjoyed over and over again, a dream that has recurred several times, that was fun, pleasant, or gave you good feelings? _____ What were you doing in that dream?_____

_____

_____

2. Do you sometimes wish you didn't have to go to sleep because you were afraid of the bad dream you might have during the night?_____ Where does it take place?

_____

Who else appears in that dream? _____

_____

3. Think back to your childhood. What dream did you have again and again that was "bad," or scary?_____

_____

How old are you in the dream?_____

Where does it take place? _____

Can you describe the room or the place? _____

What are you doing?_____

_____

How do you feel? _____

_____

Describe the other people in that dream:

Person #1: Man?_____ Woman?_____ What does
he/she look like? _____

_____

What is he/she wearing? _____

Is he/she trying to hurt you?_____ How?_____

_____

Where? _____

Is he/she holding you?_____ How? _____

_____

Person #2: Man?_____ Woman?_____ What does
he/she look like? _____

_____

What is he/she wearing? _____

Is he/she trying to hurt you?_____ How?_____

_____

Where? _____

Is he/she holding you?_____ How? _____

_____

Whom do you think Person #1 looks like? _____

Is it that person? Yes_____ No_____ Not sure_____

Whom do you think Person #2 looks like? _____

Is it that person? Yes_____ No_____ Not sure_____

How does the dream end? _____

_____

How do you feel when you wake up? _____

_____

Has that dream continued into adulthood? _____

_____

4. Have you had a "bad" dream in your adult life that
has happened several times (and is a different one from
the one you described in #3 above)?_____ How old are
you in the dream?_____

Where does it take place? _____

Can you describe the room or the place? _____

What are you doing?_____

How do you feel?_____

_____

Describe the other people in that dream:

Person #1: Man?_____ Woman?_____ What does
he/she look like? _____

_____

What is he/she wearing? _____

Is he/she trying to hurt you?_____ How?_____

_____

Where? _____

Is he/she holding you?_____ How? _____

_____

What are you doing?_____

How do you feel?_____

_____

Person #2: Man?_____ Woman?_____ What does he/she look like? _____

_____

What is he/she wearing? _____

Is he/she trying to hurt you?_____ How?_____

_____

Where? _____

Is he/she holding you?_____ How? _____

_____

Whom do you think Person #1 looks like? _____

Is it that person? Yes_____ No_____ Not sure_____

Whom do you think Person #2 looks like? _____

How does the dream end?_____

_____

How do you feel when you wake up? _____

If you have answered questions #2, 3, or 4, place an X in this box.   □

9. REJECTION

It is a rare person who can say he truly had a happy childhood. Almost universal are early feelings of rejection, some severe enough to make successful adult relationships close to impossible.

YES   NO

____   ____   1. Did you feel as a child that your brothers and sisters got more attention and privileges than you?

____   ____   2. Did you feel that you were not loved as a child?

____   ____   3. Do you remember crying yourself to sleep at night?

____   ____   4. Did you feel that your parents didn't come to your special events, plays, recitals, performances, races, etc., as much as the other children's parents came?

____   ____   5. In your early teens, did you sometimes think of running away because no one really cared about you?

____   ____   6. Did you sometimes hug yourself in bed because you simply needed to be hugged?

____   ____   7. Did you sometimes wonder as a child why you were ever born?

____   ____   8. Did you know as early as you can remember that you were not wanted, or that your parents really wanted a boy (or girl)?

_____ _____ 9. Did your mother ever say, "If it weren't for you kids, I could have been..."?

If you answered "Yes" to two of these questions, place an X in this box.   □

10. AGE FORTY

YES   NO

_____ _____ Are you about forty years old and does your life seem to be coming apart at the seams? Are things which you have been able to keep under control suddenly appearing to get the best of you? Does your family wonder what is happening to you?

If you answered "Yes," place an X in this box.   □

11. DEPRESSION

Depression—the major malady among Christians. What is it? What can I do about it? Where does it come from? Why can't I get victory over it? There are answers; and those answers will come! First, are you one who suffers from depression?

YES   NO

_____ _____ 1. Do you frequently wake up in the morning thinking it will not be worth it to get up?

_____ _____ 2. Do you have feelings that your circumstances in life will never change?

_____ _____ 3. Is your life "out of control"?

_____ _____ 4. Do the words tense, stressed, confused, disappointed, discouraged, often describe how you feel?

___ ___ 5. Do you often feel that you're not worth anything, or that life is not worth living?

___ ___ 6. As a child would you say that you generally felt bad or depressed?

7. Which of these words apply to you?

___Passive   ___I've quit caring   ___Fatigued

___Suicidal   ___Wanting Drugs   ___Blue

___Pessimistic   ___Needing a drink   ___Unloved

___Hopelessness___Overeating   ___Insomnia

___Withdrawn   ___Loss of interest

If you've answered "Yes," or several of the words above apply, place an X in this box.   □

12. ANGER

As one of the most common emotions, anger may be defined as a reaction to that which displeases us. In its most intense state it becomes rage, evidenced by a loss of self-control. At that point it becomes essential to identify it as we search for its root. Did God give you anger at birth or was it put into you?

YES NO

___ ___ 1. Do you feel uncontrollable anger is a problem for you?

___ ___ 2. Would your family describe you as one who is easily angered?

___ ___ 3. At work, do you have a reputation for "blowing up"?

___ ___ 4. Do you tend to get mad at things that you later realize weren't all that important?

_____ _____ 5. Do your children obey you because they are afraid of you?

_____ _____ 6. Have you found yourself wildly flaring up at your children when they displease or disobey you?

_____ _____ 7. As a child, do you remember getting angry frequently?

_____ _____ 8. When you do get angry, does your face get red, does your "blood boil," or do you clench your fists?

When was the last time you really got mad?_____

_____

What got you mad?_____

What happened? _____

_____

As a teenager, what was the worst experience of anger you can remember? _____

_____

In elementary school, can you remember ever getting really angry?_____ Who or what caused it? _____

_____

Think hard to your early childhood at home. What was the *first time* you got very upset? _____

_____

Why? _____

Look at your answers to these last few questions. What

similarity do you see?_____

_____

Therefore, is anger a problem for you? If so, put an X in this box.   ☐

13. LIFE OF SERVICE

YES NO

____ ____ 1. As you were entering adulthood did you feel it was important to follow a life of service where your life could be used to help the downtrodden?

____ ____ 2. Have you served in the Peace Corps or some other low income but worthy altruistic endeavor?

____ ____ 3. Have you had a desire to go into some kind of social work, such as for battered wives, abused children, sex abuse clinics?

____ ____ 4. Have you served or wanted to serve as a missionary to a foreign land?

____ ____ 5. Do you sometimes feel that God really couldn't accept you the way you are, and you therefore must work to earn His approval?

____ ____ 6. Do you sometimes feel dirty and wonder why anyone would want you as a friend?

If you answered "Yes" to two or more of these questions, place an X in this box.   ☐

14. PHYSICAL FEATURES

Without realizing it, many of us adopt certain physical or outward characteristics as a subconscious response to previous hurtful experiences.

YES NO

____ ____ 1. Do you tend to wear your hair in such a way that it covers, or closely frames, much of your face?

____ ____ 2. Do you often find yourself looking down, mostly because you don't feel good about yourself?

____ ____ 3. As a child, can you remember either parent, or a teacher, frequently getting after you because you were always looking down, or away?

____ ____ 4. If someone else were to describe the way you walk, would they say you shuffle or drag your feet?

____ ____ 5. Are you significantly heavier than normal for your height and age and really don't want to or are afraid to lose weight?

____ ____ 6. When you are discussing deeper things, such as feelings, with someone (especially of the opposite sex) do you have difficulty looking the other person in the eye?

____ ____ 7. Did anyone ever tell you that you were a homely, plain, skinny, fat or ugly child? Who? _____

____ ____ 8. When people compliment you today do you think they are just trying to make you feel good?

___ ___ 9. Do you often feel ugly and wonder how anyone could ever love you?

If you answered "Yes" to any of these questions, place an X in this box. ☐

15. SLEEPLESSNESS

YES NO

___ ___ 1. Do you often have to take sleeping pills in order to get a decent night's sleep?

___ ___ 2. Do you find that violent, sensuous or abusive movies tend to keep you awake at night?

___ ___ 3. Have you developed your own special routine or plan to get you relaxed enough to fall asleep?

___ ___ 4. Are you apt to toss for hours before going to sleep, with your mind working overtime on mostly negative thoughts?

___ ___ 5. Upon awakening from a bad dream, are you often afraid that you won't be able to go back to sleep?

___ ___ 6. Do you have a vague feeling that something is going to happen to you during the night?

___ ___ 7. Do you tend to overreact to noises during the night?

If you answered "Yes" to one of these questions, place an X in this box. ☐

16. PAINS, MIGRAINES AND UNDIAGNOSED PROBLEMS

Deep and unresolved emotional feelings, continuing depression, frequent or prolonged anxiety or stress, are readily recognized by medical practitioners as having physical manifestations. That boiling kettle of despair eventually seeps into our physical system and causes pain.

YES   NO

____ ____   1. Do you have internal pains, aches in your joints, or pelvic problems for which you are now taking medication?

____ ____   2. Has your doctor told you after exhaustive tests that he can't find any valid reason for your pains?

____ ____   3. Are you susceptible to unexplained hurts or bleeding of the uterine area?

____ ____   4. Do you frequently have migraine headaches for no known reason?

____ ____   5. Are you plagued with colitis or bowel problems?

____ ____   6. Have you been called a "hypochondriac" because you seem to have so many aches and pains, and yet you're the only one who knows that they are real?

____ ____   7. Do you frequently feel pain during sexual relations, even after medical examination finds nothing abnormal?

____ ____   8. Are you taking depression medication if there is no known cause for your depression?

___ ___ 9. Do you have any unusual allergies that have defied medical analysis and explanation?

If you have answered "Yes" to two or more of these questions, place an X in this box.   ☐

17. PMS

YES   NO

___ ___ Are you subject to long or short attacks of PMS (pre-menstrual or post-menstrual syndrome)? PMS may be characterized by severe cramps for several days, strong emotional tensions, over-reaction to normal life circumstances, frequent crying, deep depression, loss of sleep.

If you answered "Yes," place an X in this box.   ☐

18. ASTHMA, CHOKING AND GAGGING

YES   NO

___ ___ 1. Have you been plagued with asthma since you were a child? When was your first attack? _____

___ ___ 2. Do you sometimes have an unexplained fear that you are choking or will choke to death?

___ ___ 3. Do you sometimes start coughing and feel you're going to gag, you can't swallow, or you can't breathe?

If you answered "Yes" to any of these questions, place an X in the box.   ☐

19. HATRED AND RESENTMENT

Not every person we have met in our life's journey has been kind. Some were thoughtless, some were angry, some may have hurt us, some may have been cruel. As a result of the way you were treated as a child, you developed natural feelings about various people. Some were good and loving feelings. Some may have been just the opposite — resentment, even hatred.

1. As you think of the people listed below, place a check mark next to any one to whom you have feelings of deep resentment or hatred. Write his or her name in the space:

NAME

____ Father _____

____ Mother _____

____ Older brother _____

____ Older sister _____

____ Grandfather _____

____ Grandmother _____

____ Uncle _____

____ Aunt _____

____ Cousin _____

____ Neighbor _____

____ School teacher _____

____ Sunday school teacher _____

____ Scout leader _____

____ Babysitter _____

____ Youth leader _____

____ _____

____ _____

____ _____

____ _____

2. Do you know why you have these deep feelings toward them?_____

3. Why do you think you have these feelings of hate for them?_____

_____

4. Do you think any of them might have touched you sexually, or inappropriately?_____

If you answered "No" to number 2, or "Yes" to number 4, place an "X" in the box. Did you sense any emotional reactions as you answered these questions? If so, place an "X" in this box.   ☐

20. OBSESSIONS

Obsessions are similar to compulsions, but do not involve an action; rather, they involve an attitude or feeling. They are continuing preoccupations with disturbing or unreasonable feelings. A person may be obsessed with feelings of danger and insecurity; however, that obsession becomes a compulsion if she continually checks again and again to make sure doors are locked and that no one is lurking in the closets or under beds.

Place a check mark in front of each line below that applies to you. Remember, the question to ask yourself is, "Is this a continuing and disturbing feeling, or one which I think, or my family tells me, that I overdo?"

____ Anxiety

____ Being on time

____ Claustrophobia

____ Digging into family secrets

____ Fear of being followed

____ Fear of being watched

____ Fear of dying

____ Fear of elevators

____ Fear everyone is against me

____ Fear of heights

____ Fear of leaving the house

____ Fear of medical exam of intimate areas

____ Nudity

____ Panic

____ Perfectionism

____ Preoccupation with personal health

____ Excessive personal cleanliness

____ Protecting a parent's reputation

____ Public toilet seats

____ Revenge

____ Sleeping with light on

____ Terror at night

____ Strong sense of inferiority

____ Wearing multiple layers of clothes, especially underwear

If you have checked two or more of these lines, place an X in this box.   ☐

21. COMPULSIONS

Most of us have compulsions of some kind. A compulsion is an irresistible impulse or drive to perform some irrational or uncontrollable act. It is most often something we don't feel good about doing but can't seem to avoid. Even if we "control" it one time, we fail the next. In Romans 7:15, Paul confesses, " . . . that which I am doing, I do not understand; for I am not practicing what I would like to do, but I am doing the very thing I hate" (NASB). Does that sound like the way you sometimes feel?

Place a check mark in front of those irresistable impulses below that you think apply to you. On the blank lines, add any additional ones that come to your mind.

____ Anger	____ Need for frequent sex
____ Cheating	____ Nose-picking
____ Overeating	____ Constant procrastination
____ Eating candy	____ Scratching—Where?
____ Nail biting	____ Excessive house cleaning
____ Excessive talking	____ Screaming
____ Exhibitionism	____ Sex-oriented magazines
____ Fighting	____ Sex-oriented novels
____ Snacking	____ Frequent shopping
____ Gambling	____ Unnecessary buying
____ Stealing	____ Hitting your children
____ Workaholism	____ Homosexual urges
____ Illicit sex	____ X-rated movies
____ Locking doors	____ X-rated videos
____ Masturbation	____ _____

Note: Alcohol, drugs, smoking, and drinking colas and coffee are often compulsions, but they are so often addictive in themselves that they have been intentionally left off this list.

If you have checked two or more of these compulsions or *any one* of those involving sex, place an X in this box. ☐

22. FAMILY ALCOHOLISM

Understanding the presence of alcoholic symptoms in your childhood home will open the doors to give you the insight to begin reckoning with the effects that may be lingering in your adult life today.

YES NO

____ ____ 1. Was heavy drinking in your childhood home either a fact or a frequent matter of contention between your parents?

____ ____ 2. Was either your mother or father often not able to function in the home properly due to drinking?

____ ____ 3. As a child, did you sometimes feel that your needs or feelings were neglected or ignored because of the drinking of either of your parents?

____ ____ 4. Was there a constant cover-up, denial, or refusal to deal with problems in your childhood home?

____ ____ 5. Did you sometimes feel that you had to take control or assume the "role of a parent" because of the inability of your father or mother to do so?

____ ____ 6. As an adult looking back, would you say your father was an alcoholic?

____ ____ 7. Were you afraid of your father when he was, or had been, drinking?

____ ____ 8. Is the smell of liquor on someone's breath today likely to set off emotional or physical reactions in you?

If you answered "Yes" to any one of these questions, place an X in this box.   ☐

23. EATING DISORDERS

YES NO

____ ____ 1. When going to a restaurant with friends do you tend to order a full dinner plate, then "pick at it," and after eating only a bite or two, apologize that you're just not hungry tonight?

____ ____ 2. Do you have trouble keeping food on your stomach?

____ ____ 3. As a child did anyone ever tell you that you are too fat and no one will ever love you the way you are?

____ ____ 4. Has anyone ever suggested to you that you were anorexic?

____ ____ 5. Do you know what bulimia is?

____ ____ 6. Are you bulimic?

____ ____ 7. Did your father or another strong, controlling male in your childhood, say you were too heavy and insist you lose weight?

____ ____ 8. Did you then eat all the junk food you could to be sure you wouldn't lose weight?

____ ____ 9. Did you say, "This is one area that he's not going to control"?

____ ____ 10. Are you constantly on diets or reading diet books?

If you answered "Yes" to two of these questions, put

an X in this box.   ☐

24. HIDDEN URGES

Are there strange feelings within you that surface from time to time? Feelings that you are not comfortable with, or that perhaps you think are not pleasing to God? These hidden urges, strange feelings, or nagging needs have their roots somewhere.

YES   NO

____   ____   1. Have you had desires as an adult to get into bed with, or touch intimately, a person of the same sex?

____   ____   2. As a parent, have you felt like touching your own little child to see if she would get sexually aroused?

____   ____   3. As a teenage babysitter, did you ever play with the intimate areas of the child you were caring for?

____   ____   4. As a child in the age range of seven to ten, do you recall ever getting alone with a younger child and experimenting with his or her body to satisfy some urges within yourself?

____   ____   5. Do you, at this time in your life, have urges to masturbate?

If you have answered "Yes" to one of these questions, put an X in this box.   ☐

25. PERSONAL HYGIENE

In this section you will look at your personal feelings and habits regarding your bodily cleanliness. The extent to which we go to keep clean is founded on our childhood training. It may well have roots in our emotions, how we feel about ourselves, or in the things that have happened to us.

YES   NO

____   ____   1. Do you frequently bathe or shower more than once a day?

____   ____   2. Do you "wash" your mouth with a mouthwash product more than once a day?

____   ____   3. Do you use a mouthwash after brushing your teeth?

____   ____   4. When you brush your teeth, would you say you spend more than a minute to a minute and one-half?

____   ____   5. Is it extremely important to you that your hands always be just as clean as you can get them?

____   ____   6. Are you hesitant, or even afraid, to use public toilets?

____   ____   7. Do you tend to wash your genital and/or anal area each time you use the toilet?

If you answered "Yes" to two or more of these questions, put an X in this box.   □

26. SMELLS, ODORS

YES   NO

____   ____   1. Have you sometimes gotten upset, angry or afraid over some smell or odor that didn't seem to make sense to you?

____ ____ 2. Was it a fragrance, like a man's cologne?

____ ____ 3. A certain food?

____ ____ 4. A medicinal smell?

____ ____ 5. Others?

If you answered "Yes" to one question, place an X in this box.　☐

27. ATTITUDES TOWARD SEX

Sexual differences are a gift of God. How we feel about our sexuality is often a result of what we were told, how we were treated, or the things that have happened to us, especially during our formative years. These have lasting impact into our adult years, and have figured into the development of our past and present attitudes toward sex.

YES　NO

____ ____ 1. Do you, in general, feel that sex is dirty and is not something you should think about?

____ ____ 2. Do you find yourself thinking about sexual things or feelings and wish you hadn't?

____ ____ 3. As a child, did you frequently want to play doctor?

____ ____ 4. As a child, prior to the age of ten, did you sometimes think sensuous thoughts or imagine sexual things?

____ ____ 5. As a young child, prior to the age of eight, did you often rub yourself or play with yourself sexually to make yourself feel good?

____ ____ 6. During this time of your life, did you have a desire to see or touch adult genitals?

____ ____ 7. As a teenager did you have a reluctance or refuse to take showers after P.E.?

____ ____ 8. As a teenager, did you often break off opposite sex relationships because you were afraid of what might develop?

____ ____ 9. As an unmarried adult, have you been reluctant to allow opposite-sex relations to develop from the casual to the deeper and emotional level?

____ ____ 10. If you were promiscuous as a teenage girl, were you generally attracted to men who were (a) older; (b) physically or emotionally abusive; or (c) boys who would have been considered by your family to be "not as good as you"?

11. In marriage, do any of these descriptions apply to your attitudes or feelings about your sexual relationship?

___ Avoid if possible   ___ Frigid

___ Bad flashbacks   ___ Guilt

___ Being "used"   ___ Painful

___ Bound up   ___ Prostitute

___ Causes headaches   ___ Rape

___ Disgusting   ___ Tense

___ Dysfunctional   ___ Very disinterested

___ Fear

If you have answered "Yes" to two or more of these questions, place an X in this box.   ☐

28. REACTION TO POSSIBILITY OF SEXUAL ABUSE

If someone right now were to say to you that they thought there was a good possibility that you had been abused sexually as a child, your *immediate reaction* would be (check off all that apply):

____1. That's impossible. I was brought up in a Christian home.

____ 2. No, I'm sure nothing like that ever happened to me.

____3. That's too disgusting to even think about.

____4. My father was very strict and very protective of all of us.

____5. I don't remember much of my childhood and I surely would have known that.

____6. Oh, I hope not. I doubt I could handle that.

____7. That's interesting; why do you think so?

____8. I'm not aware of any, but I'd be curious to find out.

If you checked off any one statement from #1 - 6, put an X in this box.   ☐

29. NUDITY

In some families private nudity in the home is common. In other homes there is none and even the word itself is a taboo. How a child is raised and later feels about nudity will have lasting effects on her as an adult.

1. What attitude toward nudity was practiced in your childhood home?

____ Open   ____ None   ____ Casual   ____ Taboo

2. As an adult, how do you feel about the way nudity was handled in your childhood home? _____

_____

3. How do you think it has affected your adult attitudes toward nudity? _____

_____

_____

4. Do you feel fearfully uncomfortable or very reluctant to disrobe in a medical office? _____

5. Do you feel uncomfortable or reluctant to undress in front of your spouse? Do you tend to undress in a closet, a far corner, or in the dark? _____

If you are unmarried and answered "Yes" to number 4, or if you are married and answered "Yes" to number 5, put an X in this box.   ☐

30. KNOWN SEXUAL MOLESTATION

In this section you will be asked to briefly recount any inappropriate sexual contact you can remember. It might have been with an opposite-sex person, but could also have been with a same-sex person. Inappropriate physical contact refers to any such event or relationship put upon you as a child. It does not include activities in your teen years or later when you were a willing participant with a non-family member. Also exclude any such contact as a young child with another child the same age (unless, today, you feel it really was inappropriate for that age).

CAUTION AGAIN

Some of this may be too painful to remember without the help of a loving, supporting person. If so, wait until that person is with you before proceeding.

---

1. Do you remember any inappropriate fondling or touching of you as a child? _____ If so, who was the person involved? _____ About how many times do you think it happened? _____

2. As a child do you ever remember being made to touch a man's (or a woman's) genitals? _____ If so, who was it? _____ How often do you think it happened? _____

How did you feel about it then? _____

_____

How do you feel about it now? _____

_____

3. Were there any other similar incidents as a child that you remember? _____ If so, who was it with and what do you remember? _____

_____

4. Were you ever a victim of date-rape? _____ If so, who was it? _____ Where did it happen? Were you threatened? _____ Were you instructed, under threat, to tell no one? _____ Did that victimization happen again? _____ Were you ever raped by a stranger? ____ Do you still have nightmares about it? ____

If you answered "Yes" to any question in this section, please put an X in this box. ☐

NOTE: It is normal and natural to have feelings of guilt in simply recalling these abusive experiences. Most children who have been sexually abused have been made to feel guilty and that it's all their fault. If you are having feelings of guilt, picture that victimizer in your mind right now and tell him or her that what he/she did to you, an innocent child, was wrong, vicious and abusive. Don't take the blame for what was done to you.

31. AFFAIRS

Contrary to general opinion, most affairs don't start because someone is out looking for a new sex partner but rather because they feel they are not understood at home and their emotional needs are not being met. If there has been sexual abuse in childhood, the person more readily enters into extra-marital affairs.

YES NO

____ ____ 1. Do you feel that your mate doesn't really understand you?

____ ____ 2. Do you have emotional needs that your partner doesn't meet?

____ ____ 3. Is your partner too busy or preoccupied to know you are hurting?

____ ____ 4. Were you promiscuous in your teen years?

____ ____ 5. Have you had any intimate relationships with anyone outside of marriage?

____ ____ 6. Are you currently involved in an affair?

If you've answered "Yes" to four or more of these questions, place an X in this box.   ☐

32. MULTIPLE MARRIAGES

YES　NO

＿＿　＿＿　1. Have you had more than one marriage because of divorce from a previous mate? (If your answer is "No," skip the rest of this section.)

＿＿　＿＿　2. Are you in your third, or more, marriage (not due to the death of a previous mate)?

＿＿　＿＿　3. Do you feel that differing attitudes toward sex were important causes of the breakup of a previous marriage?

＿＿　＿＿　4. Did you have sexual relationships between your marriages?

＿＿　＿＿　5. If so, did you find those experiences to be easier, or more fulfilling, than those in marriage?

＿＿　＿＿　6. Have any of your spouses been abusive, unstable, or alcoholic?

＿＿　＿＿　7. In thinking of why you went into your first marriage, did you get married to "escape"?

If you answered "Yes" to two or more questions, place an X in this box.　☐

33. LITTLE MOTHER SYNDROME

YES　NO

＿＿　＿＿　1. Did you have household responsibilities at an early age?

___ ___ 2. Were you put in charge of your younger siblings?

___ ___ 3. Did your mother leave you at home alone frequently?

___ ___ 4. Did you spend time listening to your father's frustrations?

___ ___ 5. Did you and your father become good friends?

___ ___ 6. Did you ever feel you were "grown up" at a young age?

___ ___ 7. Did you function as a little mother?

If you answered "Yes" to five or more questions, place an X in this box. ☐

34. LACK OF TRUST

YES NO

___ ___ 1. Have you been taken advantage of so many times that you think there is no one you can trust?

___ ___ 2. Did you learn at an early age that you couldn't depend on anyone else?

___ ___ 3. If you were to describe your childhood feelings about your mother, would you say, "She was never there when I needed her?"

___ ___ 4. Do you think most salesmen are basically dishonest and will charge more than they should if they think they can get away with it?

____   ___   5. Do you have a basic distrust of the mo-
tives of most men?

If you answered "Yes" to two or more of these questions, place an X in this box.   ☐

35. OTHER NAMES

Some people change their names during their life.
Others use more than one name, or use several names at
different times and places.

Write your complete name including all middle names
here:_____

Do you like your name? _____ If not, why not? _____

_____

Does one of your names remind you of someone you
don't like? _____ Who is it? _____

Why don't you like that person? _____

_____

Has he/she ever hurt you? _____ Physically? _____
Sexually? _____ Emotionally? _____

What did your parents/family call you as a child? _____

_____

What did your playmates call you? _____

_____

Did you ever change, or want to change, your name in
grade school? _____ To what name? Why did you want
to? _____

_____

Do you have an imaginary friend? _____ What is his/her name? _____

Is he/she always nice? _____ Always bad? _____ Shift with your moods? _____ What does your friend do that you like? _____

_____

What does your friend do that you hate?_____

_____

How long have you had this friend? _____ years

Do you have more than one name for yourself now?____

List all the names you have for yourself. Then, in the center spaces below, check off whether you like or dislike that other name for yourself. In the right-hand section, describe that person, and in what circumstances you are likely to use that name.

NAMES	LIKE	DISLIKE	DESCRIBE
1 _____	___	___	_____
2 _____	___	___	_____
3 _____	___	___	_____
4 _____	___	___	_____
5 _____	___	___	_____
6 _____	___	___	_____

Is one of those persons sometimes trying to hurt the other persons? _____

If you have filled in much of this section, or if you have other names for yourself, place an X in this box. ☐

36. TMJ

If you suffer from TMJ, periodic and severe pain of the jaw, and if dental examination and testing has found no physiological explanation for why you are troubled with it, put an X in this box.   □

37. OUT OF TOUCH WITH GOD

YES   NO

____ ____   1. Do you feel that God is far away?

____ ____   2. Do you try to pray and feel your efforts are going nowhere?

____ ____   3. Do you somehow feel too bad, too dirty, or too distant to talk to God?

____ ____   4. Do you feel unworthy of God's love?

____ ____   5. When others are praising the Lord in church, do you have trouble joining in their praise or prayer?

____ ____   6. Do you sometimes feel that the praise of others is insincere?

____ ____   7. Do you sometimes choke up when you try to pray?

____ ____   8. When you try to get in touch with God, do you sometimes think of your father, your grandfather, or uncle?

If you answered "Yes" to two or more of these questions, place an X in this box.   □

38. GUILT

YES   NO

____   ____   1. Do you sometimes feel dirty and not know why?

____   ____   2. When something goes wrong at home, or someone gets upset, do you often feel it must be your fault?

____   ____   3. As a child, when your parents had an argument, did you feel it was because of you?

____   ____   4. Do you think that your sins are worse than those of others, and wonder how God could ever forgive you?

____   ____   5. As a child, when you had sexual feelings or thoughts, were you apt to feel guilty afterwards?

____   ____   6. When your mother got upset, can you remember her yelling at you, "It's all your fault!"?

____   ____   7. Can you recall your father, grandfather, or some other important male figure in your childhood ever saying to you, "This is our little secret"?

____   ____   8. If so, did you feel guilty about it?

If you answered "Yes" to two or more of these questions, place an X in this box.   ☐

PART III

EXPLANATION

(Fred)

What Your Memories Mean

1. EARLIEST MEMORIES

My heart breaks when I remember the past
(Psalm 42:4, TEV).

The significance of recalling your first memories is to see when your earliest recollection begins, and to develop your understanding of how life experiences may be affecting your adult feelings. Since most people can recall scenes at two and one-half to three years of age, and some even earlier, if you cannot, that could be significant. If your first memory is at age five, it could mean that there were some ugly experiences that were deeply buried so that your emotions could get on with life.

If your earliest memories are sad or hurtful, or even evoke emotional reaction now as you think about them, you may be quite certain that you are still affected by them today. Some of the negative feelings, stress, tension or body aches and pains that you now have are most likely attributable to those earliest emotions and whatever it was that caused them.

Most of us, however, have happy early memories. We are safe in presuming that no child is created with feelings of anger, rejection, hate or depression. God was well pleased with His creation when He created us. He did allow us to have personality strengths and weaknesses, light hair or dark hair, even physical difficulties or disabilities.

There is no evidence, however, to suggest we were created with those dark emotions. They were put into us later. The way we were treated, the things that happened to us, the acts that were done to us — all had their impact upon our childhood feelings. Our bodies grew and matured, but for many of us those emotions never did.

The hurts of childhood may still be hurting you today. They may be affecting your adult behavior far more than you might have believed. For the victim of childhood sexual abuse, or for that child who carried painful feelings of rejection into adulthood, the impact on his or her adult behavior or emotions can be devastating. This is where a knowledgeable professional counselor can and should assist in the process of recognizing the pains of the past, working through them at a pace which is comfortable for you, giving you all the time you need to work through your anger and hurt, providing you with practical strategies to help your recovery. Your ultimate hope is in the healing power of the Lord Jesus Christ. God has promised to comfort, to cleanse all defilement of flesh and spirit, to heal your hurts and emotional wounds. The Scriptures tell us (2 Corinthians 1:7) that we can have a part, a role, in this cleansing process.

2. MEMORY GAP

Their minds indeed were closed (2 Corinthians 3:14, TEV).

Some people have very clear memories of their entire childhood, starting as early as two, and some even back to age one. Hard as it may be to believe, some have sensed emotions or feelings in the womb!

Many others, especially women, remember nothing at all of portions of their childhood, or for the first five or six years. For others the memories in their "gaps" are very spotty. They can recall brief pieces of a scene and there is a blank.

I can remember my own childhood home vividly. I can remember every detail of the house, the yard, the surrounding neighborhood, my grade school, my playmates. However, I can remember very few incidents or events in that period, and virtually none of my feelings or emotions connected with them. As a child, the nature of my upbringing never allowed me to express real feelings. I had to bottle them up inside. I was often unhappy, and frequently cried as a little boy. I even remember consciously building a "wall" around myself so that I couldn't be hurt anymore.

Similarly, the person who has memory gaps has built a wall around the painful, hurtful experiences of childhood. They have suppressed those hurts deeply into their subconscious. They have covered them up in the garbage can of their early life and put the lid on them tightly so as never to be confronted again.

Without exception, every woman with whom we have met to comfort, counsel or console, who has had gaps in memory, also had many of the other symptoms of childhood sexual abuse. It is never a pretty picture to face. Gaps in the memory always (with the possible exception of amnesia due to an accident) seem to be a clear indication that a child's body (and hence her emotions) was defiled by sexual abuse. It was the child's body that suffered so deeply and in some cases repeatedly. With that suffering came intense damage to her emotions. As she grew up her body healed and matured. However, the damaged emotions of the little child were hidden away, sometimes so totally suppressed that even the circumstances that caused them have been completely forgotten, buried in the child's past, too painful to ever face again. Those hidden emotions never had a chance to heal and mature. They have been smoldering for years in that tightly sealed garbage can, causing, in adult years, manifestations of fear, anger, intense jealousy, guilt feelings, obsessions, pains and aches, asthma, and weight problems, to name just a few.

The problem is first compounded when the victim feels guilty over an anger or jealousy she can't control and doesn't understand. It is further worsened when the victim is told by a family member, husband, pastor or counselor that she must learn to control her anger.

It's true, she must. The problem is that she can't. Its source is deeply imbedded in her emotions. You can't simply treat the symptom and expect a healing, any more than you can put salve and a bandage on a boil on the back of your neck and expect it to go away. The pus comes from within. You have to treat the source to heal the boil.

There are many indications in the Scriptures that the Lord required the person seeking Him to focus on the inner source of the problem rather than on the symptom. Peter, in Matthew 14, started to sink while walking to the Lord on the water. He was looking at the wind, the *symptom* of his problem. The Lord told him the *source* of his problem was his faith.

The Canaanite woman in Matthew 15 came to the Lord because she couldn't stand to live with her daughter. The daughter was the *symptom* of her problem. The Lord answered her "not a word" until she bowed down before Him, and said, "Lord, help me." She was the one who needed to be changed; she was the *source* of that poor mother-daughter relationship. The Lord in His perfect wisdom knew it, and waited until she acknowledged that the problem was hers, she was the one who needed help, she was the *source* of the problem. "And her daughter was healed from that very hour."

Heidi called recently from Seattle. She had just read Florence's book, *Blow Away the Black Clouds,* and wanted to know if we could recommend a counselor for depression in her area. I asked her why she thought she needed a counselor. She described her symptoms, which in addition to depression included TMJ, stress, overweight, hypoglycemia, incapacitation due to a back injury, and abdominal pains. She was soon to have exploratory surgery for the pain. Just as my own senses suggested sexual abuse, she added, somewhat matter-of-factly, "and I was date-raped when I was eighteen." As we talked a few more minutes, I strongly suspected the rape, the known victimization, was not the only one. I recommended that she try to locate Jan Frank's book, *A Door of Hope*, at a local Christian bookstore. The very next morning she called again. The Lord had miraculously provided a copy of the book the day before, after her two local bookstores each had just sold their last copy! She had already read almost all of the book, and her husband had been reading as well. She cried through much of it and saw herself in it. She acknowledged she had practically no memories of her childhood from age two and one-half to fifteen. It seemed the lid of her garbage can was ready to be lifted. She was alone at home, however, and since reliving the hurts could be so painful, I suggested we wait until Sunday evening when her husband Steve, whom she said was very supportive, would be available.

On Sunday evening, despite two hours of probing into the dark recesses of her faint memories, we were not able to release the lid. A number of very significant pieces of the puzzle, however, were uncovered. At the end of our conversation, Steve said Heidi had been so afraid the last three days about what she might find, that she wasn't sure she wanted to know. She had tightened the lid down that had seemed so ready to be released. We agreed they would call again Wednesday evening, and that we would all pray that the Holy Spirit would guide Heidi into all truth and bring back to her remembrance those suppressed years.

On Wednesday evening it took only fifty minutes for the smoldering stench of that garbage can to blow off the lid. She was able to remember her father's attempted rape of her when she was two and one-half. She even remembered his anger at his failure because she "was too small and you'll never be able to have babies." After four years of marriage, she has not yet had a child, and the planned exploratory surgery for abdominal pain was to look into that matter as well. At this point, she dropped the phone and ran upstairs screaming. I urged Steve to hang up the phone and go up immediately to comfort his wife. Half an hour later I called back to see how she was. She was doing better, and was in the shower, but Steve said she had remembered many more times when her father had victimized her.

Early the next afternoon Heidi called me again. She had now remembered many additional times to the age of fifteen when she had been molested not only by her father, but by her uncle and grandfather as well. Her mother, for whom she had deep feelings of hate (resulting only partially from frequent vicious beatings as a child) had caught the father on several occasions and only made him promise never to do it again!

Heidi's husband Steve had been calm and comforting the night before. Today he was full of anger and wanted to "punch out his father-in-law," a Bible college graduate and sometimes pastor. Heidi was feeling guilty today over all the problems she was causing! I told her that her feelings were perfectly natural and that she was not the guilty one; she was an innocent victim as a child, starting at the age of two and one-half.

Later that afternoon Steve called. We discussed his anger and the healing process for both of them. He also told me that Heidi rarely slept well, but the night before when he expected she would be awake until at least 3 o'clock because of all the turmoil, she went right to sleep and had her best night in ages! She had already begun the healing process. She will not be able to wipe out twenty-three years of pain in one night, but she and Steve both are trusting the Lord to heal the damage from those years of brutal victimization that Heidi had totally blocked out of her conscious memory.

Heidi and Steve are very committed Christians. They love, worship and serve the Lord Jesus. But Heidi was still entangled in the unknown web of her emotions, a result of brutal victimization by those who should have protected her. Telling Heidi to cheer up, pray, get on with life and get over her depression would only have been treating the symptoms. It was essential to get to the source of her problems. There is little question that many, if not all, of her physical symptoms will disappear as the Lord completes His healing of her emotions. Together Heidi and the Lord will work on her cleansing process. As Oswald Chambers writes, "Deliverance from sin is not deliverance from human nature."

3. BAD ROOMS – BAD HOUSES

He will bring to light the dark secrets and expose the hidden purposes of people's minds (1 Corinthians 4:5, TEV).

A call came into the office one morning recently from Corpus Christi, Texas. The woman on the line was asking for help with her marriage problems. She told me that both she and her husband had been seeking help from a variety of counselors without any visible success or improvement. When her husband called a couple days later, he said he was feeling better because his counselor had told him he "must assert his position of power in the home."

Both husband and wife indicated they were Christians and were getting Christian counseling. I couldn't think of any place in the Scriptures where a husband is directed to "assert his position of power." The truth is exactly the opposite. Husbands are to love, to give, to submit (Ephesians 5:21-25), to nourish, to cherish, to provide for, to protect, to honor, to regard the other as more important, to be selfless!

As I began to share with the husband what the Scriptures say his role should be, he suddenly became "rushed," thanked me for my time and concluded the call. He simply did not want to know what he could do to help his wife through the real source of their marriage problems, the truth his wife had uncovered during my conversation with her.

As the wife shared with me some of the characteristics of their relationship (stress, tension, anger, sexual dysfunction) it seemed clear that there was sexual victimization somewhere in her childhood.

We began reviewing her homes, and quickly arrived at the first home she remembered, her house in Wyoming. She couldn't remember it well, but as we began to walk through her memories of it, room by room, she recalled that there was a porch on one side of the house, with a door from the porch to her room. She remembered three very significant things: First, she didn't like that porch; second, she could not go to sleep unless the light was lit on the porch; and third, she always insisted that the door between her room and the porch be locked.

Suddenly, and quickly, we had uncovered important evidence of a bad room in a bad house. Next I asked her to try to picture any person she didn't like or was afraid of in that room. Without a moment's hesitation she said, "It could have been my uncle, or that weird boy who lived next door!" In an instant she knew that one of them had come into her room one night, through the porch door, and molested her. That explained why she was afraid of the dark, always wanted the door locked, why her room was a bad room. Within less than twenty-five minutes the Holy Spirit had led her into the remembrance of that which all her hours of counseling had never even approached. She had now uncovered the root cause of their marriage problems.

It was as though she had a new lease on life. She had prodded her reluctant husband to call two days later, but tragically he had no interest in knowing what his role must be in the recovery of his wife's emotions and the restoration of their marriage relationship. He was not willing to see that he was the *secondary victim* of his wife's childhood sexual abuse. Most such men have no idea how deeply such trauma affects their wife's emotions, and their ability to have normal and healthy physical, as well as emotional, communion. Their wives have been mindlessly deprived of the gift God originally gave them at birth. They no longer have the ability to respond to their husbands. It has been stolen from them — until it is restored in the healing process of the Lord.

Without such restoration, there is disappointment, frustration, and dysfunction in virtually every marriage where one of the partners has been victimized, and these frequently end in divorce, remarriage, and divorce again. Men need to recognize and accept the fact that they, too, are victims — secondary victims. Don Frank, high school teacher, college basketball coach, father and husband (of Jan Frank, author of *A Door of Hope*) has an excellent tape entitled, "Are You a Victim of Your Wife's Past?" Don is not a psychologist or a trained counselor, but he has the warm wisdom of the Lord, and the compassion of having been there. His tape is a must for every husband who is a "secondary victim." It is available from both our office and Jan and Don's Free to Care Ministries.

Is there a house, or a room, in your childhood that you

can't remember, a "bad" room? It holds the key to what will unlock the mystery of your hurts and pains. Ask the Holy Spirit to guide you into the truth of the room. It may be painful to uncover the locked-away memories. You may not want to face them. That is normal and natural. No one wants to go looking for pain and hurt. But, "it is God who works in you to will and to act according to his good purpose" (Philippians 2:13, NIV). It is His will that you find "truth in the inner parts . . . wisdom in the innermost place" (Psalm 51:6, NIV) and He will reveal it to you if you ask. "The Lord my God will enlighten my darkness" (Psalm 18:28). But, you must ask. " . . . ye have not, because ye ask not" (James 4:2). Finding the truth is the first step in your healing journey.

4. MENTAL FLASHES

I have seen a vision of cruel events
(Isaiah 21:2, TEV).

Turn back to Part II, Section 4, "Mental Flashes." Did you remember any as you came to that section? If not, re-read those questions. Proceed slowly, allowing the Holy Spirit to search your memories. Does anything come to your mind now? If so, answer those questions before proceeding further.

Mental flashes are instantaneous images that occur in our mind relating to some experience in our deep and distant past. They can be a very significant clue to some incident that was so hurtful or destructive that we have totally suppressed it in our memory bank. We use the term to describe those pictures which have a painful or negative association.

Recurring mental flashes, somewhat similar to recurring bad dreams, are apt to be suppressed pains surging for an outlet and seeping into our conscious thought. Paying attention to what they are trying to tell us can readily lead us to an understanding of the trauma that may have been suppressed.

Ira and Iris came to our office from Colorado seeking help from a lifelong problem. Though both had been active and committed Christians for many years, their marriage was in trouble. Iris felt she could no longer cope with Ira's bisexuality. By virtue of sheer self control, Ira had managed for the past five years to avoid any homosexual encounter, but the temptation was always there. He was a good and attentive husband in the area of daily life. It was in the emotional and physical realm that distance raised its discordant head. Ira had no almost desire for his wife of thirty years.

Five years before, Ira had spent two four-week sessions as an in-patient at a Christian psychiatric clinic, and Iris as the supportive wife had been through two of those weeks for joint therapy. They gained a good understanding of Ira's problem, but no victory other than the success he had at controlling those urges.

In our intensive sessions together, Ira was able to clearly recount his initial seduction at the age of sixteen when his Sunday school teacher took him to the symphony in Cleveland. As they started the three-hour drive home, the teacher asked Ira if he would like to drive. Certainly! Wouldn't any young boy savor the opportunity to be trusted to drive home at night? After some pleasant conversation, Ira felt the teacher's hand on his leg, then gentle massage. It felt good. Then he felt the hand move to his crotch. Next his pants were unzipped, then came fondling, eventually followed by sodomy. Ira was able to relate this sequence of tragic events somewhat casually. It was only the first of many encounters that were to follow in later years, as Ira became both the initiator and the recipient.

I was concerned that Ira had seemed to have no natural internal defenses to this first seduction. I have never had his problem. There have been times in my life when I had sly, but recognizable propositions, which I determinedly discarded. I pictured myself at sixteen in Ira's position. Despite my own feelings of being unloved, of rejection, I would have forcefully pushed such a hand away, or stopped the car, gotten out and hitchhiked home. I knew I would not have tolerated such activity for an instant! Why did Ira? What had happened to his instinctive protection mechanism? I just felt there had to be more.

As we continued to probe into the dark recesses of Ira's childhood memory, he casually mentioned that he saw one picture in his mind, one mental flash, every day of his life. Every day of his life? That had to be significant. I asked Ira to describe it. He also mentioned that he had made the same statement at the clinic, but no one picked up on it, so he dropped it. "What do you see in that picture, Ira?"

"It's just a brief instant, and then it's gone; it's a dark, private part of a woman."

Here was a clue. This is not a normal or natural picture for a man to have every day of his life. We probed further and further back, focusing on the homes of his early childhood. We arrived at an apartment house in Detroit, when he was about three years old. His apartment was on the third floor. More memories began to unfold. One day, as he climbed the stairs alone to his floor, he could see a woman standing in the doorway of the first apartment.

"What was she wearing?"

"Nothing but a garter belt. In fact, I can see her breasts are bare, and the rest of her, too."

The memories became clearer. "And I can see she has a leering look."

"What happened next, Ira?"

"I don't know; that's all I can remember."

"Ira, I want you to try to remember the next or later times when you walked up those stairs by yourself. How did you feel?"

"Oh, I was afraid. I had to get past that door to get to my apartment. I stayed as far from it as I could, and ran."

Now, revulsion swept over my emotions. I sensed in my spirit what had happened. It seemed most likely that this unknown woman, forty-seven years before, had distorted little Ira's natural mechanism and ruined his life forever. She had lured him into her apartment, seduced him, rubbed his little three-year-old innocent head into herself and very likely orally abused him as well. There seemed to be no question what she had done, and I shared with Ira what I felt had happened. As Ira contemplated the impact of this revelation upon his life, although he could not specifically remember any more of the incident, he knew in his heart that this was true. The Holy Spirit gave us a significant breakthrough. Now it was clear why he did not resist the Sunday school teacher thirteen years later. His natural defenses had been weakened, or destroyed, by this early childhood sexual abuse.

It was exactly the same for Heidi, later, when we talked on the phone. Why had she not been able to disentangle herself from the "date-rape" at eighteen? Her defenses had been destroyed by years of sexual abuse, of which she had no memory whatsoever.

That revelation of his childhood seduction was the first step back for Ira. *Awareness is the first step to freedom.* The healing process of the Lord Jesus on Ira's emotions is well underway. Just recently Iris met us at another conference and she said, "Things are much, much better" — and that little twinkle in her eye revealed what she could not bring herself to verbalize. "And we can't thank you enough for what you have done for us."

I had done nothing but be available and willing to use the insight that I know only the Lord gave me. I rejoice because I know that there is hope for victims of sexual abuse. I know that only in the Lord Jesus is there healing, for "the world" offers no hope whatsoever. I know, because He has healed me of my "minor" sexual suppression. Minor it might seem, but it had devastating effects on my adult emotions and behavior. I rejoice, because I know that if you are a victim, He can, He wants to, and He will heal you as well.

5. CHILDHOOD PHOTOS

What we see now is like a dim image
in a mirror (1 Corinthians 13:12, TEV).

Looking at a group of her childhood photos was the

beginning of the breakthrough for Heidi. She had almost no memory of a full thirteen years of her youth, from ages two and one-half to fifteen. All she knew was that they moved often as her father traveled around the country to various construction jobs. She couldn't remember the houses and only vaguely remembered cities or states. A scene here or there is all she could recall.

As Heidi and Steve carefully examined all the pictures they could gather, they clearly saw an unhappy, hurting child. Seeing the dresses and clothes she had on helped bring some repressed memories into focus. In addition, each picture was taken someplace. As they studied the surroundings of each one, the room that was shown, the furniture, the yard, the swing, the car in the picture, the family and relatives, all became important factors in lifting the lid of her long-forgotten past. The photos were a key ingredient in allowing the Holy Spirit several days later to bring back to her remembrance the horrible things that had been done to her as a child. Those photos had been used to guide her into all truth about herself.

As a younger teen I never enjoyed watching our family movies. Why was I not anxious to see them? Because I was always crying, and my family, including my parents, laughed at me and called me "La-La." Why was I always crying in family movies? Because I was an unhappy child and extremely sensitive, frequently thinking people were picking on me, yelling at me or making fun of me—which in fact they were often doing!

Why was I so unhappy, so sensitive? Why did I feel left out, ignored? As I looked back at my early childhood, it became very clear: I never really "felt loved"; I never felt anyone cared about me. Self-centered? Surely! But remember, I was only a child, and it would be another thirty years before I would meet Jesus. My own photos and family movies helped me remember my feelings as a child.

As you look at your own childhood pictures or family movies, allow the Lord to help you remember the people, the circumstances, the places, and the feelings of your past.

In a "Memory Journal" list each picture separately, and describe everything that comes to your mind as you study it: all the people, the places, your clothing and how you felt at the time. Especially record any emotions that rise up in you as you look at each picture today. Even later, as additional memories come to your mind, go back to these same pages in your journal and write them down. These may be vital steps in God's plan of restoration for you.

6. EYES

The eye is the lamp of the body (Matthew 6:22, RSV).

It is not uncommon for a person who has suffered trauma as a child to reflect that residual hurt in her eyes. The most frequent type of look we see is:

Pained Eyes

This person may presently be going through a very painful, seemingly hopeless or traumatic time of life with a load that seems too big a burden to bear. On the other hand, she may have endured a sexual victimization, either known or suppressed, that has left deep wounds which have not yet been healed. We frequently see pained eyes at conferences when women come up after a session to ask questions. Recognizing this enables us to quickly get beyond the "presenting problem" to the "real problem," thereby helping them to focus on the source of their hurts, rather than on the symptom. Pained eyes in a woman who is also very much overweight has proven to be, in our experience, an indication of one who is bearing the burden of sexual abuse.

Kate was the Saturday evening singer at a retreat and although she had a beautiful voice her eyes were filled with pain. I could hardly appreciate her music as I watched her and wondered what had caused her hurts. When she returned to her seat, I moved over next to her and began to talk about her musical ability. The more we conversed the more I was convinced that she was carrying a bucket of burdens. Since our time at dinner was limited, I decided to ask her an opening question. "Where does the pain in your eyes come from?"

She flinched and replied, "What pain?" I then explained how the Lord had given me insight to see pains of the past in hurting eyes. Once I'd explained that the eyes are the mirror of the soul and that when we care about people we can tell from the pain in their eyes when they are in need, Kate started to cry. "If you can see inside of me like that, I might as well tell you that it's my mother. When I was a little girl my father came home one night and found my mother in bed with another woman. He threw them out and they grabbed me out of bed and took me with them. I remember the screaming that went on as they shouted back and forth. I loved my dad but I was never allowed to live with him again. Instead, I spent the next ten years with my mother and her girlfriend. What still hurts me is that she's a Bible study leader and my father has left the church. No one seems to see anything wrong with my mother's living arrangements and they think it's nice that she and her friend are so close."

Kate recounted many bizarre practices that her mother had led her into. Kate had become promiscuous as a teen and had dabbled in drugs. She has been married three times, she swings in and out of different personalities and her current husband says if she doesn't stabilize, he's going to leave.

Kate's life has been badly damaged by her mother's choices and she has to take the burden of her mother's behavior from her shoulders and place it on her mother where it belongs. We prayed together that she could leave these pains of the past with Jesus and that He would free her mind from the memories that bind.

Dead Eyes

This is the look of a person who has already given up hope. She is resigned to live forever with seemingly desperate circumstances. Often, this person has no true sense of why she feels the way she does, why life seems so

hopeless. Even the Christian, who intellectually understands the blessed hope that she has in Jesus, will be incapable of internalizing that truth to reflect the joy to
which she is entitled. It will be difficult for her to accept
the fact that Jesus can, and will, heal her of the deep, deep
pain that is the result of this cavalier defilement of her body
as a child. Often this person will have been the victim of
long-term subjugative penetration, causing her emotions
to die and leaving her without feelings.

Frightened Eyes

This person has probably suffered an attack trauma.
She might have been raped at any age, as an adult or as a
child. This assault on her mind and body was such a shock
that the frightened look is evidence of an understandable
fear of a recurrence at any time without warning. She is always on guard, looking for an escape, almost expecting to
be victimized again. This intense fear of re-attack, even
when it is unknown or unnamed, frequently leads to
phobias, often to agoraphobia, literally fear of the market
place. In practice, fear of the outside world.

Eyes are the mirror of the soul. Sparkle reflects joy.
Serenity reflects inner peace. Conversely, sexual trauma is
reflected by pain, deadness and fear.

7. PERSONALITY SPLITS

*If then your whole body is full of light, having no part
dark, it will be wholly bright (Luke 11:36, RSV).*

Our personality traits are God-given to us, as much as
our physical traits, by birth. He created us and He is well
pleased with His creation. In our studies of the personalities over the past twenty years, we are convinced that
God never created His image and likeness with incom-
patible personalities.

Looking at this simple diagram, the non-blending
combinations are those represented by the broken line and
are diametrically opposite. We do not believe God ever

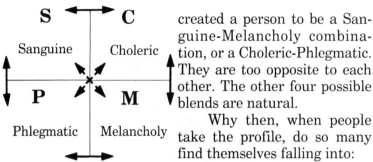

created a person to be a Sanguine-Melancholy combination, or a Choleric-Phlegmatic. They are too opposite to each other. The other four possible blends are natural.

Why then, when people take the profile, do so many find themselves falling into:

a. one of the two unnatural combinations;

b. a combination of three which therefore must include one unnatural combination; or

c. an even combination of all four which then includes both unnatural combinations?

If you found yourself in one of these unnatural blends, the first thing we would suggest is that you retake the profile analysis and as you choose the appropriate word, think of yourself as a young child. With each line, ask yourself, *Which word fit me best at about five or six? Which of the words would my playmates have used to describe me at that time?* That reassessment alone may give you a very different and probably more accurate scoring. If there is no significant change, or if you can't remember that early portion of your childhood, review your profile with a close friend, spouse, or adult son or daughter, who knows you well. They may have a more objective view of the real you.

What then is the reason for differences? Why do you perceive yourself differently today than you did as a child? Why do your friends see a different you? The answer rests in a number of possibilities:

a. You were brought up in an alcoholic home and were forced to play a role that was unnatural.

b. You are a victim of severe rejection and in order to be accepted, approved or liked, you put on a "mask" that was not you.

c. You had at least one highly domineering parent who required you to live up to their expectations instead of maturing in your own natural personality.

d. You were sexually abused, and along with the other distortions, your personality traits took on many opposite characteristics.

e. You have married a mate who expects you to live up to his standards of what kind of person you should be in order for him to accept you and to be happy.

f. Your earlier life may have been so traumatic that you really just do not know who you are.

g. A combination of several of these possibilities may figure in the reason why you see yourself as you do.

After hearing me speak, Rosalind wrote the following letter:

> Your open sharing of the pains and struggles of your life meant so much to me. I was particularly grateful that you spoke openly about childhood sexual trauma. I was a victim of incest and physical torture by my father until I was twelve years old. I first attempted suicide at the age of nine. My sister succeeded in killing herself at age forty and my brother and my mother both went insane.
>
> For years I struggled to keep my sanity. I used to watch children I considered "normal" and then try to act like they did. Being a Sanguine, play-acting came naturally . . . but I grew up not knowing at all who I was, and bearing a terrible stain of guilt inside me for being a "soiled" person.
>
> I used to feel that my body was loathsome beyond words, and that it was constructed of a thin, brittle shell over a black Secret. My real self was the Secret, and what everyone else saw was a veneer which could crack at any moment, because I knew I had constructed it myself out of bits and pieces of other people's reality.
>
> Even as I write these words I weep, but not in the same way that I wept for many years. I have done a good job in constructing a real Self over the years. I know I can function; I have accomplished many things. But thanks to you, out of my experiences this past weekend (when I discovered that I'm not really a failing Melancholy but a repressed Sanguine-Choleric), I have now found out that the little Sanguine girl inside of me can come out and play . . . That it's safe to come out and play now.

Further discussion of why we wear personality "masks" will be found in *Your Personality Tree*, which you will find suggested in the fourth week of the ten week plan.

For the moment, notice the importance of the effect of rejection and abuse. In order to be the real you and to heal those memories that are keeping you in bondage, it will be essential to remove the mask, take it off with joyful abandon and live life as God intended for you.

8. DREAMS

Tell us your dream and we will explain it to you
(Daniel 2:4, TEV*).*

"O, I have passed a miserable night,
So full of ugly sights, of ghastly dreams,
that, as I am a Christian faithful man,
I would not spend another such a night,
though 'twere to buy a world of happy days."
— King Richard, Act I, Scene 4

We don't talk much about dreams in the church, yet the Scriptures make it very clear that God often speaks to us in dreams. Dreams may be symbolic of a message from God. Joseph had the gift of interpreting dreams even as a child. Some dreams are happy dreams. Some are bad, scary or hurtful dreams. Some dreams only happen once, and some recur again and again, sometimes with great intensity. Dreams can be our repressed emotions or memories trying to find expression, searching for release. Understanding our own dreams can be an important confirmation of childhood feelings or the key that opens the door of locked-away experiences of which we have no memory.

For Heidi, one such recurring bad dream was a significant factor in the identification of her trauma and her resulting breakthrough. In the dream that she had over and over again, beginning in her early teen years, she could see herself running and running, trying to escape. Eventually she would approach the town and the hoped-for safety. There always reared up just in front of her a sandy hill that had to be climbed. She would get almost to the top, but not quite make it before she slid down to the bottom. As she looked up there was a man standing in front of her in a dark striped suit with a hat on. But he had no face. Someone else was holding her hands behind her.

As she recounted the dream, I asked her, "What do you feel in that dream?"

"I'm being hurt."

"Then what happens?"

"I die. Each time I had that dream I died."

"Then what happened?"

"Nothing, that's all there was. That was the end. Nothing else happened."

Even though Heidi has had this dream many, many times, there was never a face on the man in the dark striped suit, and she had no idea who it might have been.

I felt it must be significant that she had "died" in the dream. Only once before had I ever heard of anybody dying in a dream. In Marilyn Murray's dream, she literally placed herself in a little coffin and died from the excruciating pain and vicious assault of her gang rape. A new little Marilyn then walked home, the past totally forgotten. I remembered my own "bad dreams." If I was falling off a cliff, I always woke up before I hit bottom. If I was being chased by "bad men," I always woke up just before they would have caught me. Waking up saved me. Heidi told me she died in her dream. Remember, Heidi had virtually no memory of her childhood from about age two and one-half to fifteen.

As Heidi looked back through all the childhood photos she could find, there was one that reminded her of the man in the dream. It was her grandfather. That would later become very important.

The Lord did not allow Heidi to remember too much at one time. It would have been too devastating to her already-fragile emotions. She did uncover the attempted rape by her father and later remembered many more eventually successful incidents. About a week later when I talked to Heidi and Steve again, a new horrible memory had surfaced.

She now remembered very clearly that at the age of twelve she had gone with her parents to another part of the state to a big family wedding. On the day before the big event all the women of the family had gone off to a bridal shower. For some unknown reason, Heidi had been left at the home of the groom with all the men who were having a stag party. During the course of the afternoon, with someone holding her arms and legs, she was pinned down on the floor and forcibly raped by all but two of the men. Most of the men were relatives. She remembered her father making a mild protest. Her grandfather wanted to get in on the game. Her father said "No." She remembers her grandfather saying, "If you try to stop me, I'll spill the beans on what you've been doing with her for years!" That ended the protest. A fifteen-year-old cousin wanted to play. He was told he would have to wait until last since he was the youngest. Only two uncles, she remembered, refused to participate. They stayed in the kitchen. A tragic violation of an innocent, defenseless child.

Later that evening I asked Heidi about the bad dream. Who was the man in the suit with the hat? Without a moment's hesitation she said, "My grandfather."

"And who is holding your arms behind you?"

Just as quickly and with certainty, she replied, "My uncle."

The bad dream that Heidi had experienced for so many years was her horrible, suppressed memories, periodically stirring within, trying to find expression, searching for release.

Look back at your own answers to the questions on dreams. What secrets, what fears are searching for expression? What memories need to be unlocked and cleansed? What are your dreams trying to tell you?

9. REJECTION

The living stone rejected as worthless by men,
but chosen as valuable by God (1 Peter 2:4, TEV).

A child not only thrives on love, but a child also desperately needs love. It is difficult enough for that child who loses one or both parents to death or divorce, but it is far worse for that child who lives with parents who never love her, never nurture her, never cuddle her.

Consider the confusion of that little one who loses a father to divorce, clings to her mother as her only security, and later sees a new father come into the household who takes away the attention and love she depended upon from her mother. Picture the trauma to that little girl if this new father sexually molests her. One of two things is apt to happen. Either she is threatened, "Do not tell your mother," and she doesn't tell mother because mother doesn't seem to be paying any attention to her anyway. Or, she does tell her and Mother doesn't believe her and does nothing to protect her or prevent another recurrence.

The mother, in the latter case, may have been forced to make the choice of protecting her child or protecting her relationship with her new husband upon whom she now depends for emotional, physical and financial security. It is not uncommon for a mother to opt for her own needs, especially if she was molested as a child herself. Unaware of the great damage that has been done to her own emotions, she reasons that she survived and her child will as well.

Not every child who suffers emotional deprivation and who feels rejected has been sexually abused. However, we have never met an adult who was victimized as a child who did not also feel rejected.

Our ability as parents to successfully meet our children's needs is based first on the quality of parenting we received as children, and second, on the knowledge and teaching we sought as adults to supplement what we learned from our own experiences. Cecil Osborne writes, "Ideally, parents should be well-integrated, loving persons with experience and training . . . Most infants are born to parents who are not fully qualified to be parents"[2]

We once heard Dr. Henry Brandt, the respected Christian psychologist, state, "Becoming a qualified parent takes twenty-one years, and by then you're out of a job!" Why doesn't every father and mother then read every possible book on child rearing they can get their hands on? Is it because we are so busy trying to provide the things we perceive they need such as a bigger house, new furniture, better clothes, music lessons, a newer car, that we have no time to provide what they actually require: love, time, attention, ourselves? Your Christian bookstore is full of excellent books on child rearing. How many have you read? An excellent one with which to start your urgent self-training course is Florence's book, *Raising the Curtain on Raising Children,* published by Word, Inc.

We must break the cycle of rejection that seems to be handed down from generation to generation, the result of adults who are physically able to become parents but emotionally unqualified to parent. All of our schooling seems to be designed to teach us only how to make a living. How then are we to learn how to live?

I have learned only in the past year the value of reading and studying. I have probably read more books in this year alone than in the past ten years together. Is it too late, since my own children are grown? No, it's never too late, for everything I have learned is part of my rapidly filling reservoir of useful knowledge, gained from the insight and wisdom of others. Since I am a victim of rejection and the form of sexual abuse we call suppression, my adult emotions and behavior, my relationship with my wife and my three children were seriously affected. Only recently did I learn the basic truth that Barbara Taylor recounts: "You will never feel good about yourself until you reach the root of your problems."[3] Her book was a major building block in my own healing process, and is therefore an essential ingredient prescribed for your own restoration journey.

To be restored from your own feelings of childhood rejection, you, too, will need to read, study, and pray. Read and re-read all the resources you can find, study God's Word voraciously each day, and pray. Pray and pray until you know God better and love Jesus more than anything else on Earth.

Only when you can accept that what you see in your

mirror as worthless is of value to your heavenly Father, will you be free of the pains and rejections of the past.

10. AGE FORTY

This is a time of panic, defeat, and confusion
(Isaiah 22:5, TEV).

We don't have an answer for it yet, but so often when women call our office seeking help, we ask, "How old are you?" We cannot tell you the number of times the answer is forty, or in that range. Marilyn Murray, a professional counselor, confirms that high incidence rate. In her own life, that was when the headaches became so intense, though it was several years before she found the cause.

Florence uses the example of standing in a swimming pool trying to keep a bunch of beach balls under water. You can do that only so long before one tries to pop up. You try to recapture control of that one, only to find another has slipped out of place. Reaching for the second one loosens a third from its secure position. As you grab for it, a fourth escapes until all are popping up all around you and you give up in desperation. Does your life sound like this? Many women who have been victimized manage to keep most of their emotions fairly well under control until about the age of forty, when all the beach balls seem to let go at once.

Dear Mrs. Littauer,

I am forty years old, divorced and unemployed. I am the mother of a wonderful twenty-year-old son who is stationed in Korea, and a beautiful eighteen-year-old daughter who just graduated from high school and lives in the metroplex. I am the eldest of five daughters and have a wonderful mother and father who love God and are my strength. So many wonderful things to be thankful for and I am. I thank God every day.

My problem is me. I am in a pit of depression. I am angry with myself, I feel I have no value to anyone, and the hurting is becoming unbearable. Last fall I rededicated my life to Jesus Christ. There have been many times since last September that the Lord was all I had and all I needed. Every day I spend the mornings reading the Bible, watching TBN, praying or reading books such as yours. I have no friends, no one to call on other than my parents. I have tried not to lean on them too hard because of their age and there are four other daughters who need them also. I would really like to go to Mena, Arkansas and live with them. I feel I could hide there and be safe like a little girl.

Instead I sit in this apartment in Garland alone everyday. I don't know where to turn. I don't know where to go. I have identified all of my symptoms as listed in your book and I want to do something. I am willing. I want to be of some use to someone. I want to be involved. I feel led to help other women. I have asked the Lord to show me clearly what God's plan for my discouraged life is. I know He must want me to do something because I cannot find a job or for that matter I can hardly get an interview in my previous profession.

For eighteen years I have been in banking. I never looked for a job in the past. Other banks would call and offer me more opportunity and money and away I would go. Last May I quit a job that paid $70,000 a year. I was successful, respected and in demand. I never thought there would be any problem in securing employment with my successful background. I quit because the bank changed leadership and the hours I worked along with the stressful situation were making me ill. Since that time the bottom has fallen out of banking in Texas but still there are jobs. Jobs for everyone but me.

Many times in the last year doors have opened wide and just as I stepped through they were slammed tight. I have prayed diligently concerning this and I believe the Lord is closing those doors. I do not think He wants me to go back to banking. They have opened so wide so many times and then closed so quickly. I see people who were fired finding jobs in one week. I do not understand but I am trusting the Lord to lead me through this. I had a beautiful home and I lost it (sold it at a loss). Soon I may not be able to pay what few bills I have.

I want God's will and I want Him to use me in any way He wishes. I need a prayer partner. I need a friend to talk with to pray for me and with me. In my old days I was a woman with a lot of friends but one by one they have gone. I have found I really had few and none who loved Jesus. I would like to be involved with a women's group that meets more than once a month for two hours. I want to attend Bible studies.

I do need help and I can say it out loud. My life has come apart at the seams. An alcoholic husband and a wasted life. I want to use the rest of my years doing what God wants me to do.

11. DEPRESSION

*Ahab slept in the sackcloth, and went about gloomy
and depressed (1 Kings 21:37, TEV).*

The predominant plea of all the letters and calls to our
office is from people seeking relief from depression, often
described as our nation's number one disease. Modern
medicine seems to have no solutions.

Marjorie's daughter asked me during the lunch break
of a women's retreat if I would speak with her mother.
Later that afternoon, Marjorie and I sat down for an hour.
She had been under psychiatric care for the past three
years, receiving regular treatments of medication and
shock therapy.

She told me that most of her life had been a turmoil,
but the last three years had been a "living hell." Was there
a cause for her depression? Was she being treated for the
source of her problem, or merely for the symptom? As we
searched through her life we found nothing that seemed to
be significant, except that she had no memory of her early
childhood.

As we then tried to dig into the dark hole of lost experiences, probing and searching, she finally came up with
just one scant picture. She was four or five years old, living
in New Jersey. She remembers a man in her house. He was
known to the family, but she had no idea who he was. In
her child's-eye view, she could see his pants open, and he
was exposing himself. That's all she could remember.

I was sure she had finally arrived at the source of her
years of turmoil, depression, "living hell." We weren't able
to learn anything more in that hour, but she did have a
sister who was two years older, and I suggested that she
ask her sister to call me. A week later, her sister did call
from Los Angeles. Oh yes, being two years older, she
remembered the situation very well. The man was known
to the family. He was their next-door neighbor, and it didn't
happen once, it happened at least four or five times. And
he didn't only expose himself, "he sometimes had us play

with him. But, that is all it was, and I don't think it has really affected either of us."

No, it hadn't affected them much at all . . . It only had all but destroyed Marjorie's life. And her sister? She said she was just then in the process of terminating her third marriage! Otherwise she had led a normal life. Were we to get deeper into her emotions and memories, she would no doubt have been able to see that the sexual molestation had indeed affected her life and no doubt was a key factor in three failed marriages.

That childhood sexual abuse had devastated the lives of two little girls. Each sister had suffered very differently from the same trauma. For Marjorie it was the source of her life-long battle with depression. No one seemed to know the cause or how to treat it. Marjorie's present condition took forty-five years to develop, so it will also take time to heal. Now that the truth of her past is known, the healing power of her Lord Jesus can be applied to cleanse and heal.

Here are excerpts from a letter we just received from a Tulsa woman, Marlene. She had just heard Florence speak on depression on the radio program, "Hope for the Heart."

Dear Florence,

I realize that depression has played a large role in my life for a long time . . . I went to a psychiatrist for a year and did a lot of crying and dumped a lot out, which has helped some but that was all that was happening. I started bleeding and we couldn't stop it. I had to go in for surgery. If it doesn't stop now . . . the next thing would be to take my uterus out and I don't want that! I am so knocked down now. I feel it was God's will that you were on at this time and I heard you. (Usually I am at work at that time.) I feel this has gone as far as it can go. I have to come back up.

You had more insight and understanding than I have ever heard. I am a Christian and need that input.

The reason I wrote to you—Do you know someone really good on this subject here in Tulsa that I could go to?

My depression started years ago . . . I have an eating problem—Have gone through being extremely tired, and affecting my periods.

I really need help—I am 49 and on my own and have to keep

working. I had to work but I became explosive at work.

The stress of counseling and not getting anywhere is why I am in this condition. Please help. I have not spoken to my mother for a year and a half — which makes me feel guilty and I have been afraid the stress of it has caused my condition to worsen. I have to learn better coping behavior than I have learned. I didn't mean to tell you all this in detail — but I guess I hoped it would help you recommend someone.

Look back carefully at Marlene's letter. See if you can find these many symptoms of sexual abuse: long-term depression, uterine bleeding, "knocked down," eating problem, extreme fatigue, menstrual problems, explosive emotions, stress, guilt, fear, coping with the symptom (rather than the source).

Recognizing that what Marlene needed was not depression counseling, but an awareness of a very probable childhood sexual abuse, we contacted her and arranged a telephone appointment.

The evidence was so clear, and yet Marlene could not recall an inappropriate act. She had no memory gaps, but seemed to have clear recollection of her childhood even to a very early age. So clear that even as a little child she knew she hated her mother. That is not normal. Little girls run to their mothers for comfort when they are hurt. Today, Marlene still has a love-hate relationship with her mother. That anger and hate, despite Marlene's best efforts to love and make amends, still controls her emotions. Her emotions are still those of a little child, unmatured, still not cleansed of that childhood hate. She is now just beginning the healing process of forgiveness and cleansing (1 John 1:9), that will free her from her depression, as well as from her anger and hate.

Please understand that every depressed person is not necessarily a victim of sexual abuse. However, many, many victims do in fact suffer long-term and often debilitating depression. When coupled with even one or two of the other symptoms, it may be a clear sign that such a trauma did in fact occur.

Even though Marlene seems to have so many of the

symptoms, she may not be a victim of sexual abuse. The Holy Spirit will guide her into truth, the Father will comfort her, and the Lord Jesus will heal her. That is a promise.

For further study on the subject of depression we would strongly recommend Florence's excellent and highly praised book, *Blow Away the Black Clouds.*

12. ANGER

If you become angry, do not let your anger lead you into sin; and do not stay angry all day (Ephesians 4:26, TEV*).*

C. S. Lewis explains that the psalmists showed anger and resentment and suggests we not condemn them but understand their reasons for anger.

> The natural result of cheating a man, or "keeping him down" or neglecting him, is to arouse resentment . . . their hatreds are the reaction to something. Such hatreds are the kind of thing that cruelty and injustice, by a sort of natural law, produce . . . Not all the victims go and hang themselves like Mr. Pilgrim; they may live and hate.[4]

Yes, victims live and hate and some of us wonder why. We give them verses on love and forgiveness and can't understand why they can't put the past behind them and get on with it.

Anger is appropriately the first reaction of an adult who suddenly faces the reality of sexual abuse in his or her childhood when the long-suppressed memory is finally brought into focus. It is natural and right to feel angry that "anyone could do such a thing to me." When I first heard Marilyn's testimony of her vicious gang rape by a group of soldiers when she was eight, I reacted with intense anger. When the lid first released on the garbage can of Heidi's memories as she focused in on her father's attempted penetration of her when she was two and one-half years old, she dropped the phone and ran upstairs sobbing. Heidi was tempted to throw herself off the second floor balcony until she remembered, "He's ruined the first part of my life; I'm not going to let him ruin the rest of it!"

Intense anger, suppressed or not, is one of the most frequent adult symptoms of childhood abuse. Some of us don't think we have any anger. Others admit they have a lot of anger in them. Whichever position you might be in, it is essential to find the source of the anger. To tell yourself or someone else to "get over your anger," and to "pray about it" is an exercise in futility.

When you can identify the source of your anger you have taken the first and key step to healing. "Awareness is the first step to Freedom." If you are not aware of any victimization in your life, but are now acknowledging some of these symptoms, it is vital that you continue to seek out the truth. On the other hand, if you are aware of victimization in your childhood, it is equally vital that you recognize that the emotional manifestations you are experiencing, such as anger, have their roots in that trauma.

If you have been victimized it is right that you feel angry about it. That is "righteous indignation." You have just as much right to be angry for a crime that was committed against your body and emotions, as you would for a crime that was committed against some other innocent little child. Heidi has a right to be angry that her father tried to forcibly penetrate her at the age of two and one-half, and that most of her relatives, including her father and grandfather, did in fact do so when she was twelve. I get angry, too, thinking about it.

Don't let anyone tell you that you shouldn't be angry, that it isn't Christian! Jesus, too, was always angry at sin. He loved the sinner, but He hated the sin. You may not be ready yet to love the sinner. You alone can never love the sinner. Only when you fully comprehend the agony the Lord suffered for you on the cross can you begin to "have that attitude in you which was also in Christ Jesus" (Philippians 2:5, NASB) when He said "Father, forgive them; for they know not what they do" (Luke 23:34, KJV).

Once you have identified the source of your righteous anger, then phase two becomes operative, the healing of that anger. "The acid of anger eats away only at the container." You are the container, and you will be eaten alive by it, until you are willing and able to bring it to the Lord for cleansing. "If we confess our sins," those we committed (#1), as well as those that were committed against us (#2), "he is faithful (#1) and just (#2), to forgive us (#1) and to cleanse us (#2) from *all* unrighteousness" (1 John 1:9).

He is faithful to forgive us for the sins we committed.

He is just to cleanse us from the sins that were committed against us.

Anger that has never been identified, that has never been dealt with, that has not been healed, can be a frightening emotion.

In December 1987, David Burke, an angry discharged employee of PSA Airlines, boarded its flight 1771 to San Francisco. Also on board was Raymond Thomson, the customer-service manager who had fired Burke after he was caught stealing $69 from flight cocktail receipts. The flight never reached its destination. It disintegrated as it crashed into a hill in the San Jose mountains, killing all forty-three persons on board. From the grisly remains the FBI reconstructed the horrible multiple murder. David Burke walked into the cockpit and shot and killed the pilot and copilot in order to get revenge on Raymond Thomson for firing him. "Most incriminating was a note, written in Burke's hand, on the outside of an air-sickness bag. It read: 'Hi, Ray. I think it's sort of ironical [sic] that we end up like this. I asked for some leniency for my family, remember. Well I got none. And you'll get none.' "[5]

After the tragedy, more about David, his life, and his emotions unfolded each day in the newspapers. The $69 theft was only the final factor in a stormy employment history. Fellow employees said Burke was subject to *fits of rage*. He had never married, but had fathered seven children by four women. As a child, his mother had lived with a series of different men. We ask the question, "Why? Why was he subject to *fits of rage*?" It would only seem all too clear that one or more of the "series of different men" viciously and violently abused him, physically and very likely sexually. He was a victim himself as a little boy, who vented his adult anger in "fits of rage" and ultimately in making victims of the forty-two other innocent persons on the plane. While David Burke is evidently guilty of his heinous crime, the initial perpetrator is the one(s) who victimized him as a child. Unresolved anger can be a fearsome thing, and a competent therapist can help you find appropriate ways to release it before it can become destructive.

Anger is not a gift of God, nor are we born with it. Somewhere in life it was put into us. Circumstances or people do not generally make us angry. They stir up the anger that is already inside us. You can be healed of your anger if you are willing to acknowledge its existence, search for and identify its source, and bring it to the Savior.

Because I have experienced the healing of the Lord of my own anger, rejection, and hurts, I know that He can and will heal the hurts of your heart. It is not platitudes to which I commend you. It is the miraculous healing power of the Lord Jesus Christ.

13. LIFE OF SERVICE

I know your love, your faithfulness, your service and your patience (Revelation 2:19, TEV).

Men and women who have faced significant feelings of rejection in their childhood and who have also been abused sexually have a strong tendency to devote themselves, at an early age, to a life of service to God or to mankind. It is one way they feel they can make up for their low sense of self-esteem.

Because victims often feel they have been dirtied and are not worth much, it is natural to be drawn to worthy endeavors such as missionary work, the Peace Corps, full-time Christian service, ministry and priesthood, social work, and helping the hurting or down-trodden. By living a life of sacrifice they feel they can make themselves acceptable to God.

A couple of years ago we were speaking at a pastors' conference in Phoenix, Arizona. In the course of our presentation I made the statement — startling to some — that fully one out of four women in this country has suffered from some form of sexual abuse. At the coffee break, a distinguished looking gentleman in a three-piece suit approached me to discuss our statistics. He identified himself as the president of a Christian college in California. He said they had recently completed a survey of the women at the college, many training for lives of Christian service. Forty percent of them were victims of sexual abuse. Another authority with whom we have spoken feels that probably 50 percent of women in missionary work, in para-church organizations, or in Christian service are victims. At one small ministry office eight of the last nine women employed there had suffered such abuse. One young wife who came to us seeking help and who had many of the symptoms said her mother refused to discuss anything of her own past with her. "It's not important," the mother would say. The mother works at a child sex-abuse clinic.

This pattern doesn't mean that every woman who devotes her life to selfless service has been sexually abused. However, it is significant that such a large percentage of full-time Christian workers have been victimized as children.

14. PHYSICAL FEATURES

God, I am too ashamed to raise my head
in your presence (Ezra 9:6, TEV).

All of the questions asked in this section of Part II are characteristics of a person who was sexually abused as a child. Some are signs of protection, some are the result of very low feelings of self-worth, and some are a combination of both.

The girl who regularly wears her hair closely around or partially covering her face does so as a protection, often unconsciously hoping she will not be found or noticed. She wants protection from a repetition of something she cannot explain. Many a significantly overweight woman has told us the weight is a defense, so that no one again will ever find her attractive and attack her again. On the other hand, many others have told us they lost fifty, eighty, even a hundred or more pounds, and felt so terrified, so stressed, so uncomfortable, they had to put the weight back on! You would expect a person to feel good about herself for losing so much weight. Not the victim. Even without the knowledge of what happened to her, she feels miserable, afraid, disoriented, and finds her only solace in the return of the weight. Then she feels safe!

If you have difficulty looking people in the eye, if you tend to look down, if you often shuffle your feet as you walk, it could be that you also don't want to be noticed. Persons who tend to look down or away have a generally low sense of self-worth and feelings of guilt. Virtually all victims of childhood sexual abuse have the coupling characteristic of low self-esteem. They feel dirty, unwanted, used and unlovable.

At a women's retreat, Gina came to see me in the prayer room. She felt terrible about herself and was hoping I might give her some guidance. She was sure she was not really a victim of sexual abuse, even though she acknowledged several symptoms. What else could have caused them? After about twenty-five minutes, I said to her, "Gina, do you realize that during the entire time of our conversation, you have not once looked me in the eye?" That stopped her and made her think. She knew it was true.

Shortly after we returned home to California, we received the letter from Gina quoted earlier. In part, she wrote, "Fred reminded me that in the thirty-forty minutes we spoke, I could hardly look him in the eye. I feel very self-conscious talking eye to eye with men, but I crave their friendship and knowing they accept and approve of me. You are the only one who has ever believed me and I will always be eternally grateful for that."

Do you identify with some of these features? It is not

only important, it is essential for you to uncover the past in order to be restored in the present. Gina's husband, though loving and supportive, wanted her to "forget it and quit living in the past." Searching for truth is not living in the past. Psalm 18:28 promises, "The Lord my God will enlighten my darkness," and in Joel 2:25, "I will restore to you the years that the locust hath eaten."

15. SLEEPLESSNESS

Even at night your mind can't rest (Ecclesiastes 2:23, TEV).

Coupling two Scripture verses confirms for us that restful sleep is the natural state that God in His infinite wisdom has planned for you and me: "Thou will keep him in perfect peace whose mind is stayed on thee, because he trusteth in thee" (Isaiah 26:3) and "When thou liest down, thou shalt not be afraid: yea, thou shalt lie down, and thy sleep shall be sweet" (Proverbs 3:24).

Do those verses describe your sleep? Do you have the perfect peace that when you lie down you are not afraid? Is "sweet" the way you feel about your sleep? If sweet sleep is a promise of God for each of us, why does our drug industry sell so many sleeping and sedative pills? Apparently our "minds are not stayed on Him." Apparently when we "liest down," we are afraid, tense or angry.

To miss a good night's sleep now and then because of the pressures of the day's circumstances is common for all of us. To lose out on that sweet sleep night after night, forever and ever, is not what God intended. It takes the likes of deep pain, continuing stress, or suppressed rage to deny us what is rightfully ours. The victim's normal emotions are so distorted by the deed done to her, that perfect peace, sweet sleep, and the ability to relax are perennially beyond her grasp. The result is night after night of sleeplessness. Hurting persons lose sight of the possibility that there will ever be anything different for them. They feel doomed to a night of dread, and to a dread of night.

When the lid blew off Heidi's garbage can of suppressed memories, her husband Steve expected her to be up most of the night. So accustomed to his wife's sleeplessness, he was prepared to stay up once again to offer love, support and care. Wasn't he shocked when Heidi promptly fell asleep like a little baby and had her best night's sleep in quite some time. The identification of the forgotten released some of the pent-up pressure that had been churning inside her for years.

If you are beginning to identify something you never suspected before—that you have several of these symptoms of sexual trauma—take hope in the experience of Heidi and countless others. Release from inner turmoil comes with recognition, and restoration comes with the Redeemer! It is possible, then, to give "thanks always for all things unto God and the Father in the name of our Lord Jesus Christ" (Ephesians 5:20). It may not seem like it now, but one day you will see His hand in all of this!

16. PAINS, MIGRAINES AND UNDIAGNOSED PROBLEMS

Peace of mind makes the body healthy
(Proverbs 14:30, TEV).

Kathy was allergic for as long as she could remember to both the sun and to any kind of outdoor work. No medical analysis could find a cause, and no medication helped. When her husband Burt, with the miracle assistance of the Holy Spirit, was able to lead her back into her childhood memories for answers to other emotional manifestations, Kathy found the answer. She had been victimized by her father at the age of four. Only two months after this discovery, Kathy was able to share her joy over the phone with me that she had just spent eight hours working in her garden, in the sun, with no allergic after-effects.

Our interest, attention, and rapidly growing understanding of this all-pervasive problem of sexual abuse among Christians was first sparked by our very dear friend Marilyn Murray. If ever there was a woman of God who had a dynamic personal ministry that so deeply affected the lives of hundreds of women, it was Marilyn. She was never too busy to encourage, to help, to write a letter. That was all in addition to the thirty-five or so weekly cell group Bible studies that were thriving under her leadership. But Marilyn had headaches that had been growing in intensity for several years. She had been to doctor after doctor, clinic after clinic, seeking relief, searching for causes.

She had even tried acupuncture, acupressure, chiropractic, every holistic hope; you name it, she tried it. No one had any answers; no one could give her relief. Twenty-four Excedrin a day and packing her head in icebags was insufficient to still the raging pain. So intense was the unremitting throbbing pain in her head that she prayed for death to take her. When hope was gone, a friend insisted she go to a certain counselor (name available on request) who was an expert at uncovering unknown childhood trauma.

After ten days of intensive therapy, the truth one day exploded. Marilyn was able to relive the horror of a gang rape at the age of eight when she lived in Kansas. That little girl, left for dead by her attackers, so totally buried her own emotions that she would never even be able to remember that assault, until the incurable headaches forced her to try one last option—prying into her forgotten past.

After her horrible discovery, it took seven more weeks of four-hours-per-day therapy, plus eighteen months of weekly follow-up, for Marilyn to fully come to grips with her anger and despair. *It is never an easy, instant process.* But it is worthwhile, for Marilyn is today free of her pounding pain.

Many, many women have been brought to awareness and set on their healing journey as a result of Marilyn's unfolded agony. This book would never have been thought of, no less written, were it not for Marilyn's experience. She is today one of our dearest friends, free of former physical symptoms. We eagerly await the publication of her own book.

Undefinable pains and aches stand high on the list of possible symptoms of childhood sexual abuse.

17. PMS

Your heart and mind are sick (Isaiah 1:5, TEV*).*

A certain amount of monthly stress, tension, depression, or other disruptive feelings may be considered normal. It is when these symptoms become especially oppressive, severe or long-lasting—either before or after the period—that they become significant. Since childhood sexual abuse is a distortion of the normal physical and emotional sexual mechanisms, it is only logical to consider the effects it might continue to have in the natural cycle in adulthood.

Dr. Joe McIlhaney, in his book *PMS* writes, " . . . though stress does not cause PMS, it can increase premenstrual symptoms. Then, PMS can actually create new stress, and the increased stress can make PMS worse."[6]

Several women with whom we have talked, including those with known molestation as well as those with symptoms only but not yet confirmed abuse, were also victims of severe PMS. Linda frequently missed several days of work each month, and she admits that those days that she did drag herself to her office were not very productive. She denied any possibility of sexual abuse in her childhood, (she was sure she would have remembered it), despite the indication of several significant symptoms. Some time later we saw Linda again. She now confirmed what had earlier been suspected. The Holy Spirit, she said, had shown her husband that she had been victimized. Suddenly, under His guidance, it all became clear and she was able to acknowledge it.

Even if you have no knowledge of any such abuse in your past, but have suffered severely from PMS and have noted other symptoms on these pages, you will want to open your mind to the possibility. Then the Holy Spirit can guide you into all truth about your past. "Ye shall know the truth (about your past) and the truth (Jesus) shall set you free" (John 8:32).

18. ASTHMA, CHOKING, AND GAGGING

I hear the cry of Jerusalem gasping for breath
(Jeremiah 4:31, TEV).

There is a hidden reason somewhere to explain why a person suffers from an intense fear of choking or gagging, or has recurring bad dreams of suffocating to death, or has frightening attacks of asthma. One does not have to search very far into childhood to recognize that a fear or dream of suffocating may well have come from either the threat or the actual placing of a pillow over a child's face during a sexual assault, or the hands of an adult on the throat put there to overcome a child's resistance. Choking, gagging or bouts of asthma recreate the sensation of oral rape, a form of assault on both little boys and girls that is far more common than even most professionals would begin to suspect.

Marilyn Murray is one of those children. Her mother confirmed that she never had asthma until she was about eight years old. She suffered with it, along with the headaches, most of her adult life, until she had her "volcano" and uncovered the fact of that gang rape in Kansas when she was eight. Her first asthma attack was that evening. Marilyn has never had asthma since her healing.

Marilyn now remembers that as a child she woke up in the night crying, deathly afraid that the drapes on her windows were coming after her and were going to strangle her. During her frequent nightmares she felt she was drowning in white glue.

19. HATRED – RESENTMENT

Their hatred smoulders like the fire in an oven
(Hosea 7:4, TEV).

Hatred is a deep emotional feeling of intense dislike

for someone. If you hate a person, if your dislike is that deep, there is most likely a valid reason for those feelings. Stormie Omartian tells of being locked often in her closet as a child for long periods by a mother who was not in control of herself. Heidi hated her mother because of the excessively violent physical beatings she received as a little child. The Lord is in the process of giving her victory over those feelings. George Johnson in Kentucky loved his mother and was very close to her, but he hated his father and didn't know why. All he knew was that he had always, ever since he was three, hated his father: "He was disgusting." George, now a Christian, is struggling. He is a homosexual. George was orally raped by his father when he was three, probably several times.

We tend to remember most forms of childhood physical or emotional abuse that lead to hatred. We know when they happened and who did them to us. Sometimes a person can remember sexual abuse that resulted in hatred. As we learned in the "Memory Gap" section, a child, as a means of emotional survival, frequently will totally block from her memory the sexual abuse experienced as a child. While the act is therefore unknown, the resulting hatred, anger, fear, or stress remains. It generally remains forever, until exposed to the light of truth and the source is uncovered, and the healing of the Lord can begin. Feelings of hatred when you don't know why you hate someone is, therefore, an almost certain symptom of severe sexual abuse. "Ye shall know the truth[7] (about yourself) and the truth[8] (Jesus) shall make you free" (John 8:32).

20. OBSESSIONS

All things become visible when they are exposed
to the light (Ephesians 5:13, NASB).

Patti sought help when she realized she was beset with feelings that were controlling her life and her thoughts. Despite a vital, abiding and dependent relationship with the Lord, she could not seem to gain the victory over the fears that had obsessed her for so many years. Instead of diminishing, they were becoming more frequent and more disruptive to her emotional stability and the family relationships. A loving and supportive husband cared for her too much to watch her continue to suffer as she did.

In addition to an increasing number of "panic attacks," she had ever-present fears: of being raped; of finding someone in her house when she came home alone — she had to check each and every room every time; of leaving a door to the house unlocked; of being attacked when her husband was away on a business trip; of periodic medical examinations; of leaving her daughter with her parents to babysit; of being alone in public places. Patti's life clearly was dominated by obsessions — continuing preoccupation with disturbing or unreasonable feelings that rule the emotions. In this brief list, notice the direct or indirect connotation of things sexual. It would seem that one would not need to be too much of an expert to search for sexually based sources to understand and cure these symptoms.

Nevertheless, current professional treatment continues to focus on the *symptom* rather than on the *source*, as indicated in this excerpt from a recent article in the *Los Angeles Times* entitled "The Orderly Disorder — New drug trials and therapy offer hope for those suffering from obsessive-compulsive behavior."

> Nearly five million people in the United States suffer from this disorder at some time in their lives . . . there is no standard treatment for its victims. However, a combination of interpersonal "behavior therapy" and a new drug approach suggests a more optimistic picture . . .
>
> According to the official manual of psychiatric diagnoses, the primary feature of obsessive-compulsive disorder is anxiety . . . the combination of obsessive thoughts and compulsive rituals often begins during childhood or adolescence. Many victims are ashamed of their behavior . . .
>
> Freud conceived of obsessions and compulsions in his patients as complex psychological defenses used to deal with unconscious conflicts.
>
> A successful treatment appears to be behavior therapy. In fact, says psychologist Edna Foa of the Medical College of Pennsyl-

vania, . . . behavior therapy should be the first treatment offered to obsessive-compulsives; only if it fails should (the new
drug) be considered.

Behavior therapy consists of supervised exposure to anxiety—
provoking situations and prevention of compulsive rituals, often
with the help of a patient's friends and family. For example, a
therapist will observe while a patient touches a doorknob that he
fears is infected with germs and then discusses those fears with
the patient. Then the therapist will recruit friends and family to
follow up on these sessions and make sure, for instance, that the
germ-fearing patient doesn't take more than one shower a day.

The latest study, reported by Foa at the psychiatric meeting
finds that after three weeks of behavior therapy—a total of fifteen
sessions, each about two hours long (i.e. thirty hours of therapy
at approximately $100 per hour, or a total of $3,000)—sixteen of
twenty-one obsessive-compulsive patients improved markedly for
at least three months. [The new drug] may help the thirty percent
of . . . patients who do not respond to behavior therapy, Foa
said.

National Institute psychiatrist Joseph Zohar said, "We think
a combination of (the new drug) with behavior therapy would
probably be the most effective treatment for obsessive-compulsive
disorder."[9]

Does $3,000 for three months of improvement with
the prospect of a 30 percent failure rate strike you as a good
investment in a temporary solution? Nowhere in the article
is there any reference to the cause of the problem, even
though childhood origins are several times mentioned!
Even in the hypothetical example of the germ-infected door
knob, no one asks the "why" question. Why was the patient
obsessed with a fear of catching germs from a door knob?
What might have occurred in his childhood to provoke such
a fear?

Why did Patti have such an obsessive fear of being
raped, of being attacked, of finding someone in her home?
Should Patti have a relative enter the house with her each
time to assure her that there is no one there, no one under
the bed? What if she lived alone and there were no relatives
or friends available? If she had such a friend available,
would repetition cure the deeply held emotion? Would the
obsessive fear return after three months, or when the

friend tired of the game? Should she resort to a life-long dependence on the "new drug"? Patti was the victim of childhood sexual abuse of which she had no knowledge or memory whatsoever—until she began prayerfully searching her childhood for answers. She found the source of her problems, and in finding those answers, her fears began to disappear.

After three hours of probing with Patti, we found no answers, but we did find many symptoms in addition to the obsessions already mentioned. She had no memories of her childhood before the age of about five. She could remember kindergarten and going to her grandmother's house, but nothing of her own house. She was brought up in a "totally non-loving atmosphere." As far back as she can remember, she never did have a good relationship with her mother; they were always angry with each other.

She couldn't remember her brother Freeman as a baby, who was born when Patti was two, but she remembered being "pushed aside" when he came along and feeling "really rejected." When she was ten she found out that she had been conceived out of wedlock, and that her mother had tricked her father. She recalled her mother always "talked dirty about sex." Patti felt sure she had not been raped as a child, for she was a virgin on her wedding night. Her parents were not spiritual, even though they attended church regularly. Patti remembered that early in her life, and many years before she became a Christian, God was very important to her and she prayed frequently.

Patti knew she was hurting. For years she had prayed and asked God to heal those hurts—hurts that she didn't understand and whose origins she couldn't identify. Now, however, instead of denying the possibility, she acknowledged she had many of the symptoms of sexual abuse. In addition, her brother, who was always obsessed with sex as a boy and teenager, was totally "messed up" in his adult life. Her younger sister weighed about 250 pounds. Patti was spared this symptom.

She went home determined to ask the Lord specifically to reveal the truth about her past to her. She wanted "total freedom from the bondage" she was in. The truth came speedily and over the next four weeks in the form of three painful and frightening "flashbacks."

She started by having dreams of her mother abusing her. Later, she could see herself lying nude as a baby on a desk or table. She was nine or ten months old. Her mother and father were looking at her, but not just looking! They were ogling her little body. At that tender age she was able to perceive the manner in which they looked at her, the attitude in their hearts!

Then came flashback number one: As a little girl, perhaps three, she remembered playing on the lawn, in a small pool or large bucket. She might have been nude. Her mother was sitting on the porch. Little Patti got out of the pool and walked up on the porch, and her mother reached down and fondled her. This revelation was devastating to her adult emotions.

Flashback number two came several days later. The picture is hazy, but was with her mother and the words "oral sex" kept coming through to her. She remembered that a while back, when she and her husband Walt were reading a Christian sex book, she told him she thought "oral sex is disgusting." She suddenly knew her strong "reaction" was significant.

A couple of weeks later on a Saturday morning, she woke up sobbing uncontrollably after flashback number three. A picture came into her mind of seeing her mother's father, Patti's grandfather, lying nude on her parent's bed . . . and Patti was sitting on top of him. She thinks she was about three years old. Patti commented, "That morning I allowed myself to be really angry with my grandfather!"

Patti suspects these events happened several times until about the age of five. With what she knows now, she feels sure her mother was also victimized as a child. Since those flashbacks, Patti's recovery has been rapid for several reasons.

She was and remains deeply committed to the Lord, spending priority time daily in the Word and in prayer.

She earnestly sought the truth of her past, and God allowed her to see it. She was ready.

She had strong and tender support from her husband who also read Jan Frank's book *A Door of Hope* and has listened to Don Frank's tape.

She didn't quit at the first revelation, painful as it was, but continued to search for more.

She remained in constant communion with her Lord who gave her the strength to see it through. As promised, He released her from the bondage of her past.

Patti told us that if she didn't have the Lord, she thinks she "would have jumped off a cliff. I know now why so many people are in mental institutions and have mental breakdowns." She has a friend who had similar panic attacks, was given tranquilizers, and became addicted to them.

Patti's fears have been healed. Recently she had to go to the Greyhound bus station to pick someone up and only later realized that she had gone into the terminal and out and never even once thought about protecting herself from the possibility of rape. Shortly after, her husband had to be away for several days at a business conference. When he returned home, she was joyously able to tell him she slept soundly each night! These are major milestones for Patti. She does not presume to be fully healed. *She knows complete restoration will take time. It is a process.* She is being cleansed of the defilement of her flesh and spirit. Already she is being used as a comforter to others who are hurting. She has been amazed at who the Lord is sending to her for help.

Obsessions can be healed, not by treating the symptoms, but by uncovering the source of the emotional conflict. The pains of that childhood abuse or rejection can be healed by the One who came to set the captive free. "All things become visible when exposed to the light" (Ephesians 5:13).

21. COMPULSIONS

*You strongly desire things, but you can not get them,
so you quarrel and fight (James 4:2,* TEV*).*

Sandra weighed 225 pounds as she sat weeping before me. "I can't stop eating and I'm so depressed. I look in the mirror and I hate myself. I'm so stupid. Why did I ever think I could do anything right?"

Sandra had a pretty face but pain-filled eyes. She obviously had no self-worth and had contemplated suicide several times. In checking her current situation, I found relatively few obvious problems, except for a recent bankruptcy. When she cried out, "We lost it all," I assumed she blamed her husband. But upon my questioning she sobbed, "It's all my fault. I went on a buying binge. I was trying to cheer myself up and I bought everything I could get my hands on." Everything included dresses several sizes too small and exercise equipment she had never taken out of the crates in the garage, making it simple when the men came to repossess them.

Since I know compulsive behavior is rooted in some childhood problem that may be repressed from the conscious mind, I asked about her childhood. On the first question, "Where did you live?" Sandra began to cry and as she told her story, she went from tears to rage. She had grown up in a town full of "very religious Quakers" and her parents had run a 24-hour truck stop. In school she was teased by the other children and looked down on as low-class. Every day she hated to go to school and when she told her mother about her problems her mother said to ignore them, be brave and grow up. Sandra wanted some loving understanding of her situation but her parents were proud of their truck stop business and couldn't see why it bothered her.

As Sandra poured out how embarrassed she was to live over a garage, to have no yard or front door, and to be surrounded day and night by huge semis, I thought back to how humiliated I had been as a teen to have to live in a store, not realizing how grateful my parents were to have any business that would support us through the Depression.

Sandra's emotions had kept her from doing well in school and her mother had sent her to a counselor in a neighboring town. When she came home after answering what she felt were very personal questions, she asked her mother why she had made her go to the counselor. The mother answered, "I'm trying to find out why you are so dumb."

I'm sure that's not the worst statement a mother ever made, but it branded Sandra as eternally dumb in her own mind. In high school she worked hard to impress her mother, but her mother never changed her evaluation of Sandra, who still feels "dumb."

One other problem Sandra had was her lack of appropriate clothes. Her mother's flashy taste did not fit the Quaker image and the teens ridiculed her and called her a hussy and other unprintables. From that time on Sandra buried her anger toward her mother, who never has understood why she didn't like the exciting life with the truck drivers or the bright clothes she so generously gave her. Sandra pushed down her deep hurts from the high schoolers and she tried never to talk about these feelings again.

Unfortunately, repressing our feelings doesn't deal with them and sooner or later they spring up in some personality disorder. For Sandra it was compulsive eating. She weighed 100 pounds more than when she was married. She hated how she looked and was constantly depressed. Her childhood loathing of her clothes presented itself in a compulsive need to buy clothes and her revulsion with her weight made her buy ones too small to wear in a wishful hope she'd somehow shrink down to fit them.

Dr. Cecil Osborne, in his book *Understanding Your Past: The Key to Your Future*, writes of the experiences he has had counseling compulsive personalities and how he has found that

> All excessiveness, all compulsive, obsessive, phobic behavior
> have roots that go back to those first few years . . . A compul-
> sive act — nail biting, over-eating, compulsive talking, working,
> drinking, smoking — is simply an unconscious effort to relieve
> anxiety. The solution is not to attack the symptom, but to try to
> relieve the anxiety.[10]

Before we can relieve the anxiety, we have to find out
where it originated. No amount of Bible reading or
prescription drugs will wipe out the source of the problem
and until we find it, medicine or Scripture become only a
Band-aid over a deep wound. Osborne continues:

> What possible connection can there be between compulsive
> spending and having inadequate parents? The answer is, of course,
> that when we repress a strong emotion and deny the truth, a dis-
> tortion takes place in the personality. In Dorothy's case [the case
> history he is discussing] the distortion took the form of severe
> anxiety, which she relieved temporarily by going on a buying
> spree. Other people experiencing similar anxiety might have dis-
> charged it by excessive drinking, compulsive eating, or in a score
> of other ways. Each of us unconsciously chooses our own neurotic
> manifestation.[11]

Oswald Chambers writes, "A man's disposition on the
inside — what he possesses in his personality — determines
what he is tempted by on the outside. The temptation fits
the nature of the one tempted and reveals the possibilities
of the nature."[12]

With Sandra, her unexplained buying binges had
nothing to do with current needs or even conscious desires.
Her personality had been fractured from her childhood experiences and her mother's lack of understanding of what
she was going through. Children can handle almost anything if at least one parent can lovingly understand their
feelings.

Sandra's behavior fit the nature of the deep desires
she had boiling within her. It's what is inside that sooner
or later pushes out and leads us into some kind of temptation that may have no logical explanation. When these
negative patterns emerge they do fit the nature of our personal background and they "reveal the possibilities of the

nature," what we may be capable of doing in a pattern of self-destruction!

Sandra had the additional problem of a desperate need to be approved of by her mother. Since her mother was of a Choleric nature and totally consumed with running her 24-hour truck stop, she didn't have time to affirm Sandra as a child and when Sandra cried out with her hurts and rejections her mother told her to grow up and get on with life. To Sandra this was one rejection on top of another and instead of making her cease to seek attention and understanding, it made her crave these even more.

Now as an adult, Sandra calls her mother every single day. There is surely nothing wrong with calling one's mother, but for Sandra it is a compulsion. When I asked her what she hoped to hear from her mother, she replied, "I hope she'll tell me I'm all right."

"Does she?" I questioned.

"Not yet," she cried.

Unfortunately, the odds are poor that this Choleric mother will, without understanding the need, ever give praise to Sandra. More unfortunate is the fact that when we emotionally sense someone is after praise, even desperate to receive it, we have a bad little voice of independence that says "Don't give it." The more needy others are the less giving we tend to be.

In looking at Sandra's case, what can mothers learn? That every child needs love and understanding. That when it's not given, emotions shut down. That emotions will spring up somewhere later. And when they emerge, they will strangely fit the nature of the original distortion.

22. FAMILY ALCOHOLISM

Do not get drunk with wine, which will only ruin you
(Ephesians 5:18, TEV*).*

As a nation we have been well aware for generations of the impact of alcohol addiction on the family. It is only in recent years, however, that the Christian community has been willing to begin to recognize the magnitude of the problem. In the surveys of family problems and traumas that we have conducted over the past eight years at each CLASS, with approximately six thousand responses, invariably almost half of these men and women indicated that alcoholism was a significant problem in their immediate family.

The all-pervading effects of alcoholism on the family and the everlasting impact on each member involved is of such importance that we would urge you to make this whole problem an area of intense separate study if you checked off even one of the questions in this section of Part II.

We would like to highlight three very significant and often inevitable results of growing up in an alcoholic family.

1. The child who must "take over" because one or both parents is not functioning matures at an early age, but later is apt to be victimized by anger, tension or depression — a result of the normal childhood she never had.

2. The child who is raised in an alcoholic home misses out on the natural nurturing and attention that every child should receive. The result is feelings of being unloved, "nobody cares about me," and rejection. Then these unmet emotional needs later seek fulfillment in adult and married relationships. The grown child now places upon her spouse the unrealistic expectation to fill this never-satisfied childhood vacuum. Dr. Cecil Osborne's book, *Understanding Your Past — The Key to Your Future,* is an excellent resource for understanding the workings of these emotional dynamics. (See the order form at the back of this book for information on obtaining it.)

3. Children of alcoholic parents have a higher than average incidence of sexual abuse. It is important to recognize that alcoholic mothers may be found to be molesters as readily as are alcoholic fathers. This can be understood when we realize first that alcoholic mothers are alcoholics for a reason. They themselves are often childhood victims and have turned to alcohol as a reprieve from the trauma

that has resulted from their own sexual abuse; secondly, women who are victims themselves become victimizers at close to the same rate as victimized men. The effect then of the alcoholism becomes very significant, in that it lowers or obliterates the normal inhibition that would otherwise preclude such a devastating act upon a child's body and emotions.

David Peters, in his highly recommended book *A Betrayal of Innocence,* reports on the findings of a respected researcher in the field of child sexual abuse, and states that there are "four preconditions that had to be met before an adult could sexually abuse a child:

1. The adult must have sexual feelings about children,

2. Any internal inhibitors, such as conscience, must be overcome,

3. Any external inhibitors, such as the presence of other adults, must be dealt with, and

4. The resistance of the child to the act of abuse must be overcome.

"Alcohol was one effective means of overcoming internal inhibitors to sexual abuse."[13]

Alcohol is equally effective in removing external inhibitors. While the women of the family were off at a shower for the bride, twelve-year-old Heidi was gang-raped on the floor by her grandfather, uncles, cousins, et. al., at a drunken stag party. We wish we didn't have to add the number of women who have told us of having been molested by a father, even in the presence of—or worse, with the participation of—a mother or older brother! Peters continues:

> While the use of drugs and alcohol is by no means a prerequisite for sexual abuse, it often does contribute to the problem. A person normally having enough internal control to resist abusing a child may go over the line with even minimal amounts of alcohol or drugs.
>
> Once conscience is removed as an obstacle to sexual victimization of children, it is little problem to create opportunities to molest a child and even less of a problem to overcome the resistance of the child. Children, in their innocence, have no defense against being hurt by those they love and trust.[14]

Alcoholism in the childhood family is a problem of the greatest magnitude. It does lead to the discomfiture which results from a lost childhood, and to serious adult behavior manifestation due to feelings of childhood rejection and emotional deprivation. Alcoholism in the family in itself is not a symptom of childhood sexual abuse. However, if you have some of the other symptoms described in these pages and were brought up in an alcoholic home, even though you are sure you were not abused sexually you should at least open your mind to that possibility. Sexual abuse is rampant in alcoholic homes. It might have been in yours.

23. EATING DISORDERS

You must keep control of yourself in all circumstances
(2 Timothy 4:5, TEV*).*

When a child's body is violated, one of the reactions is a need for control over the body. Because these children are initially too small to defend themselves, they find a form of control in what they eat. As they grow up, those victimized as children often have what is currently termed as eating disorders.

There can be many reasons for the different types of abnormalities in eating, but for our purposes we will look at how molestation can be the source of such problems. As the child internalizes, *I have no control over myself—I must find something I can control,* she often turns to her eating patterns. In a dysfunctional family, little emphasis is put on positive dinner-time conversation and the pre-teen or teen can be far into an almost irreversible problem before anyone seems to notice.

Anorexia—refusing to eat and playing with the food given—causes the individual to lose weight rapidly. Initially the victim may be praised for dieting successfully and this much-needed affirmation encourages her to continue until she is extremely and dangerously thin. By the time some nurturing person (not necessarily the parents, who are often too bogged down in their own dysfunctional ways to notice) suggests the individual is in serious trouble, the habit may be set to the degree that resident therapy is needed.

As I have questioned anorexics, I have found that each one had some kind of abuse in childhood and that some male figure—usually the perpetrator—has made a comment such as: "If you weren't so fat, you'd be more popular;" "I hope you'll lose weight when you grow up;" "Men never like women with big hips." Often anorexia is coupled with excessive exercise, an added compulsion to become the slim, trim perfect person these women hope will be acceptable. So much of the victim's emotional energy goes into a lifetime search for acceptance.

Telling the anorexic to eat more usually turns her away from all food as the person pleading with her becomes a potential controller; anorexics resist any outside power. As with so many of the child abuse symptoms, anorexia will only improve when the initial cause is unearthed and brought clearly to the surface. Our purpose here is not to write a treatise on the harmful, sometimes deadly, effects of starving one's self, but to alert you to the possibility that anorexia could be a symptom of child abuse.

Bulimia is an eating disorder where the person binges or eats more than she needs and then withdraws to the bathroom or restroom and vomits it. This self-induced "purging" is both a way to eat while losing weight and a control of what goes in and out of the body. This leads to inflammation of the esophagus, abnormal tooth decay, and an inability to keep any food in the stomach. The person, in effect, is training her stomach to reject any food as she herself was rejected, and when she wishes to stop the purging she often finds the pattern irreversible. Food in triggers food out.

In both of these disorders, control is the issue, but as the problems and side effects increase, the person begins to see she has no control over what she felt she was controlling. This leads to increased self-loathing and the verification that her whole life is beyond control. Every day becomes a battle of the will and once again the victim is helpless.

Treating the symptom of the eating disorder without first identifying and then treating the source may be an exercise in futility. If you suffer from these disorders and find other symptoms as well, thank God that He is guiding you into all truth about your past, and that *the* truth will set you free (John 8:32).

24. HIDDEN URGES

People will appear whose lives are controlled
by their own lusts (2 Peter 3:3, TEV).

As Christians, we must recognize that the inner drives or urges within us have their roots somewhere. Even the drive to achieve financially probably has its origins in childhood. This would not be considered a negative or discomforting drive, unless the individual is so driven as to virtually ignore the needs of his family.

There are other drives, however, that we have within us — hidden urges that bother us from time to time, needs to see or do that we are not comfortable with, feelings that we wish we didn't have or can't seem to control. All of these hidden urges are a result of something that happened to us in life, especially in childhood and in our formative years or as a result of feelings about the way we were treated.

In this section we are particularly looking at those urges which have sexual connotations, and which are aberrations or distortions from what is generally considered normal behavior or feelings.

We do not believe any person was born with homosexual tendencies. The Bible clearly indicates this. As Christians we have no choice but to fully accept all Scripture as God-given, God-ordained, God-directed. "All Scripture is given by inspiration of God, and is profitable for doctrine, for reproof, *for correction,* for instruction in righteousness" (2 Timothy 3:16). Since God himself so clearly states that all Scripture comes from Him, for us to question, discount, or even discard any portion of Scripture puts us in the absurd position of judging what our holy, all-knowing God has ordained. The creation is never in authority over the Creator. In order to judge God, we must be of higher rank, above God. Because we do not comprehend something is no reason to appoint ourselves as experts and judge God.

What does God say about how He made you, and about incest and homosexuality? Genesis 1:27: "So God created man in his own image, in the image of God created he him; male and female created he them." Genesis 1:31: "And God saw everything that he had made, and behold it was very good."

After the Fall, the Lord said to Moses, "None of you shall approach to any that is *near of kin* to him, to uncover their nakedness: I am the LORD." "Thou shalt not lie with mankind, as with womankind: *it is an abomination." "You shall therefore keep my statutes and my judgments, and shall not commit any of these abominations"* (Leviticus 18:1,6,22,26).

For a clearer picture of God's statutes regarding incestual and homosexual relationships, take a moment and read all of Leviticus 18. You will have a clear answer for the standard homosexual pronouncement, "You don't understand, I was born this way." (See also 1 Corinthians 5:1, 6:9-20.)

We in the Christian community have a tendency to look down at homosexuals as unrepentant sinners, as aberrants not worthy of our time or compassion. The Lord Jesus loved the sinner, while hating the sin. Because of my own childhood deprivation, but for the grace of God, I might have become an incestuous father, or been seduced by someone into homosexuality. Let us therefore look with compassion upon those who were not born that way but were innocent victims of vicious crimes against their bodies and emotions. They need the healing hand of the Lord Jesus — no more, no less, than you and I — in order to be restored and cleansed; in order to break the shackles that keep each one of us in some form of bondage; in order to be fully cleansed vessels more fit for the Master's use.

Lana asked to see me for a different reason at a recent conference. She knew she had been sexually abused by a cousin several times at about the age of ten. As a teenager she had participated in some homosexual relationships. At the age of twenty she committed her life to the Lord Jesus.

Serious about her faith, Lana went to Bible college. As a result of a thorough investigative history, her past experiences and present tendencies came to light and she went through a spiritual deliverance which did succeed in lifting her above her past. Now a happily married mother who enjoyed normal relationships with her husband, she had an unusual question. When she was twelve she had her little three-year-old niece fondle her while babysitting. Knowing how damaging such activity can be, she wondered, "What, if anything, should I do about that niece, who herself is now seventeen? Should I tell her?" Further sharing also showed that while she had made progress on her own healing journey, she did sometimes still have thoughts of going to bed with a female friend, even though the idea never gained control of her.

How would you handle that question? I knew my role was only to show her possibilities. The Holy Spirit must guide her decision. We discussed what the effects of the revisitation of her own molestation might have on her now teenage niece. She might be suffering the same confusion of identity, the same distortion of normal sexual feelings that Lana had faced at her age. She most likely would have no knowledge of what had happened to her at three, and therefore, no understanding of why she had feelings today that she couldn't rationalize or no indication of the source of the emotions that might be raging within her. As we parted, Lana was committed to trusting the Lord for her own further healing, as well as for the clear answers to if, how, and when she should confess to her niece and ask her forgiveness. Awareness is the first step to freedom, and Jesus said, "I have come to set the captive free" (Luke 4:18).

A desire to touch or get in bed with a person of the same sex is clearly not God-given. It is an abomination. It is inevitably a result of some sexual activity in childhood which was not normal, not part of the natural growth process that is part of God's plan.

A mother who tries to sexually stimulate her infant child, does so because her own sexual mechanism was distorted as a child. A couple of years ago, a woman called our office from Oklahoma seeking help. Even though she had been in weekly Christian counseling for three years, she didn't feel she was making much progress. After only fifteen or twenty minutes, she had presented several symptoms of having been sexually abused as a child. As she thought about it and focused on her past, she acknowledged that it was true. In her three years of counseling it had never been discussed. Then she said, "And what bothers me the most, I'm afraid I'm abusing my two-year-old son!" At that point I was dumbfounded. What could a *mother* possibly do to abuse her *infant son*? I dared to ask, and she responded, "I try to get him aroused."

Not only is the mother a victim of sexual abuse, but now her little son is as well. The sins of the fathers were revisited unto another generation. Can you imagine what that little boy's life will be like as he grows up? His natural sexual mechanism has already been greatly distorted by premature arousal. Without early help and healing, we can project one or more of the following very certain patterns of behavior: rapist, homosexual, bisexual, child molester, incestuous father, abusive husband, alcoholic. When one of every four women in this country (and an even higher percentage in the church) and one of every eight men are victims of some form of child abuse, it is clearly the number one scourge of our nation, and of the church as well!

If you answered "Yes" to even one of the questions in this section of Part II, that may be taken as a fairly clear indication that your inner sexual responses were inappropriately activated at an early age, even if you have no knowledge of any such experience.

25. PERSONAL HYGIENE

Whoever has taken a bath is completely clean and does not have to wash himself (John 13:10, TEV*).*

Personal cleanliness is surely a desirable characteristic for all of us. It is the norm for civilized living. Why then would the subject even be discussed in regard to freeing the mind from the bondage of repressed memories?

Excessive emphasis on personal hygiene is simply an unconscious effort to relieve some hidden anxiety, an anxiety of which the individual may not even be aware. She has probably practiced her special form of cleanliness for so long that it has become second nature to her. She does not think she is doing anything unusual. All the questions in the Part II section on personal hygiene are designed to identify habit patterns which most people would not consider normal.

Treating the symptom without identifying the source will miss the heart of the matter. The cause of the anxiety must be identified. Telling someone that she spends way too much time brushing her teeth will not suddenly initiate a change in her behavior any more than hiding her toothbrush will cause her to stop brushing her teeth. The question is "Why?" Why does she have this obsessive need to make sure her teeth are so clean? What is the anxiety she is trying to relieve?

A pastor friend of Florence's presented this very question to her one day as they were discussing the general subject of abuse. He described his wife's sister-in-law, the daughter of a well-known Christian leader of a generation ago. In addition to being extremely thin and having a very low sense of self-worth and a deep hate for her father, she had brushed and rebrushed her teeth so much for so many years that she had actually worn the enamel off her teeth. Could there be any connection between this obsession for clean teeth and sexual abuse? The answer: a resounding "Yes."

There would be little question that her life had been

marred by childhood sexual abuse. It is not very difficult to retrogress to her childhood and project the form of abuse to which she was subjected. A victim with a cleanliness phobia tends to focus on that part of her body that was violated. All her life, she had been unconsciously trying to relieve the anxiety that resulted from her victimization. Because most victims feel they are forever "unclean," it is easy to understand why they make a life-long fetish about personal cleanliness.

26. SMELLS, ODORS

The Lord opened her mind (Acts 16:14, TEV).

If certain smells or odors incite an emotional or physical reaction in you, you need to look for the reason. Your reaction is an identification with something in your past that was traumatic enough then to cause that response today. The smell of motor oil, of cigarette breath, of new-mown grass, or of men's cologne may trigger a flashback of something that gives rise to intense fear, tension, or even physical pain such as a migraine.

Jan Frank, a counselor with understanding, compassion and God-given wisdom (and a victim herself) writes in her powerful and anointed book, *A Door of Hope*:

> When in bed with my husband one evening I sensed his desire to be intimate. In the midst of love-making, I became rigid, frozen, unable to move. Because I had learned through therapy to process what was happening, I mentally investigated why I was reacting this way. Finally, after ruling out certain conditions in our environment, I hit on the cause of my intense reaction. It was my husband's aftershave. He was wearing the same fragrance my stepfather had worn for years. My subconscious had made the connection. When I've shared this example with victims, they invariably recall similar happenings.

Listen to what your reaction to any smells or odors is trying to tell you. It is an insight into a memory that is trying to break through from repression to expression, and once clarified, to complete cleansing.

27. ATTITUDES TOWARD SEX

You may be innocent and pure as God's perfect children
(Philippians 2:15, TEV).

An infant is not brought into this world with a set of standards in her hands proclaiming what is or is not normal. Whatever she is shown by her parents is what becomes the norm in the areas of eating, dressing and behaving.

Although each baby is born innocent and pure as God's perfect child, any molestation can taint the emotions for life. A child may grow up with feelings that are not at all normal, but since in her conscious memory she has always had those feelings, she has no reference point to know anything differently. Sometimes she learns later in talking with her peers that they were brought up with totally different attitudes. Some only learn as adults in talking with a counselor while seeking answers and help for their known discomforts.

Recently at a conference in Orlando, Florida, Laura asked me some questions about her Personality Profile. She had scored evenly in all four columns, a frequent sign of an obliterated personality. When we looked at her husband's profile, it was a more balanced score of Melancholy and Phlegmatic. As we discussed some of the possible reasons for her scoring similarly in all four columns, we began to focus on her childhood.

In a very few minutes we uncovered several symptoms which suggested the possibility of childhood sexual abuse. I then asked Laura if she had experienced sexual feelings as a child. She said she had and volunteered that she had often felt "sensuous." I asked her at what age she began to have these feelings. She answered, "Oh, probably from about five on up. I even remember playing with myself in the bath tub."

I asked her husband, Dave, at what age he had started developing sexual feelings. Dave said, "Oh, probably, sometime after ten." Sexual feelings are normal in a pre-teen. They generally start at puberty, somewhere between ten and twelve. But "sensuous" feelings are not normal in a five-year-old child. Laura had no idea until then that all children did not experience those same feelings at that age. I suggested to her that there was a good chance of some form of sexual abuse in her early childhood.

She seemed relieved. For the first time she felt there might be an underlying cause for all the tension, anxiety and depression she had felt most of her life. I recommended some steps they both might take and resources they should study, and they both thanked me profusely for the new hope they had found.

Identification is only the first step, but an essential one on the road to restoration. It also helped Laura to be able to cease being "all things to all people," an unnatural and energy-draining effort. Finally she can be the person God created her to be.

Sexual abuse distorts the normal and natural sexual mechanism of any boy or girl. It arouses at a totally inappropriate age natural sexual feelings that would be perfectly appropriate at a later time. It is these distorted, premature sexual urges that are the cause of aberrations from what may be considered normal sexual feelings and attitudes. Look back at your check marks in this section of Part II. If you checked two or more of those questions, it is possible that your sexual feelings were inappropriately activated.

28. REACTION TO POSSIBILITY OF SEXUAL ABUSE

Deliver me Lord from Hidden faults (Psalm 19:12, TEV*).*

Often the abuses we have felt as children have been hidden from our conscious mind, but this lack of awareness doesn't mean that we are not still affected by them. When we have unexplained reactions to certain situations, we should question the source of these feelings.

The first time a counselor asked me about any negative feelings about my mother, I over-reacted. I loudly defended her and proclaimed that she was a wonderful woman. Later the counselor told me that my vehement denial showed him there were some hidden problems with my mother that I had refused to look at. It took more than a year before I was willing and ready to lift the veil. As the Lord began to deliver me from those "hidden faults" I was able to look realistically at our relationship.

As Shakespeare wrote, "The lady doth protest too much, me thinks."[15]

Years ago while working as an assistant manager in a Stouffer's Restaurant in New York City, I had the responsibility of tracking and stopping the large number of "walk-outs," people who would eat and then slip out without paying their check. I remember watching one group of four. One by one they left the table, none bothering to walk by the cash register. I waited until the last one got up and went directly outside. Following him right out to Forty-Second Street, I stopped him and asked him if he had forgotten to pay his check. With his lips "quivering," he insisted he had paid the bill. I asked him to check his pockets. What a surprise! He found four unpaid lunch checks. As he returned inside to settle all four obligations, he showed me his identification. He was a detective employed by the New York Central Railroad! I've never forgotten his quivering emotional reaction, the certainty that he was hiding something.

Most people who were in fact sexually abused as children and have no adult knowledge of it, have no such awareness because they have consciously suppressed or sub-consciously repressed all memory of it. The absence of any memory therefore does not indicate an absence of a violation. The energy that you have expended all these years to repress those emotions is likely to boil over any time someone comes close to "tapping in" to those protected and private areas. In this section of Part II, questions one through six are designed to trigger an emotional reaction. That emotional reaction may be a sure sign that something has in fact been suppressed. *Our emotions remember what our mind has forgotten.*

29. NUDITY

*I was afraid and hid from you, because I was naked
(Genesis 3:10,* TEV*).*

When God created man and woman "they were naked,
the man and his wife, and were not ashamed" (Genesis
2:25). When you arrived in this world, you were also naked
and unashamed. Your attitudes today toward nudity were
formed by your parenting, by religious practice and by life
experiences.

When a little girl, or boy, is a victim of incest or other
sexual abuse, their normal sexual emotional mechanisms
are inevitably distorted. Their feelings about themselves
are affected as well — feelings of self-worth and misgivings
about the appearance of their own body. Carried into adulthood and the marriage relationship, these distortions then
significantly affect their feelings about nudity. If you feel
nervous, reluctant or uncomfortable for your husband or
wife to see you nude, it is probably not because your family raised you that way. Such feelings usually result from
childhood sexual abuse. By far, the largest number of
women, and men, who have come to us for help with the
trauma or stress related to sexual abuse were raised in
homes with strict attitudes or practices against family
nudity.

Katherine was molested by two hired hands on
separate occasions when she was between the ages of three
and eight. She was also raped by her father when she was
eleven. Katherine managed to bury these events in the
recesses of her mind until she was thirty-five. Even though
she was not consciously aware of her victimization,
Katherine has always preferred to undress in the bathroom
rather than in front of her husband. She recently admitted
to me that she even has difficulty disrobing in department
store dressing rooms.

When Katherine was deeply involved in journalizing,

counseling, and interpreting frequent mental flashes this past year, there were times she awoke in the morning and found that she had slept on top of the covers, fully clothed, with even her shoes still on. She then remembered she often slept that way as a child. When I asked, "Why did you sleep with your shoes on?" she commented, "I felt I always had to be ready to run."

Even though Katherine could not remember her victimization until recently, it still affected her attitudes toward her own body and nudity.

30. KNOWN SEXUAL MOLESTATION

They used her and defiled her (Ezekiel 23:17, TEV).

It is an interesting paradox that men and women who were sexually abused as children, but have no knowledge of it at all because of repressed memories, are aware of deep hurts, anxiety, or stress in their lives. But they have no idea why they feel that way. On the other hand, those who are able to remember molestation in their childhood often have identical or similar symptoms, but are very reluctant to even consider that there may be a connection. Their usual attitude is, "It was no big deal" or "I don't think it has affected me at all." The truth is that whether you remember the abuse or have no remembrance of any such thing, adult behavior and emotional manifestations may be exactly the same.

If you are one who does remember molestation or inappropriate activity in your childhood, allow the Holy Spirit to show you that it may very well be the root cause of the hurts or frustrations which you are feeling today.

As an adult, I was well aware that any normal sexual inquiry was suppressed in my childhood. I remember either feeling guilty or being made to feel guilty anytime any sexual activity or sexual connotations occurred. But I had no idea how this suppression affected my adult emotions or ignited inappropriate sexual responses. I also remembered how, after my father died, I became my mother's roommate at eighteen, which continued until my marriage six years later. I remembered my mother coming into my separate bed at night and "cuddling" me, providing the nurturing I had so desperately craved and missed as a child.

As I looked back on those experiences knowing there never was any sexual contact whatsoever, I could not see how what appeared to be a basically positive experience could have such a negative result. I had forgotten that for those six years a young man at the height of his natural sexual drive had to totally suppress normal feelings while in bed with his mother. Those suppressed emotions, coupled with my deep feelings of rejection and my denied feelings of low self-worth, eventually created unrecognized distortions of my marital, family, and even business relationships. I cannot wipe out all the past mistakes, my own hurts or the hurts I unknowingly inflicted on others, but I can praise the God who today has healed my hurts of the past, and in addition given me wisdom and understanding to help guide others into His restoration process.

When Molly and Ron came to us seeking insight for their constant marriage squabbles, we found that in ten years they had sought the help of thirty-two different counselors. This was no new problem. In twenty years of marriage they were further apart than ever before. She was living in their big house with their three children. He had been living for most of the past two months on his boat. They both professed love for each other, but couldn't stand living together. The fights, both emotional and physical, were simply too frequent and too intense.

In talking with Ron, he admitted to an uncontrollable rage, which he feels he usually is able to keep under control. At home, it usually flares up when Molly cuts him off or will not allow him the opportunity to express his feelings: "I'd get in three to seven words, and she'd cut me off, and we'd be into screaming and yelling."

Twice Molly had to call the police, and once Ron was arrested and spent six hours in jail. As a self-employed video engineer, he has to be available when his clients need him.

"Molly has no consideration for my job," he complained. "I rarely work a weekend. She doesn't want me to work weekends, but I can't tell a customer 'No.' She finds fault with every job I've had."

Ron remembers his mother as very domineering. He felt "smothered and wronged" as a boy. His mother always took up his battles for him. He felt his mother was prudish, and remembered that there were fights at home every day of his life.

At age five he was molested by a young neighbor boy who taught him to do things that five-year-old boys would never dream up on their own. At seven, while his eighteen-year-old sister was babysitting him, she asked, "Do you ever touch yourself? Would you like me to touch you?"

"She had me come into her room, lie on top of her and put myself into her. I think this happened about three times.

"My sister, whose life is pretty screwed up, recently told me she was assaulted by my dad."

"When I was about twelve, I remember being home sick from school one day. My mother came in the room, saw that I was aroused and got into bed with me. I felt embarrassed at first about it, and then later I didn't.

"When I was in junior high I wasn't popular and was usually overweight and didn't have any girlfriends, so a friend and I sometimes got into bed and touched each other.

"When I was about thirty, I was very frustrated in my marriage. I went out one night to a bar. I wanted to find someone who would find me attractive. I met a guy there who invited me to his apartment. I felt as long as what we did was below the waist, it was okay, it would not be homosexual. Kissing would have repulsed me. I later felt very disgusted with myself."

Today Ron has a driving need to be found attractive, and even though he once weighed about three hundred pounds, he keeps himself trim and has cut out his heavy drinking and kicked his four-pack-a-day cigarette habit.

Ron's emotions are filled with feelings of rejection and

anger. Ron knows he was molested but he never saw the connection with his marriage problems. Apparently, neither did any of his counselors. They were aware of his anger but never probed into the source.

Molly acknowledged to me her anger, but insisted to Ron that she had none, that it was all his problem. Molly's driving need is to control and to be in control. That is a little difficult for a Sanguine-Choleric living with a Melancholy-Choleric who also wants control. Molly agrees they are committed to each other and to loving each other. Molly is easily angered (and can become almost as violent as Ron), has an obsessive fear of heights, doesn't like to get her face wet, has severe PMS, has had asthma since she was twelve, which increases just before her cycle time. She has both a compulsive need to cover up her body at certain times, and to display it at other times. She is subject to bouts of depression, and has a great need to be non-sexually touched. She doesn't remember crying as a child, but recognizes that when her emotions flare up it is anger that comes out.

Molly remembers masturbating with a sanitary napkin when she was six years old. From then until she was about fourteen, she remembers her brother playing sexual games with her. It was the only time he paid attention to her and it felt good. She also remembers being left at a family friend's on several occasions with their teenage son to babysit her while the parents went out together. She remembers very clearly that what he did to her was oral rape.

At eight, "I started sleeping with my eyes open. I was afraid something might happen to me while I was asleep."

When she was seventeen, and "was already a woman inside" she called some college boys who were home and said, "If you want it, come on over and get it." They sped over. This continued for about four months. "I did sex for sport. I was willing to sacrifice and take the risks for the few minutes of being held. I was looking for love, but I felt angry. It was very unfulfilling."

Molly has many more cases of known sexual abuse in

her childhood and promiscuity in adulthood. She never felt her mother was there for her and has "real anger toward her today." Her older sister seemed to get everything: "She was so pretty, I always felt like a mudhen."

31. AFFAIRS

Husbands and wives must be faithful to each other
(Hebrews 13:4, TEV).

It doesn't seem logical that women molested as children would ever want anything to do with sex again but the amazing truth is that they frequently become promiscuous in their teens, seeking love in the only way they know it.

Toya, a strikingly attractive oriental, approached me with her story. She was born of a Korean mother and an American soldier father who was never heard from again. Because of her mixed blood (a disgrace to her family), Toya was taken to an orphanage when she was six months old. She was adopted by American missionaries who returned to the States when she was ten. From that time on her brother raped her regularly. When she complained to her father, he said she was lucky to have a nice home and that she should cooperate with her brother. Later the father molested her and when Toya told her mother, she replied stoically, "Boys will be boys."

Toya told me, "Because I was foreign, they looked on me as a pet—like a dog they could kick around."

Toya became promiscuous during her teen years even though she was in church every Sunday and was a leader in the youth group. She married the youth pastor, settled down and had two little girls who are one-fourth Korean. Her husband threw himself into his work and she felt he put the church ahead of her.

Her marriage should have been the end of her loose lifestyle brought on by her childhood abuse, but as is typical she began to have an affair with a man in the church who was known as a playboy. She knew this man was worthless and in the time she had been seeing him he had been through several other affairs. When I asked her why she would risk her marriage for this man, she thought a moment and then said, "I guess he's about as worthless as I feel I am."

Her husband had become suspicious and she had confessed her infidelity. As a pastor, he had to seek counsel out of town and they had been taking a weekly trip into the nearest big city. Toya, an adorable Sanguine, winked at me and said, "I know just what to say to please my husband and to fool the counselor. They both think I've changed my ways and just yesterday the counselor told me he was so proud of me and I could stop coming. I've sort of graduated, but what neither of them know is that I'm still seeing that other man. My husband told me he'd divorce me if I ever cheated again. Why am I still doing this?"

Why is Toya driven to sex outside of marriage? Because she feels worthless and can only find excitement in sex when it's forbidden. If we didn't know Toya's background we might label her as a loose woman who has made bad choices, but when we know how she was treated as an animal by people who were preaching Christian love, we can see how she fits the pattern of the victim. We are not to condone her secretive lifestyle, but we can understand where the pattern comes from. Behavioral counseling, telling her to refrain from her extra-marital affair, has had no effect. Toya needs to peel away layers of her past hurts, face the abuse squarely, and deal with the source, not the symptoms.

Because she doesn't want to lose her children or ruin her husband's ministry, she is now willing to seek help. But her compulsions are strong. What a tragedy that so many lives are in jeopardy over what two Christian men did in sport throughout Toya's childhood.

Often in the homes of Christian workers we find that preoccupation with the "Lord's work" leads to emotional neglect on both sides and becomes a downhill cycle. If the male has received any sexual abuse or even comments about being a sissy when he was a child, he may have underlying feelings of inadequacy as a sex partner. This person often "escapes to ministry" to keep himself holy and away from worldly temptations. He easily becomes absorbed in the problems of others and emotionally neglects his family while mouthing platitudes about God's care and protection.

The children in this "All for God, nothing for you" home frequently turn from the Lord and want nothing to do with a church that has robbed them of their father.

The wife in this home either becomes withdrawn and depressed or is at least open to any form of seduction. One adorable Sanguine lady with a saintly husband in a supervisory denominational position told me that she had housed many traveling evangelists in her married years and had been happily seduced by many of them. She smiled as she said, "If I told you the names you'd know some of them. If it hadn't been for my flings with them, I wouldn't even know what sex is."

Sometimes the male partner in the dysfunctional Christian home feels so spiritual that he ignores any quiet stirrings within him. He and his wife live like brother and sister. Then one day he is counseling some poor distraught woman who falls into his arms in tears and all his latent sexual potential comes bursting forth. Some are frightened off at this point; others "help" the poor lady with her problems. As we travel, we are constantly amazed at how many women tell us of their hidden affairs with Christian leaders. Certainly one doesn't need to have been a victim to have an affair but an abused background seems to remove some of the normal restraints.

32. MULTIPLE MARRIAGES

He must have only one wife, be sober, self-controlled and orderly (1 Timothy 3:2, TEV).

Whenever we meet someone—especially a woman—who has had two or more marriages because of divorce, we ask the "why" question. It invariably seems to reveal significant clues. Divorce and remarriage is simply a prevalent fact in the "throw away society" that exists even in our Christian community.

The added tragedy of childhood sexual abuse is that the victim, now an adult, is almost doomed to unhappiness and dysfunction in marriage. This results in maintaining a frustratingly unsatisfying relationship, or the alternative: losing or switching to new mates, constantly seeking but rarely finding the right partner who will be caring and patient enough to accept the victim's often strange behavior patterns.

Our nation's divorce rate at present is running at better than one out of every two new marriages. Long-term relationships are the exception. When we consider the stunning impact of sexual abuse on marriage relationships, we can begin to understand one of the major underlying causes for marriage failure. A major factor, but one that is rarely ascribed its rightful position in the chamber of horrors.

33. LITTLE MOTHER SYNDROME

Children should not have to provide for their parents
(2 Corinthians 12:14, TEV).

David Peters, in *A Betrayal of Innocence*, well describes the transition from little child to little mother.

> As sexual abuse continues within a home, a massive confusion develops within the child's mind. At one moment, she is an object of sexual desire, to be wooed and courted. She even has some degree of control over the adult while advances are being made. Then, immediately following the abuse, she again becomes a dominated child—without control—subject to the orders and discipline of adults. This lover-child confusion is an almost universal outgrowth of incestuous relationships. The victim is robbed of her right to a clearly defined role within the family and instead is forced to float between the adult world and the world of children.
>
> Often going hand in hand with the lover-child confusion is...the "little mother syndrome." The fact that most non-offending caretakers (usually mothers) were sexually molested themsel-

ves as children contributes heavily to this phenomenon. Because of her own molestation as a child, the mother often suffers from difficulties in regard to intimacy and sexual adjustment. Rather than fight the developments in the family, of which she is often vaguely aware, she may choose to remove herself gradually from the role of mother. As this transition takes place, the child often takes on an increasing number of motherly duties, including care of the younger children, a larger share of the household chores, and the position of emotional confidante to the father. Assuming the role of his sexual partner seems almost to be a logical step in this progression of errors.

The little mother syndrome is an important indicator of sexual abuse and is seen with shocking regularity in sexually abusive families. Yet such behavior is too often overlooked or dismissed as being indicative of a "very responsible young lady who cares about her sisters and brothers."[16]

34. LACK OF TRUST

Give me some sign that I can trust you (Joshua 2:12, TEV*).*

From infancy a child depends totally on her mother and father to supply all of her needs. She has to be loved, fed, changed, and nurtured. The infant can do nothing for herself. She trusts her parents completely. As she grows and learns to do some things for herself, that trust relationship also grows until that day when sexual abuse comes into the child's life.

Then, in one mindless action, the trust bank becomes insolvent and total bankruptcy takes place. If the trust relationship between that parent and child is over, the child's emotions are thrown into utter confusion. Almost as often, the relationship with the non-offending parent is damaged as well. "Why didn't mommy protect me?" or "Where was mommy — why did she let this happen to me?"

Even if a child has no memory of any sexual abuse in her childhood, she may still feel she never can trust anyone. Because a parent's abusive actions destroyed that little child's God-given feelings of trust, she may not feel she can trust the Father image of God! What a devastation it must be to want to love God but not be able to trust Him. What a shame it is that when a parent betrays the automatic trust of a child, he also wipes out that child's ability to trust anyone, including God, and sends that child into a lifetime of suspicion and anxiety. No wonder so many women today are crying out, "Give me some sign that I can trust you."

35. OTHER NAMES

A good name is better than precious ointment
(Ecclesiastes 7:1, KJV)

A person who filled out much of this section of Part II, who does have several names for herself and who functions at times in the different personalities of these other names, has developed what is known as multiple personalities. The most frequent and most probable cause of this development is a childhood sexual victimization of such magnitude and/or frequency that this defense mechanism had to be constructed simply to cope and survive.

Many persons with multiple personalities have one that is hateful and dangerous, often trying to kill off the others. It is a fact that they literally sometimes succeed.

If you feel this symptom may apply to you, we would urge you to seek out a qualified therapist as quickly as possible. A qualified therapist is one who, when you ask "Have you had significant success in working with multiple personalities?" is able to answer with an unhesitating "Yes." He or she should be highly recommended in this field. We regret to advise that in working with anyone else you will likely be either wasting your time and money or educating that counselor or therapist at your expense. Simply stated, it is a very specialized field with precious few qualified professionals available.

36. TMJ

Consider my affliction and my trouble (Psalm 25:18).

Many people suffer from the jaw disease commonly

known as TMJ who apparently have no distortion or irregularity of their bone formation. In quite a few cases, there seems to be no medical explanation for the unquestioned discomfort and intense pain. From our understanding, the symptoms are most prevalent during periods of stress, and TMJ is often considered to be a stress-induced malady.

It is most interesting to note the connection in several women with whom we have talked who were diagnosed as suffering from TMJ, who also suffered from attacks of stress and who were later determined to be victims of sexual trauma. We do not presume to imply that everyone suffering from TMJ has been sexually victimized, but there does seem to be strong evidence that with adult levels of stress resulting in TMJ, the root cause of that stress may be childhood sexual abuse—particularly oral sex. If confirmed by other key symptoms described in this section, this conclusion should give new hope to many TMJ sufferers. Identifying the original source of the stress, then experiencing the restoration of the Lord Jesus Christ, could bring freedom from the physical pain of TMJ.

37. OUT OF TOUCH WITH GOD

My God, my God, why hast thou forsaken me?
(Mark 15:34)

Not everyone who has trouble relating to God is a victim, but those who have been abused often feel that God has deserted them. Coupled with other symptoms, our detachment from a vital relationship with God gives us a clue. There may be a barrier in our spiritual life that may indicate some pains of the past that we have not yet overcome or uncovered.

We can readily understand how the adult who was abused or who felt rejected as a child could take on the cloak of depressive loneliness, guilt, and of being soiled, unworthy or unacceptable. She was made to feel that way as a child. Especially tragic is the adult who attempts to face the reality and bring it into the open among family or before the Christian body, expecting to find compassion and tenderness but meeting disavowal and further rejection. Where can one turn after finding one rejection after another? The hurdles on the upward road seem insurmountable. *Where is God? Why does He let all this happen to me? Has He abandoned me?*

Jenny had every reason to feel abandoned, rejected, out of touch with God. In her letter, she wrote:

> I just wanted to thank you for writing such a beautiful book, *Hope for Hurting Women.* It has helped me so much in many of the healing processes that I have had to go through in the past three years. Two years ago I was in a state psychiatric hospital for severe depression resulting from twelve years of sexual abuse from my father. I have spent the last two to three years trying to make a life for myself away from my family, who have disowned me for telling the "family secret."

Jenny is a victim of repeated abuse and multiple rejection. Is it possible to identify with a Father God when you have suffered years of abuse and been rejected again and again by your earthly father, family and friends? For some this is exceedingly difficult. Intellectually the victim can draw the distinction, but emotionally, it may be almost impossible to trust a loving, merciful, protective Father God, when for years the image of father has instead been demanding, hurtful, and destructive.

Any of us can feel "out of touch with God." It may simply be a result of misplaced priorities or unconfessed sin over a period of time. But for the one who is a victim, a subtle barrier can block the establishment of the bonding and abiding relationship with the heavenly Father. If you answered "Yes" to two of these questions in Part II, there must be a reason why you have difficulty sensing His presence. Look to your childhood for the reasons.

38. GUILT

Our guilt has mounted up to the heavens (Ezra 9:6, RSV).

Guilt is the natural result of sins we commit. It is the way the Holy Spirit pricks our conscience to let us know that we have displeased God. Guilt is healthy and normal, for not one of us is without sin. It is part of our cleansing process. As we become aware of our shortcomings, we have the knowledge of those areas of our life that we must submit to Him. We are cleansed of the guilt by confession of the sin.

Guilt is also the unnatural result of the sins that were committed against you. Unexplained and underlying feelings of guilt are typical of the adult who suffered sexual trauma as a child. If you answered "Yes" to several of the questions in this section of Part II, even if you have no memory of any such abuse, there is significant likelihood that you were innocently used to satisfy someone else's compulsive needs.

If you are one who is aware of and does remember early childhood sexual activity and are carrying a burden of guilt to this day, you may feel safely sure that it is the basic cause of your feelings of guilt or unworthiness.

RECAPPING YOUR SYMPTOMS

Turn back to the beginning of Part II, "Identification." Wherever you put an X in the box, put an X on the line of the corresponding symptom that applies to you.

___ 1. Earliest Memories

___ 2. Memory Gap

___ 3. Bad Rooms —
Bad Houses

___ 4. Mental Flashes

___ 5. Childhood Photos

___ 6. Eyes

___ 7. Personality Splits

___ 8. Dreams

___ 9. Rejection

___ 10. Age Forty

___ 11. Depression

___ 12. Anger

___ 13. Life of Service

___ 14. Physical Features

___ 15. Sleeplessness

___ 16. Pains, Migraines,
Undiagnosed
Problems

___ 17. PMS

___ 18. Asthma, Choking
and Gagging

___ 19. Hatred and
Resentment

___ 20. Obsessions

___ 21. Compulsions

___ 22. Family Alcoholism

___ 23. Eating Disorders

___ 24. Hidden Urges

___ 25. Personal Hygiene

___ 26. Smells, Odors

___ 27. Attitudes Toward
Sex

___ 28. Reaction to Possibility of Sexual Abuse

___ 29. Nudity

___ 30. Known Sexual
Molestation

___ 31. Affairs

___ 32. Multiple Mar-
riages

___ 33. Little Mother
Syndrome

___ 34. Lack of Trust

___ 35. Other Names

___ 36. TMJ

___ 37. Out of Touch
with God

___ 38. Guilt

TOTAL NUMBER OF SYMPTOMS
YOU MARKED = _____

PART IV

RESTORATION

(Fred and Florence)

The Steps to Freedom and Peace

1

THE PROMISE OF RESTORATION

Have you sensed that you may have been a victim of sexual abuse? At this point in your personal search for wholeness, it is possible you've discovered that your body and emotions were defiled, and you are beginning to see how that trauma has affected so much of the way you feel and act today.

Another possibility is that you may have seen that you do have many of the symptoms, but that is all you know. Your eyes have been opened to the possibility, but you still have no memory of any abuse, and, perhaps, still question that such a thing is even possible or that it would have any effect on you today. The third possibility is that you may have found you have virtually none of the symptoms of abuse. You may have escaped, by the grace of God, the childhood trauma to which so many millions in our country today have been subjected. If you were spared, that alone is enough for you to sing praises to the Lord as you have learned how devastating it has been to so many others.

Perhaps you found that you are a victim of emotional deprivation—that you have experienced the hurtful feelings of rejection. Rejection, which invariably accompanies the feelings resulting from sexual abuse, can be equally destructive to happy, healthy, adult emotions. In looking back at your feelings of rejection, you will see that the steps to restoration which follow apply equally to those victimized by sexual abuse or by emotional deprivation.

Look at the symptoms that you marked with an X in Part II. Are there some in your life today from which you would like to be freed — some emotions that are binding you from being all in Christ and for Christ that you would like to be? As we study the New Testament, we see that our Lord Jesus never set out each day to see if He could find someone to heal. The persons He healed took the first step. They went looking for Jesus, or someone else went in their behalf. A theme which you will find recurring again and again through the Bible is "If we . . . then He."

> *If my people* . . . shall humble themselves, and pray, and seek my face . . . *then* will *I* hear from heaven and will forgive their sin, and will heal the land (2 Chronicles 7:14).

The first step is up to us. If we come to Him . . . then He will hear, forgive and heal.

> *If we* confess our sins, *he is* faithful and just, to forgive us our sins, and to cleanse us from all unrighteousness (1 John 1:9).

We must come to the Lord first, then He will forgive us of the sins we have committed, and He will cleanse us of the sins that have been committed against us!

As you search both the Old and New Testaments you will find this theme constantly coming to your attention. It is a basic truth of the way God demonstrates His Grace for us.

Therefore, if you have many of the symptoms, take steps today to begin seeing a competent counselor who knows how to help victims of childhood trauma.

The Healing Fruit of Freedom

It is never pleasant to relive or uncover past pain in our lives. That is why it was buried in the first place. It was simply too much for the child's emotions to deal with. Now, as adults, we must search and pray diligently to release those memories in order for the healing process of the Lord to commence. "No chastening for the present seemeth to be joyous, but grievous; nevertheless afterward it yieldeth the peaceable fruit of righteousness" (Hebrews 12:11). Likewise no cleansing of painful memories is pleasant, but afterward yieldeth the healing fruit of freedom.

Heidi found immediate relief each time additional painful memories came into focus. Both physical and emotional problems lessened or began to disappear. She actually laughed during one of our conversations! What joy it was to hear her personality sparkling for the first time. And immediately the Lord began to give Heidi a ministry of compassion and understanding for other victims.

Only a week after Patti's discovery, her husband told us with deep appreciation and excitement that he had a "new wife." Patti herself told us she had gone alone to her local bus depot to pick someone up, and only later realized she hadn't been afraid of being raped — for the first time in her life! She also had been freed of the need when she entered her house to check each room carefully, and under the beds, to make sure no one was there. And these were only two of the obsessive traumas of which the Lord had already healed her.

What made the difference? Heidi and Patti earnestly sought the Lord in prayer and asked the Holy Spirit to bring all things to their remembrance (John 14:26) and guide them into all truth about themselves (John 16:13). They found the answer because they sought Him with all their heart and soul (Deuteronomy 4:29). As Christians they knew there is only one way with God, and that is *all the way*. Nevertheless, they were afraid, and they didn't like what they found. It was painful and hurtful. How could Patti's mother and Heidi's father have done such things to them? But they believed that Jesus would restore to them the years the locusts had eaten (Joel 2:25) and He is already doing so!

Awareness is the first step to freedom, and then the Lord can begin His restoration process. He has also shown that 1 John 1:9 is operative in this situation. "If we confess [acknowledge] our sins," those sins also that were committed *against* us, "he is faithful to forgive us," [of the guilt we often feel] and "*cleanse us*" from the unrighteousness done to us. How can we acknowledge a sin committed against us if we have no awareness of it?

Denial

On the other hand, some will be tempted to *deny* that any abuse could ever have taken place, or even if it did, "that it could have any effect on me today." A mother recently asked us at our booktable if we had a book that would be helpful to her daughter who would be going away to college soon. Naturally, we asked something of the daughter's needs in order to be able to recommend an appropriate resource. After hearing of the emotional stress in her daughter's life, Fred asked, "Have you ever considered the possibility of sexual abuse?"

The mother almost defiantly answered, "That's impossible!"

Fred asked, "How can you be sure?"

"Because I'm her mother and I've never left her alone with anyone!"

"Did you have any babysitters for your daughter?"

"Yes, but I only had girls!"

It had never occurred to her that girls, or women, could also be victimizers. Just this week we have spoken with two different young men, both of whom had been abused as children by girl babysitters. The one clearly remembered when his thirteen-year-old sitter abused him when he was five; the other by his seventeen-year-old sitter when he was ten. Both young men admitted to being born-again Christians, but with many problems now in their adult life, including drugs.

The mother was not even willing to consider abuse as a possibility. If indeed one out of four women and one out of eight men are victims, it is important that we be alert to the possibilities. When you add the presence of symptoms to statistics, it is a wonder that anyone would deny that they might have been victimized. As you study your Bible, watch for the number of verses that do, or can, refer to the sins that were committed against us.

If you have no memory or proof of such sin committed against you but do have identified symptoms, open your mind and let the Holy Spirit guide you into all truth. Don't further punish yourself by being "in denial."

Discovering the Truth

If you have identified a number of the listed symptoms as being present in your life but still have no conscious memory of anything happening to you as a child, you now must commit yourself to finding the answers you are searching for. Your search may uncover the desired truth quickly, or it may take some time. The first thing you should do is seek out a knowledgeable counselor who can give you professional guidance in uncovering the truth.

You will also want to find a trustworthy support person. If you are married and your partner is supportive and understanding, he or she would be the best choice. The key criteria are *supportive* and *understanding,* for this person will need to be available to be with you, pray with you, comfort you, and encourage you in the days ahead. Except for a husband or wife, your support person should be of the same sex and deeply committed to the Lord Jesus.

Share with your counselor and supporter what you are facing, what you are searching for, and that there may be deep emotional times ahead as your lid of memories begins to release. Ask them to commit to see you through, to be willing to pray diligently with you that the Holy Spirit will bring all things to your remembrance. Since you will likely have some deep emotional bonding in the next few days, it would be well if you could share these pages with them, including your journalizing and your written answers in Part II, so that they will have some knowledge of your feelings and be prepared to be compassionate. By sharing your symptoms with your counselor and supporter, you make them partners to your innermost feelings and deepest confidence. Therefore, they must be people you know you can trust, and with whom you will be comfortable.

Prayer

Come to the Holy Spirit in prayer—earnest and diligent prayer. We speak not of little blurbs sent heavenward now and then but of a deep pouring-out-of-your-soul-on-your-knees prayer! You may even find it necessary to ask the Lord to strengthen your desire to find the truth.

We encourage you to start a prayer journal — perhaps as a section of the journal you are already keeping. In it, each day, write out to God your pleading to find the truth of your past, no matter how painful it may be. Write out your prayers, word for word, just as though you were writing a letter to God, asking Him to come and help you.

Do not rush your prayer time. Plan on at least an hour each day! Do not wait until you have the time to pray. Make the time! It must come before and above all else. The best time is early in the morning when you are fresh. "Seek ye *first* the kingdom of God and his righteousness; and [then] all these things shall be added unto you" (Matthew 6:33).

If we . . . then He!

This prayer search should become the major thrust of your life for these days. If it is necessary to take a day or two off from work, by all means do so. Clear your daily calendar of all that is not absolutely essential. Plan to spend *hours* in Bible study and prayer.

Keep in close daily contact with your supporter. Share everything that God is unfolding to you. Answers, or glimpses of answers, may come during prayer, during study, or even in "flashes" as the day goes on. Be prepared to jot down on a piece of paper any such flashes that come to your mind. Focus on them and see what else comes into the picture as your mind dwells on these flashes. Fervently plead to the Holy Spirit to show you the whole picture.

When Patti did this, a picture of herself as a tiny little girl came to her mind. She was sitting in a play pool on the lawn, and she thinks she might have been nude. Then she could see herself walking up on the porch where her mother was sitting. Then it happened. The first repressed memory came in to focus. Her mother reached down and molested her. Patti was shocked and hurt. How could her mother have done that to her?

This was only the beginning. More and worse came

later. But God answered her prayers. The Holy Spirit gradually released these buried memories and she was at last, after thirty-nine years, ready to start on her healing journey.

Keep a record in your journal of *every memory* of your childhood that comes to your mind during these days. Some of the memories may be happy ones or seem insignificant, but they may lead to the ones you are seeking. You may see a pattern developing in your written notes. You may see fear developing, or anger, or one person may continually come into focus. Your answers may come in bits and pieces, or in cascades of long-forgotten memories pouring over you. As the pieces of the puzzle begin to fit into the picture, be sure to share with your support person what you are learning. Your supporter can only be supportive to the extent that you share your discoveries with him.

If after a week or two of this intensive prayer your memory bank is still bare, we would recommend you spend a day in fasting and prayer. Set the entire day aside to spend with the Lord, allowing no other activities to distract your mind or attention from the task for which you asked the Holy Spirit to help you. The Lord reminded the disciples in Matthew 17:21 that there are some things which can only be accomplished through fasting and prayer.

If your answers don't come, do not despair. Do not quit. Don't let an outsider tell you this is foolishness, or let some well-meaning but uninformed friend tell you to forget about this "business of your past" and to "get on with your life." Awareness is the first step to freedom, and God will give you the awareness. He knows all and knows you may need a little more time. He already *knows* what you are searching for!

Keep on keeping on. If you have not yet done so, now is the time to locate a knowledgeable Christian counselor to help you through the recognition and restoration process.

The first rule, before going to any counselor for help, is to ask point blank, "What experience have you had with victims of sexual abuse?" This is still a very specialized field, and there are relatively few who are informed, skilled, and also Christian. Any answer that gives you less than full confidence probably indicates a counselor to avoid. A sincere and competent therapist will probably arrange your visits to give you two to three hours at a time. A one hour visit, which is in actuality forty-five to fifty minutes, is simply not enough time for you to get deeply into discovering emotionally repressed memories.

The Glorious Promise

This is not the end. This is really the beginning of a new life for you — a dynamic life in Christ, full of new opportunities, new joy, and a new sense of purpose in life. One day you will even be able to say, "Praise God for all that has happened to me. I may have wished I never had to go through it, but now I can rejoice and praise my God for what He has given to me today!" Yes, there is a bright new world coming for you.

But there is one catch! You have to be a Christian to enjoy it, to experience it!

If you have read through this book this far, and right now you are not sure that you can answer a resounding "Yes" to these three questions:

1. Are you a Christian?

2. Have you received the Lord Jesus Christ into your life?

3. If you died before this month was out, are you sure you would go to heaven?

. . . then turn to Appendix A at the end of the book and be sure.

For the Christian, there is the Glorious Promise. For non-Christians, sadly, it all ends at this point. They have identified their problem. They are better off than they were before. They have achieved awareness and have taken the first step to freedom. Unfortunately, for those who live without Christ, that first step is also the end of their journey. We are utterly convinced that there exists no healing

of the emotional residue of sexual abuse without the healing power of the Lord Jesus. He alone can and will heal your
broken emotions. There is no healing "in the world." All
the psychiatric or psychological help that excludes the Lord
Jesus Christ can only take you so far. But He can take you
all the way to complete healing and restoration.

In Luke 4:18, quoting from what was written about
Him in Isaiah 62:1, Jesus said, "I have come to heal the
broken-hearted, to set the captive free, those who are in
bondage." The victims we have been discussing are the
broken-hearted who are in bondage to the defilement of
their body and emotions. Jesus said He came to set us free.
He will set you free. That is the Glorious Promise!

A well-known secular "authority" on sexual abuse, a
counselor and victim herself, was reported to have recently said on a national television talk show that sexual abuse
was the unpardonable sin. A woman in the audience,
probably a Christian, asked, "Where does forgiveness come
in?" The answer, sad to say, was that there is no forgiveness for the victimizer.

Of course, that isn't what the Bible says, but that
wasn't an issue on the program. Since human forgiveness
must come from the victim, that means the victim must
bear the burden of carrying that hatred, anger or resentment for the rest of her life. How unfair that, according to
this counselor, the victim must carry the burden! The "acid
of anger eats away only at the container." That not only
doesn't sound fair, it doesn't even make sense. The wrong
person is carrying the burden. Jesus has made it possible
for the victim to be healed. Jesus can set the captive free.
"You shall know the truth, and the truth [Jesus] shall set
you free" (John 8:32). What a Glorious Promise!

Not only will Jesus heal you and set you free. There is
more. Remember the Holy Spirit's part, to guide you into
all truth, and bring all things to your remembrance? Now
comes the role of God the Father. Look for the role God has
planned for *you* in these verses:

Blessed be God, even the Father of our Lord Jesus Christ and

the God of all *comfort*; Who *comforteth us* in all our afflictions, that *we may* be able to *comfort them* which are in any affliction, by the comfort wherewith we ourselves *are comforted* of God (2 Corinthians 1:3-4).

Even while we are being comforted by God, we will be able to comfort those who are also afflicted. That's exciting! That ignites our sense of purpose on this earth. Ten million sexually abused Christians in this country waiting for us to be comforters. What a mission field! Almost immediately after Patti and Heidi found their hidden traumas, the Lord began sending hurting Christians to them. Picture the joy they felt in being able to have a positive impact in the lives of others so quickly. Kathy, who discovered her victimization in February, was already in July starting to minister to her second group of victims. The comforted became comforters. This is not to say that Patti, Heidi, and Kathy were already fully healed. But neither is it the blind leading the blind. For they have received a comfort which they can share. They can give hope and encouragement to others who are searching. The apostle Paul in Philippians 3:12-13 acknowledged that he was not yet perfect but he nevertheless reached out to press forward. We might call this "service while in the process."

The Glorious Promise is that Jesus is available and ready to heal you. That healing, however, is up to you. It is not up to Jesus. He is the constant. He is always there. We have to come to Him. In terms of our healing, then, the progress is up to us. We are the variable. We are to have a very significant part in our own healing process. The rate of your healing, then, is very much in your own hands. If Jesus is the healer, your role will be to totally align yourself with Jesus, to immerse yourself in Jesus.

If you were suddenly told you had serious cancer of the stomach and without immediate and concerted action on your part there would be no hope, would you not quickly and earnestly do something about it? If surgery were prescribed, would you not want to go to the finest stomach cancer surgeon in the world? If you are a victim of sexual abuse, you also have a similarly serious cancer. It is "emotional cancer" and it, too, requires the finest surgeon in the world. Fortunately, despite His unique skills and experiences He is not overbooked. You do not have to wait six months for an appointment. He is available now. You only have to go to Him. His name is the Lord Jesus Christ, the *one* who can heal your hurt, your anger, your depression, your lack of self-worth, your compulsions, your feelings of rejection. But you must go to Him. He will require that you make Him the first, foremost, most important thing in your entire life. Is that too much to ask to be healed of cancer?

If you treat your recovery process casually, you may expect a casual recovery or even no recovery at all. The extra blessing is that this intense alignment with your Lord is something you will never want to give up for the rest of your life. It will be that meaningful to you. You will have a richer understanding of the truths of Proverbs 3:13-15:

> Happy is the man that findeth wisdom, and the man that getteth understanding.
> For the merchandise of it is better than the merchandise of silver, and the gain thereof than fine gold.
> She is more precious than rubies: and *all the things thou canst desire are not to be compared unto her.*

As you proceed through your healing process you will gain more and more of the wisdom and understanding of the Lord. As you find it you will never want to relinquish hold of it or return to the baser unfulfilling ways of the world. The lures of the world never satisfy. You always need more and more to "recapture the feeling." The wisdom of the Lord is fulfilling and nothing can even equal the joy of it.

A Double Blessing

So you will receive a double blessing. You will be healed, and you will be lifted to a higher level of understanding and relationship to the Lord Jesus. We oftentimes need the low times in our life in order to reach to the pinnacle. It has often been said, "There is no growth on the mountaintop, the growth only comes in the valley." Oh, Lord, if that be true, may we never leave the valley!

The Bible also tells us we can and must have a very significant role in our own recovery process. That means you can do something about it. You don't simply have to stand by, watch and wait for the healing to take place. God intends for you to be an integral part of freeing your mind from memories that bind.

As Fred was in the midst of his own healing process of the pains of anger and childhood rejection, his attention was redrawn to 2 Corinthians 7:1. It had been his prayer verse for the preceding year.

> Let us cleanse ourselves from all defilement of flesh and spirit, perfecting holiness in the fear of God (NASB).

Fred had focused on the last phrase, "perfecting holiness." Above all else, he desired holiness in his life: "I wanted to please my Father in Heaven. And the Lord was helping me throughout the year to perfect that holiness, to see those areas that were not pleasing to Him. My healing and my own personal desire for holiness became even more effective when I recognized that my controlled—but deep-seated—anger resulted from my childhood feelings of rejection, coupled with that form of sexual abuse we describe as suppression."

It was during this time that the Lord refocused Fred's attention on 2 Corinthians 7:1. Imagine his spiritual excitement as he examined the first phrase:

> Let us cleanse ourselves from all defilement of flesh and spirit.

After some confirming research, it became clear that the verse was referring to defilement of the body and of the emotions. Further, it was referring to the defilement that was done to us, the sins that were committed against us.

The first part of the phrase says, "Let us cleanse ourselves." That means that we can have a part with God in the cleansing of our emotions. We already know that God will "cleanse us from all unrighteousness" (1 John 1:9). Jesus told us to "take my yoke upon you." Now we can be joined to Him, work side by side with Him, to cleanse all defilement of our flesh and spirit, our body and emotions.

The progress of our healing, then, will depend in large part on how effectively we fulfill the role God has assigned to us. That role is to make the Lord Jesus Christ preeminent in our life, first and foremost in every respect. The following plan of restoration will give you specific recommendations for achieving that relationship.

2

THE PLAN OF RESTORATION

Your part of the restoration plan will require time, effort and action. Since we have already learned that it is a partnership, it might be considered foolish to expect God to do His part if you do not do yours. If you have agreed that you have emotional cancer, is it not reasonable to presume that you are ready to take all steps necessary to be healed of that cancer?

If you can find a knowledgeable Christian counselor who will give you the extended session time you will need and who is skilled in gently guiding clients through the process of uncovering and healing painful memories, we recommend you work closely with him or her. At the same time, we suggest you implement the twelve recommendations in this chapter to lend strength and focus to the restoration process. If you do not have access to a qualified counselor, these steps can give you a good start toward restoration.

Your role in the plan of restoration starts with your daily quiet time alone with the Lord. It is recommended that you make every effort to set aside sufficient time for this in the earliest part of your day. Most adherents agree that their most effective times are early in the morning when their minds are alert and not yet distracted by the activities and pressures of the day. You will have to work out whatever schedule can best fit your family or work responsibilities.

The important thing is that your time with the Lord be given the highest priority. That means putting the Lord first, rather than trying to "work Him in somewhere." Plan on at least an hour a day. Can you allocate one out of twenty-four for your Savior?

1. Focus on the Centrality of Jesus Christ.

Start your daily time with the day's reading from Oswald Chambers, *My Utmost for His Highest*. This has been for the past fifty years an all-time bestselling daily devotional. There is a reason. The all-pervasive theme of his writings, each built around a Scripture verse, is the centrality of Christ Jesus in your life. The writings are clear but not simple. You will want to have a highlighter or underliner to mark key statements each day which have impacted your thinking.

2. Study the Word.

If his key verse for the day speaks especially to your heart, you may want to look in your Bible to see the full context of it, or to compare other chain verses with a similar theme. This can sometimes be so rewarding that you may spend your entire Bible study time hunting down, studying, and meditating on such verses. Many Bibles have chain references. We particularly recommend the *Thompson Chain Reference Bible*. It comes in King James or the New International Version translations, and in addition to chain references, has an excellent system of Bible Study Helps with index and a reasonably complete concordance.

Also highly recommended is the New American Standard Bible (quoted frequently herein) with cross-references. Not all editions of the NASB have these cross-references, so be sure to get one that does. In addition to being a modern and easily comprehended translation, it gives in the margin numerous other verses with similar content, thought, or words. When you are meditating on a given verse or thought, comparing these cross-references can be a treasure trove in itself.

Use your highlighter liberally in your Bible as well. It will help make your Bible personal to you. Do not hesitate to make notes in your Bible of your own thoughts, outlines, or "words from the Lord." The pages of your Bible are not too sacred to write upon. Plan approximately one-half hour or more for your daily Bible study.

Another suggestion for your Bible study is a daily sequential study in the Psalms. Most of these are prayers written by David, and the person searching for healing of emotions will quickly identify with the torments of David's soul as expressed in his prayers. After pouring his heart and hurts out to the Lord, he invariably ends with ecstatic praise as he sings out the thanksgiving of his heart. Studying the Psalms will lead your heart and your prayers into praise and thanksgiving as well.

There are many forms and types of Bible study. The important thing is not what you do, but that you do something! Unless you have never studied the Bible before and are not really familiar with it, we would not recommend for you at this time one of the many excellent Bible study programs, ten-step plans, etc., that are available. These are designed for new believers to get them started. You will probably be more energized by your own independent study of wherever the Lord leads you.

3. Communicate With God Through Written Prayer.

Following your daily period of Bible study, you will want to spend an average of thirty minutes or more in prayer. Does that sound like a lot of time, more than you have spent before? Are you wondering how you can possibly think of enough things to tell or ask your Father in heaven to spend thirty minutes doing it? Fred understands because he, too, would have thought that before. Now, he rarely prays for less than thirty minutes and has, on numerous occasions, prayed for two hours or more. "Obviously," he says, "in some of those longer sessions God and I had a lot of things to talk over!" How does he do it?

"I write out my prayers, word for word. Being half Melancholy, I even punctuate and capitalize properly. Probably doesn't make a bit of difference to the Lord, but

I feel good about it. I feel the Lord deserves the best I can give Him. Writing out my prayers has so improved and altered my prayer life and my relationship with my Father in heaven, that I believe I shall do it virtually every day for the rest of my days that the Lord chooses to leave me on this earth. I believe it is the major factor in my own healing process.

"It was writer and speaker Becky Tirabassi who was God's instrument in getting me to write out my prayers. Becky has been a special friend for several years, and I've known that she practices written prayer. Somehow it didn't touch me until I saw Becky sharing this on Christian television. That day God spoke to me! I started just a few days later, and have been doing it ever since. I use an 8" x 11" spiral binder and just write in it each day until my prayers are finished. I like to date each page, and also indicate the scriptural passages I studied that day, for they are often reflected in my prayers.

"Praying has now become an indescribable blessing, never the 'chore' that it sometimes was in the past. I cannot write fast enough to keep up with my thoughts, so there is never a lag. No longer am I sending up ten cent prayers and expecting million dollar answers! No longer does my mind wander, as it formerly did, when I am praying. No longer do I 'doze off' as has happened before, especially in the early morning.

"Instead of praying *to God,* I have found that I am often having communion *with God.* God has spoken to me clearly during these prayer times. On several occasions He has told me truth which I later found in His Word during my study time. That was so exciting, it was supernatural! On other occasions the Lord has lifted me to levels of prayer I had rarely experienced before.

"One of the great blessings has been to go back and read my prayers from a previous day. That is a 're-blessing.' I have been thrilled with the sense of spiritual energy and power I found in my own previous prayers. The writing of my prayers has also greatly deepened my love for the

Lord, the sense of adoration I have for Him, my desire to praise Him at all times. Surely it has greatly strengthened my faith.

"Another advantage of written prayer is that because I date each day's prayer I can immediately tell if I have missed a day or two. It therefore helps my discipline to stay with my daily program, and is more difficult for the devil to interfere.

"Since I have been sharing this concept from the platform for many months now, urging others to do the same, I have received the extra joy of people coming up to me saying they heard me suggest it several months ago, and when they started writing their own prayers they experienced the same blessings! Finally, just recently the Lord showed me that this plan is scriptural as well, for didn't David also write out his prayers, many of which we now know as the Psalms?"

In your written prayers it will be very important that you pray specifically for the needs and hurts of others. Not only is this part of God's scriptural provision for prayer:

> And the Lord *turned the captivity* of Job, when he *prayed for his friends* . . . (Job 42:10)

. . . but it also does one other very important thing which is pleasing to God. It gets your mind off yourself and your problems (which is when depression and self-pity are nurtured) and on to thinking of others. God will use your love and prayer for others to help free you from the bondage of your own past hurts. The importance of your prayer communion with God cannot be overemphasized in your restoration. It is the divine key to your healing, and to establishing an ever more intimate relationship with your Lord Jesus.

4. Become an "Expert" on Your Situation.

You will want to begin a "college course" of reading on the subjects that are of special interest to your personal needs. For example, if you are a victim of any of the forms of sexual abuse, you will want to read as much as you can on this subject, especially the good Christian books that are now being published. Look over the resource list of books in the appendix. You will find many that will be of great benefit to you in addition to those in our recommended reading program.

The adult emotional results of childhood sexual abuse are so little understood that you will want to become an expert on the subject. You will want to learn as much as you can about how your trauma has affected you. The God who comforts you wants you to also be a comforter, so you will want to understand as much as you can about the pains and hurts that others are facing. The more you understand, the more capable and the more compassionate a comforter you will become.

After you have finished reading this book and learning all you can from it, you will want to begin reading, studying and re-reading Jan Frank's excellent book, *A Door of Hope* — probably the most authoritative and helpful book available on the subject. Also published by Here's Life Publishers, it should be available at your Christian bookstore. If not, ask them to get copies for you and for all the others you know who will benefit from it. It can also be ordered from our office, as we regularly keep an ample stock on hand. Ordering information is included at the back of this book. Once again, with *A Door of Hope* and the other books we will recommend, keep your highlighter and your underliner handy to mark up the book. Make notes on everything that strikes you as particularly significant.

As you meet another person whom you think would be helped by our book or by Jan's book, you will be tempted to give them your copy. But as you know, the problem with "loaning" books is that they frequently fail to find their way back home! Your personally marked copy may be gone forever, unavailable to you for future reference or study. You should try to read *A Door of Hope* during the second week of the Ten Week Plan described later.

The next most essential book to read is *Understand-*

ing Your Past: The Key to Your Future, by Dr. Cecil Osborne. This book will help you to more fully understand how your childhood experiences have affected your adult emotions and behavior. This book is no longer generally available in bookstores, but is available through our office.

Since most people feel the results of childhood emotional deprivation or rejection, and virtually all victims have feelings of rejection, Barbara Taylor's clear and very helpful book *From Rejection to Acceptance* is most important for you to study. It will help you to anchor in your mind God's complete acceptance of you, thereby dispelling even the most subtle feelings of rejection you may have. Fred found this book to be exceptionally beneficial in his healing process. It is published by Broadman Press, and should be available in bookstores.

If you have not already read Florence's bestselling book on the four personalities, *Personality Plus,* published by Revell, and her newer, very insightful book, *Your Personality Tree,* published by Word, these must be high on your reading list. Both will give you a new and rich understanding of the personality traits God gave you at birth, and *Your Personality Tree* will show you how some of these characteristics may have been modified by life's experiences, parental training, abuse, or marriage. This whole fascinating subject has only been touched on in *Freeing Your Mind From Memories That Bind.* Further reading and study on the temperaments will be especially important to becoming free to be the person God created you to be.

You cannot read or study too much. There is much valuable wisdom and knowledge locked between the covers of good books. It is all available to you, but only if you avail yourself of the opportunity. Furthermore, we believe such reading to be a vital part of your total healing process.

5. Be Accountable.

As we talk with individuals who are working to overcome addictions, we find that many who do not yet have spiritual victory are hanging on by sheer will power to tough it out one day at a time. In Alcoholics Anonymous, the oldest successful support group in existence, the person has to admit he is helpless and call on a "higher power" as he perceives that divine being to be. Although the organization is not preaching the gospel, believing Christians in the local groups often have an evangelistic influence on individuals seeking a power more specific than some vague grand-daddy in the sky.

Whatever a person's problem may be, the first step is to admit that there is a situation that self-effort has been unable to correct and to seek divine healing. The second step, which has been the heart of the Anonymous groups' success, is their insistence on accountability. You must constantly keep in touch with at least one other person who has been where you are and will talk you through your temptation at the moment. Many have told me that without a specific individual holding them accountable, someone who cared enough to check in with them and encourage them daily, they never would have made it.

As you work through the pains of your past, realize how important it is to have a close friend, a prayer partner, a confidant, who is willing to hold you accountable. Usually a close family member is not the best choice as often they are sick of your problems and lack the patience to help you. Someone who has been dealing progressively with her own emotions is usually the most understanding, but an objective, willing friend with or without similar problems can be your support person. Even if you are working with a counselor once a week, you still need someone who will call and ask specific questions: "Have you journalized today? Have you written out your prayers? What verses have you found in your Bible study that have given you hope? Could we pray together now?"

For this person to be effective you have to be willing to accept her questions and not become defensive. Defensiveness will destroy the relationship and leave you alone.

If you sign up for any of the weight reduction programs, you must agree to come in daily, sometimes

weekly, to be checked. If you are evaluated daily, this accountability will keep you eating correctly. You don't want
to face your counselor if you have been binging between
sessions. Yet without accountability it is so easy to say,
"This one piece of cake won't make any difference."

The same principle applies when we are working
through the binding memories of the past. It's easier to quit
the program than to push through a painful past in order
to free your mind for the future.

So choose a willing, trustworthy, affirming friend who
will hold you accountable daily to persistently follow the
path to peace.

6. Enlist a Prayer Partner.

Another important element in your restoration
program is a trusting relationship with a prayer partner.
Such a person only needs to be available and committed to
working and praying with you. Your prayer partner must
be someone in whom you have complete confidence, who is
a mature Christian and is compassionate and understanding, but never judgmental or dogmatic. This person's
role is to help you listen, to encourage you, to be the wind
beneath your wings. A person who is a recovered or recovering victim would obviously have an identification with your
emotions. Not only will you and your prayer partner want
to be able to get together regularly for prayer for at least
the first ten weeks, but you will also want to be able to share
your victories, discoveries, valleys, hurts and doubts. The
Lord may send someone unexpectedly to you. Or, you may
have to ask the Lord to guide you to such a person, and then
ask her to be your helpmate, carefully explaining what you
will need from her. Again, it is important that this person
be of the same sex as you.

7. Find a Compassionate Comforter.

This is a person who definitely is a recovered or
recovering victim, whom you can call or meet with when
you are struggling with memories or have questions that

you just feel you need to discuss with someone more experienced than yourself. Your comforting friend could surely be someone out of town, even out of state, with whom you might converse once or twice a week. If the Lord does not bring someone to you in the first week or two, please feel free to call our office and we will endeavor to match you up with someone or help you make a connection with such a person.

There's an old expression about the blind leading the blind, suggesting that one of us has to see to help the other. In working with adult victims of incest, we have found that often only the blind can lead the blind because only they can truly understand how the other person feels and what they've been through. The pairing of two victims to work through the restoration process can be very effective if they are both believing Christians constantly calling on the wisdom of the Holy Spirit. By working together they are able to share mutual insight as it is revealed, encourage each other during depressing times, and hold each other to some measure of accountability.

Isaiah tells us that we are to help each other out in our times of need. We are to "lose the chains of injustice and untie the cords of the yoke, to set the oppressed free and break every yoke" (Isaiah 58:6, NIV). "Then your light will break forth like the dawn, and your healing will quickly appear. Your light will rise in the darkness, and your night will become like the noonday" (Isaiah 58:8,10, NIV).

It is only right that you should be prepared to pay the telephone toll charges in calls to your comforter, bearing in mind that your comforter may likely be working with several others at the same time. In calling your comforter, also be sensitive to her schedule, her family needs, and the time zone in which she lives. Your compassionate comforter could conceivably also be your prayer partner, but there is an advantage in having two such separate persons. The role of the comforter is primarily experience and guidance, while the role of the partner is prayer, listening, and caring.

8. *Join a Support Group.*

Until recently, individual therapy has been the predominant form of recovery assistance available to abuse victims. There is simply a grossly insufficient number of qualified therapists available to guide the millions of persons needing help. Fortunately, with the new awakening to the problem, other forms of restoration are developing, and one of these is support groups. A support group is generally a weekly gathering of five to eight persons who meet for mutual encouragement and sharing of experiences and feelings. They are being found in more and more communities. Some are professionally sponsored or directed, and others are simply individual self-help groups. Jan Frank, in *A Door of Hope*, has devoted an excellent chapter on how to organize a support group. If you do not find access to one in your area, you might want to get a group together to form one.

9. *Guard Your Input.*

As part of your program to immerse yourself in the Lord Jesus Christ and make Him first and foremost, you will want to carefully consider the nature of the sound input you allow into your mind.

Several years ago Fred began to listen to country music as he drove to work each day. He enjoyed the upbeat tempo and the generally happy sound.

"I didn't pay a lot of attention to the lyrics of the songs, but gradually I became familiar with them, and found myself singing along. It was probably a year or so before I realized the moral pollution I was putting into my mind. One day, as though struck by a thunderbolt, I suddenly realized how much the lyrics actually made one think about 'running around,' extra-marital sex, drinking and drunkenness. You hear enough of that and your mind is insidiously seduced into thinking this is the norm — that it is acceptable!

"I couldn't believe what I had allowed myself to listen to. I had been duped into complacency because these stations also played a fair number of very acceptable country-style gospel songs! That day I switched the buttons on my car radio forever off all the country music I had been listening to. Now I listen only to Christian radio, and in retrospect I can see the tremendous difference it has even made in me. It has been a subliminal but very significant part of my own healing."

What kind of music and thoughts are you allowing to enter your mind? There are so many good Christian music and teaching programs available today. Fortunately for us, there has been almost an explosion of new Christian radio stations. In virtually any area of our country you have a choice of Christian radio, so you can even choose the type of programming that you enjoy the most!

We have had the privilege of traveling several times to Australia to speak and share. We love the body of Christ there. Unless there are changes we have not heard about, at the present there are no Christian radio stations as we know them, and only very limited Christian radio and TV programming on the secular stations. We rarely appreciate how blessed we are with all the freedom and opportunity we have in America. Are you taking advantage of it? We urge you to take stock of the kind of radio and TV programming you are allowing to fill your mind. Replace any that is not uplifting and Christ-centered with that which will be a blessing to you and help speed you on in the healing of the memories that bind.

10. Give Away a "Silver Box" Each Day.

One of the key criteria of our Christian life is that we put our faith into action. Our Lord never expected us to hide our candle under a basket. Faith without works is dead. Our paraphrase of 1 John 3:18 is, "Love is not a proclamation or an explanation; love is a demonstration."

It is all too easy for the victim of abuse or rejection to dwell on her hurts. This leads to either depression or frustration. The two-pronged antidote is first to fix our focus on the Lord (Isaiah 26:3) and then to "do unto others

. . . " as God has directed us to do. As part of the recommended ten-week program you will have the opportunity to do something for, or say something to, someone that will be a comfort, a help or an encouragement. A little "silver box" of kindness! Each day you will want to check off your "Daily Silver Box Project." Melancholies will enjoy that! Sanguines could easily forget to do it, especially without the helpful chart.

Some of your efforts will come naturally and will qualify. Other days you will have to plan: Whom should I go to see; whom should I call; to whom should I write a note of encouragement or love; who is in the hospital I could visit; for what neighbor could I do an act of kindness; who can I bring a word of cheer to; who can I ask over for coffee or for supper? Each day the recipients of your thoughtfulness will be blessed and you will feel good yourself, for "It is more blessed to give than to receive" (Acts 20:35). Through the repetition, such acts of kindness will become a way of life for you.

Florence has a recorded message entitled "Little Silver Boxes with Bows on Top." It will be included if you order the recommended package of resource materials, or it can be ordered separately. Once you have listened to it you will be challenged to pass out "little silver boxes" to everyone you meet. The weekly chart will help you remember to do so!

Etienne De Grellet, about 1820, is reputed to have said, "I shall pass through this world but once. If, therefore, there be any kindness I can show, or any good thing I can do, let me do it now; let me not defer it or neglect it, for I shall not pass this way again."

May that also be said for us—and we'll do it in the name of the Lord Jesus Christ.

11. Laugh Each Day.

An apple a day may keep the doctor away, but a merry heart doeth good like a medicine and may help to heal a broken spirit. As you work through the serious, difficult, and often upsetting steps necessary to take before freeing your mind, it is important that you not get so bogged down that you don't come up for some fresh air. Although you may not feel like laughing, the healing powers of humor will hasten your recovery.

Norman Cousins tells in his book *Anatomy of an Illness* that he found funny movies cheered him up and lessened his pain.[1]

Focusing on the problems of the past, although necessary, can be physically draining and emotionally exhausting. Give yourself a humor break. Watch a funny show, read a chapter from a humorous book, call a friend who always has a hilarious story to tell. Do something to pick yourself up and give yourself a laugh.

Recently our friend Cal Walker tried an experiment on us. We each held out one arm and he pulled down on them. We were able to resist his tugs. He then said, "Think of something wonderful and exciting." Florence thought of a standing ovation she had just received. When Cal tried to pull her arm down, her resistance was even stronger! "Now think of something negative and depressing." Florence immediately keyed into a night when she got off the plane and was given some bad news. Cal easily pulled her arm down to her side. We couldn't believe the difference. Exciting thoughts raised our energy; sad thoughts lowered our resistance.

Don't keep yourself so bogged down with searching through the pains of your past that you forget to take a laugh break. A merry heart truly does good like a medicine.

12. *Remember: It's a Process.*

The Lord Jesus is capable of miraculous and instantaneous healings. Generally He seems to work in the normal time patterns. If you fractured your leg in several places, you might reasonably expect to have a cast put on it, and perhaps not walk on it for as long as six months. The Lord can, and on occasion has, healed such an injury in an instant. More often, however, He allows the healing to take place over a period of time.

The very same is true of the hurts and later adult manifestations of childhood sexual abuse or emotional deprivation. It has taken time for you to get where you are today. The emotions that were suppressed as a child and never had a chance to develop normally will not suddenly blossom into a lovely spring rose. That undernourished, tightly clenched bud will need time, patience, love and understanding so that it can be gradually nurtured and eventually bloom. The pains and hurts of newly discovered sexual abuse will not suddenly disappear, nor will the fears, anger and guilt feelings that have been living in you for so many years. They *will* gradually fade, but like scars they will remain tender throughout your life. Because they do not all heal or disappear rapidly does not mean God is not doing His work any more than in the broken leg that did not heal overnight.

Remember that you are a part of your healing process. God is allowing you certain responsibilities to "cleanse yourself from all defilement of flesh and spirit." There is probably little doubt that how diligently you apply yourself to the part God has assigned to you, will in large measure determine the rate of your own restoration. "He who sows sparingly shall also reap sparingly; and he who sows bountifully shall also reap bountifully" (2 Corinthians 9:6).

3

How Can I Forgive?

The most grievous crime ever committed against the body of an innocent person in all of history was that perpetrated against our Lord Jesus when they nailed Him to a cross for no other reason but to satisfy the rantings of an angry mob. Perfect, sinless man suffered a physical agony far beyond that which you or I ever have or likely will ever have to endure. We have some idea as to how His flesh was defiled. Scripture gives us indications of the atrocities wrought against His body. It was so ugly most Christians would prefer to shut their eyes to what actually happened.

(For a deeper and clear understanding of the torture committed against our Lord's body, write to our office for "The Passion of Christ—from a Medical Point of View," a detailed description of what actually happened during crucifixion. It is powerful and heart-rending. Your life will never be the same after reading it. No longer will you simply say "My Lord died for me." That will be too callous. You will better comprehend how much He actually suffered for you. The paper is available for a small donation and is included in the package of recommended resources.)

Our minds cannot begin to identify with our Lord's very first words from the cross during His crucifixion. In the Luke account, 23:34, "Then said Jesus, 'Father, forgive them; for they know not what they do.' "

Can you project your emotions and feelings into what our Lord Jesus must have felt? The Bible tells us He "in all points was tempted like as we are, yet without sin" (Hebrews 4:15). That means He also was tempted and suffered emotionally. Can you picture for a moment how He must have felt when Peter said, "Woman, I know him not"

249

(Luke 22:57), or when the multitude accused Him of sedition; when Herod's soldiers mocked and scorned Him; when Pilate sentenced Him to death after confessing, "I have found no fault in this man"; when on the cross the very people to whom He had ministered and healed "derided Him saying, 'He saved others; let him save himself if he be Christ, the chosen of God' " (Luke 23:35). Consider what might have been your reaction had you been in His place, innocent and defiled. His response was, "Father, forgive them, for they know not what they do."

Jesus suffered physically. He suffered emotionally, yet He was able to look upon those who had victimized Him with compassion. As a victim of sexual abuse, you, too, have been in His place. You, too, were innocent and defiled of your flesh and of your spirit.

When Heidi first realized what her father had done to her when she was two and one-half years old, she was angry. She had a right to be angry. That innocent little child had been assaulted. It makes us angry, also, to think that any father could do such a thing to his own child. Hers was righteous anger, anger at the sin that was committed. Heidi, however, loves the Lord more than she loves anger, and though a relatively tender twenty-seven years old now, she knew that her Lord wanted her to have the same attitude in her that was also in Christ Jesus (Philippians 2:5).

In the days that followed, more and more horrible facts were revealed to her, gradually brought to light by the Holy Spirit. It is worthy to note that as these past horrors became manifest, instead of seething with rage Heidi turned to the Lord, perhaps more intently than ever before. The Lord answered her prayers and remained very present in her life as well as in her husband Steve's. The anger never took control of her emotions because the Lord already had. She had surrendered herself to Him, and "Greater is he that is in her, than he that is in the world."

Forgiving and "Forgetting"
Forgiveness also involves forgetting. "Saith the Lord"

in Jeremiah 31:34, "I will forgive their iniquity, and I will remember their sin no more." When God forgives, He forgets! Can we do likewise? Can Heidi now forget that which she has just uncovered which had been so long forgotten? Can Heidi forget what was done to her? Is it possible for you to forgive what was done to you? And, having forgiven, can God possibly expect you to forget?

The answer is yes and no. Because He is ruler of heaven and Earth, He can give you the ability to remember what happened to you, and at the same time give you the ability to put behind you the emotional pain and anger you feel toward the guilty sinner. He can and will give you the ability to forgive the sinner without forgetting the sin that occurred. However, in your forgiveness of the sinner, you will be able to put the pain of the trauma behind you. An attitude of forgiveness makes that possible. Without that forgiving attitude you will be an angry, vengeful person the rest of your life.

Fred still remembers the sexual abuse of suppression from his childhood, as well as the emotional deprivation which resulted in disruptive adult feelings of rejection. "But," he says, "as I have studied the root causes I recognized that both of my parents were victims of emotional abuse and deprivation in their childhood. They were victims themselves. They, too, were scarred. They did the best they knew how for me. The best, however, was stolen from each of them in their own childhood. I understand that I can forgive them. I have forgiven them. I remember the events of sexual abuse that took place in my childhood. They are part of my testimony when comforting another victim. They help me to have compassion and understanding for the pain they are facing.

"But, I have *forgotten* the pain and the anger, the rejection I felt. My God who is big enough to heal my emotions is big enough to help me forget the pain and hurt. In its stead, He has placed love and compassion. It didn't happen overnight. It was part of the restoration process the Lord has been working in me. It had to start with me. I had to be willing. I had to have an attitude of forgiveness. I had to be willing to have the attitude that was also in Christ Jesus when He said, 'Forgive them, Father, for they know not what they do.' "

The Father wants you to be able to forgive. He knows how difficult it will be for you to do so. He has suffered like unto you. He understands your pain. He cares for you. He cares so much that He sent His only Son to suffer in your place. He will give you the strength and the ability to do what you cannot do yourself. He will give you the ability to forgive if you are willing. If today the pain is too great for you to be willing, He is already at work in you to make you able and willing to obey His good purpose for you (Philippians 2:13). You, too, can forgive the one who abused you. You, too, can forget the pain and the hurt, putting it behind, once and forever. You can, and you must, if you would be healed.

Seven Steps to Forgiving Others

In an article titled "How to Walk Free," Doris Boydston, a mental health unit supervisor, gives seven steps to forgiveness:

> The first step is for you to choose to forgive that person for the specific offense(s) against you.
>
> The second step is to ask God to forgive that person. Earnestly ask that He will no longer hold anything against that person on your account.
>
> The third step is to ask God to forgive *you* for holding unforgiveness, resentment, anger, bitterness or even hatred in your heart.
>
> In the fourth step you forgive God for allowing this person to hurt you. You may think: God does not need to be forgiven. Indeed, He doesn't, but *you* need the exercise of forgiving Him.
>
> Ventilation of stored-up emotions is the crucial fifth step. Anger turned inward is a common reason for depression. Feel free to cry, sob, hit a pillow, anything to get rid of that bitterness and frustration.
>
> The sixth step is a request for God to pour His healing balm over your wounds and painful memories and to let Him fill you with His love and presence.

The seventh step is directed towards the offender. You ask God to bless him or her in every way possible, spiritually, physically, socially, financially, at home, at work, in every aspect of life.[1]

Once you have been able to forgive, then you will be able to do that which humanly seems to make even less sense. You will be able to say, "Thank You, Lord. I thank You for that experience. I thank You that through it You have drawn me closer to Yourself. I praise the name of the Lord, my God forever."

Thanksgiving is God's ointment of healing. It is the spiritual salve we put on the wound. It will work wonders in your healing process. It is God's ordained procedure for us. It works because God says to do it. You can't be angry and thankful at the same time. Thankfulness displaces the hurt and the pain. Yes, it is possible to be thankful for bad experiences. God makes it possible because He orders it in 1 Thessalonians 5:

16 Rejoice evermore
17 Pray without ceasing
18 *In everything give thanks* for this is the will of God in Christ Jesus concerning you.

And again in Ephesians 5:

20 *Giving thanks always for all things* unto God . . .

And in Philippians 4:

6 Be anxious for nothing; but *in everything* by prayer and supplication *with thanksgiving,* let your requests be made known unto God.

The next verse relates well also to this concept of the result of being thankful, despite our circumstances:

7 And the *peace of God*, which passeth all understanding shall keep your hearts and minds through Christ Jesus.

Learn to Praise God

We have peace *with God* when our sins are forgiven and we accept and believe in the One who sacrificed Himself for us. We have the peace *of God* when we abide in Him, when we are obedient and submitted to Him. We have the peace of God when we are able to "give thanks always for all things." The next time you feel upset or tense, put into practice God's plan for dealing with stress. Be thankful, truly thankful, and the blessings God will pour into your heart.

David learned to praise God, to give thanks unto His majestic name. David faced many distresses, many hurts, many enemies. He cried out to God, voicing all these pains. After he had done so, he invariably finished his prayer with thanksgiving and praise to his God. He learned the importance of cleansing himself of all defilement of his flesh and spirit, and then was truly able to rejoice and sing praises. Psalm 31 is an excellent example of David's crying out to the Lord. Listen to his pleadings:

> Pull me out of the net they have laid for me. I am in trouble, mine eye is consumed with grief, my life is spent, my strength faileth, my bones are consumed, they that did see me fled from me, I am forgotten as a dead man, I am like a broken vessel, they took counsel against me, they devised to take away my life . . .
>
> But, I trusted in thee O Lord: I said Thou art my God. Blessed be the Lord, for he hath shewed me his marvelous kindness. Be of good courage, and he shall strengthen your heart, all ye that hope in the Lord.

An attitude of forgiveness and a spirit of thanksgiving may not come easily to you. It is possible they won't come to you at all—at this present time. If your pains are too hurtful, seeming to be too heavy for you to bear at this time, tell this to God in your daily prayer time. Open your heart up to Him, and as you write, tell Him exactly how you feel. Tell Him why you can't be forgiving, why you can't be thankful. Then ask Him to do the impossible. Ask Him to give you the ability to do what you cannot do on your own.

> I love the Lord, because he hath heard my voice and my supplications. Because he hath inclined his ear unto me, therefore will I call upon him as long as I live (Psalm 116:1-2).

4

SOME WORDS OF CAUTION

Wherever the Spirit of God is working, Satan cannot be far behind. If you are sensing God's healing presence in your life, be prepared for setbacks, disappointments and discouragements. The road up will not be all smooth. The devil will come like a roaring lion or a sly fox and try to devour your progress.

There will be days when you cry out in agony, "How did I ever get into this?" There will be days when the emotional hurt will be so intense you will think you can't bear another moment. At other times you will feel so alone that it seems no one in the world really cares what happens to you. Your mind may know that all this is not true, that in a day or two you will feel better. For the moment, however, it may be very difficult to convince your feelings.

This is where your counselor, prayer partner and your compassionate comforter can be so helpful to you. This is the time you will want to contact them. Do so quickly, before the hurts get too deeply set in the concrete of your emotions. The close trusting relationship you have built up in the past will serve you well at this time, helping you to reclaim the sovereignty of God in your life.

Rewards of Repairing and Restoring

As we talked with a sex-abuse counselor, she told us her job was not only a thankless one but that often her clients would take out much of their anger on her. "Frequently they yell at me. They tell me they never were abused and that it's all in my head. I keep them probing into their childhood and they decide I have no pity or compassion. Some get angry, tell me off and quit coming for therapy, but soon I get a call asking if they can return — they're ready for more."

What a great God we have who uncovers only what we can handle at one time and then allows us some recess.

We have found that trying to gently tell a woman we think she was abused as a child is not a popular pastime. If God had not called us into this "freeing of the mind" ministry we could not have held ourselves together through the denials and anger we have received.

Fred counseled Inez at a retreat where we both were speaking. She had the typical symptoms of an abuse victim, but when Fred asked if she had been molested as a child she got upset and denied the possibility. Two weeks later we received this letter:

> Dear Florence and Fred,
>
> Fred, when I talked with you on Sunday, you suggested I had been a victim of molestation. I became angry with you and denied it all the way home. But God arranged that we had to pass through my home town (where I had been molested several times). I finally acknowledged I have been a victim.
>
> There was also much dirty joke telling and anything that was fun would have sexual connotations. I realize I need healing from this general attitude, but the anger started to rise within me as I read Jan Frank's book and when I looked at my pictures of my childhood. From the age of about ten months to four years, the pictures of me are this glassy-faced kid — not sad, not withdrawn — just no expression. I can trace molestations back to about age eleven or twelve and have become very angry as I have traced repeated victimizations. The anger multiplied as I talked with a friend and then with one of my sisters and realized that continued victimization was not a part of their growing up. I thought what I experienced was what every woman experienced.
>
> Fred, I told you about the support group we have for bulimics and anorexics and you said you suspect that our group will become one for victims of sexual molestation. Now I am seeing this is beginning to happen . . . Some of the girls in the group can identify. Eating disorders are multi-faceted problems and victimization is definitely one of the facets, but not the only one.
>
> Inez

Even though leading someone into uncovering hurts of the past may not make one popular, the rewards of changed lives make it all worthwhile. Isaiah the prophet wrote, "And those from among you will rebuild the ancient ruins; you will raise up the age-old foundations; and you will be called the repairer of the breach, the restorer of the streets in which to dwell" (Isaiah 58:12, NASB).

Homosexual Tendencies

It is not unusual for the person who has been sexually victimized as a child to occasionally have feelings, flashes, or even dreams of attraction to another of the same sex. For a Christian, this would naturally be disturbing and cause feelings of guilt, on top of the guilt you have been carrying around as excess baggage for years.

Bear in mind from all that you have already read that when you were abused your normal sexual mechanisms—both physical and emotional—were distorted. They may have never healed. They may never have normally matured. Therefore, such disturbed sexual feelings are apt to happen. It is important to immediately acknowledge the feelings. This is consistent with the ten steps Jan Frank recommends in *A Door of Hope*.

Share these feelings with your counselor, prayer partner or comforter—relieve those guilty feelings. Don't let them simmer unchecked in your emotions. Don't be ashamed to talk about them. Acknowledging them exposes them to the light. Keeping them to yourself is repressing them into the back of your consciousness, which is what you have likely done with hurting feelings for years. There is a release in talking about them, admitting their existence and sharing them with another. Keeping them within yourself is inviting the devil to work on your mind. He does not like the light. He likes to work in the dark places.

The Lord Jesus is already working in you to heal you of any such feelings. He understands. He does not judge you. He alone can heal you if those feelings have already developed into relationships. You must take the first step.

You must be willing to come to Him. You have a role that God has assigned to you. "If we . . . then He!" You have a significant part in your own cleansing process. You do your part; He will surely do His.

Confrontation

As part of your restoration to wholeness, it may be necessary at some time for you to "confront" the offender, the person responsible for the initial problems in your life. We do not believe it is a necessary step for every victim. It does seem to be necessary for some persons.

Jan Frank does specify some very clear and detailed guidelines from her experience and wisdom as to who should participate, when it should be done, and how it should be planned. Since we expect you will study her book after you finish this, we will not duplicate her well-constructed recommendations. We would make just a few points in regard to confronting the offender.

1. Do not even consider going to your offender until you have read Jan's book and clearly understand her suggestions on confrontation.

2. Do not attempt a confrontation until you are absolutely sure it is what the Lord wants you to do, and until He shows you from His high vantage point, where He can see all things, that this is the chosen time.

3. Jan emphasizes a confrontation from a position of strength. We would like to suggest that it also be a "loving confrontation," as opposed to an attacking confrontation. You may be effectively relieved of your guilt and pain by an attacking confrontation wherein you properly leave the responsibility in the hands of the offender where it does belong. However, you may also leave a path of new devastation that you never expected in the various lives that are touched by the confrontation. A loving confrontation is obviously more difficult. It requires the confirming presence of the Holy Spirit and can result in a time of healing and restored relationships. Negative emotions can so easily erupt on the part of either the confronter or those con-

fronted, and these can have long-term damaging consequences if not quickly brought to sorrow, repentance and humility.

In a loving confrontation, love between the participants is regularly reaffirmed, and the loving selfless attitude of the Lord is clearly seen and evidenced in the heart of the one bringing the confrontation. The love is not only expressed (spoken); it is evidenced (seen). First John 3:18 instructs, " . . . let us not love in word, neither in tongue: but in deed and in truth." This we have paraphrased, "Love is not a proclamation, or an explanation; love is a demonstration." Don't tell me how much you love me. Let me *see* how much you love. Before bringing a loving confrontation you will need to prepare yourself spiritually as well as emotionally. In the meeting, shared prayer is an important and vital part of the experience.

4. Not all confrontations need to be accomplished to be effective. The same thoughts can be expressed in a letter that is never sent! The results for you can sometimes be more beneficial than an actual meeting. If your offender is deceased, it is probably the only way you can gain the benefit of properly placing the responsibility where it belongs. Once you have written such a letter and put all your thoughts on paper, you will want to promptly destroy it. Do not make the mistake of thinking you need to save it. It will become a cancer to the steps of forgiveness you will want to take in order to be fully healed.

A second occasion for writing out your confrontive letter is when no matter how well prepared spiritually you would be for a head-to-head meeting, you do not have any sense of peace that the purposes could be served without an explosive and unredemptive reaction. If the presentation to the one who should properly bear the burden of guilt would only further drive an immovable wedge between you and that offender, your message may best be written in that letter you will never send. You will still be free of the guilt you have been bearing and you leave the offender in the hands of the almighty God. That's not a bad idea under any circumstances.

What About Unresolved Anger?

There will be some whose emotions were so damaged by abuse or rejection that there seems to be no hope or possibility of dealing with the anger. That anger must not be repressed or stuffed away, it must be released in an appropriate manner.

Be wary of those well-intentioned friends who counsel you that your anger is sin; that you should be rid of it by now; that there must be other sin in your life if you can't get the victory over it; that you probably aren't really a Christian because of your anger problem. The real problem is that they have never walked in your shoes. Rather than deal with their own needs and problems, it is easier for them to judge you for yours. We have generally found that most people who are dogmatic about other people's lives or problems are not willing to face their own.

As described earlier, you have a right to the anger that results from abuse or rejection. It is what you do with that anger once you have identified it and its source that is important. The resolution of that anger is now up to you. It is your responsibility to bring it prayerfully and consistently to the Lord for cleansing and healing.

What can you do with that anger if you have already done everything you know to do and there is no change? How can you release that anger in an appropriate manner? Chances are you have been venting it on the ones you love the most, perhaps even your little children if you have them. You know the incident that "triggered" the anger did not warrant the fury that came out. You end up feeling ashamed or disgusted with yourself, piling more guilt onto that baggage you are already carrying. Note that we said "triggered," not *caused*. For the anger was already in you. The milk your child spilled at the table, for example, did not "cause" your violent reaction, it merely "triggered" what was already inside waiting for an excuse to happen.

If you are plagued with this kind of anger, there are

three things you can do. All are important; all are effective.

First, you will want to follow your counselor's guidance in working through the rage you feel. He or she will help you identify the true source of your anger and face up to it at your own pace.

Having identified the true source of your anger, the second thing you might do is go to your nearby toy or full-line drug store and buy yourself a child's whiffle ball and bat. You won't need the ball. It is the bat you want. They are usually very light in weight and orange in color. The cost should only be a dollar or two. What you are going to do with this bat is to bang it on some cushion at home whenever the surge of anger starts to come up. If hurt feelings surface while you are washing the dishes, take up your bat. Go to your cushion and bang away at the cushion as much as you want. Cry out or scream if you feel like it. That is releasing the pent-up emotions in an appropriate manner. No one will be hurt by it. The cushion will not cry, and you will not feel compelled to apologize. It is far better than screaming at or beating your kids or your spouse. It is far better than taking a drink to "calm your nerves."

It is one of the most effective things you can do to physically release the rage that is in you. If David Burke had had a chance to vent his inner rage during earlier portions of his life, the forty-two people might never have lost their lives when the PSA airline crashed into the mountains. Many tragedies have occurred because of rage that was never vented.

Feel free to beat your cushion as long or as often as you wish until you get it all out of you, until you feel calmed and relaxed.

The third thing you can do—which can be done separately or in conjunction with "batting your cushion"—is similar to your "prayers on paper." When the anger feelings come, get out your prayer notebook and talk it all out to Jesus. Tell Him in writing how angry you are. Tell Him exactly how you feel, word for word. Don't leave anything out—make sure you tell Him everything. Don't worry about Him; He can take it. And He won't argue back. He won't criticize or judge you. He will not be angry with you. Instead He will wrap His loving arms around you and give you peace. He will make you feel His love. You will feel ever so much better. You will want to shout His praises, or in tears thank Him and tell Him how much you love Him. "Cast your cares upon him, for he careth for you" (1 Peter 5:7).

Repeat these physical and spiritual exercises as often as you feel you need to. We would not recommend that you only "bat your cushion." That brings only temporal help. Work closely with your counselor in resolving your anger. Keep your journal up to date. Over time, God's healing process will be at work to free your mind from the memories that bind.

What About My Husband?

A husband whose wife was victimized as a child becomes the "secondary victim" of that abuse. His life and his emotions may be dramatically affected by the events that occurred in his wife's life. One of the most frequent problems is sexual dysfunction. Unless the husband is knowledgeable of his wife's ordeal, his natural reaction to his wife's disinterest may be a questioning of his own virility, and a growing emotional frustration.

If he also is a victim of childhood emotional deprivation, with feelings of rejection, he almost automatically transfers those feelings to his wife and feels that she is rejecting him. A downward spiral is triggered, with a disheartening breakdown of communication. Is it any wonder that the divorce rate is so high?

It is amazing to find, as Jan Frank also points out in *A Door of Hope,* how often "victims marry." Each one brings his own baggage of emotional pain to the marriage. Each expects the other to fill the void in his or her life without giving much thought to how they can minister to the needs in the mate's life. Because we all have a basically self-centered nature, we tend to focus on our own needs and look to see how well our partner meets them. But our mates almost never meet them to our satisfaction and the spiral of frustration, disappointment and depression accelerates.

Since the husband of an abused female is the "secondary victim," he, too, needs to be involved in a healing process. It is most important that he learn as much about the subject as possible by reading this book as well as the others recommended. As he develops compassion and understanding, a bond of support and love will grow between you. These are deep waters in which you walk, and better to walk together than alone. "Two are better than one...for if they fall, the one will lift up his fellow: but woe to him that is alone when he falleth; for he hath not another to help him up. Again if two lie together, then they have heat; but how can one be warm alone?" (Ecclesiastes 4:9-11). God designed a husband and wife to be yokemates, to be one in Christ. "A man shall leave his father and mother and cleave unto his wife, and the two shall be one flesh" (Genesis 2:24). This little-understood truth is supported by the test of Scripture. To be one in Christ — one flesh, one mind — means united, undivided.

This speaks of the relationship that a husband and wife will have as they walk through residual hurts of childhood. The partner who is the secondary victim then must be as informed or perhaps even more so than the actual victim. Knowledge leads to wisdom and wisdom to compassion and compassion affirms commitment.

Don Frank, high school teacher, basketball coach, and husband of Jan Frank, delivered a compassionate and enlightening message entitled "Are You a Victim of Your Wife's Past?" at a recent large conference. It is a message that every husband whose wife was victimized should listen to if he wishes to gain an understanding of his wife's trauma and the stress that it most likely is now placing on the marriage. The tape may be ordered from our office. With all this knowledge, wisdom, compassion, and commitment, the husband becomes an integral part of his wife's restoration, and by that personal involvement he may discover some areas in his own life which can be brought to the Lord for healing.

Victims Marry Victims

As we sat at lunch with Peggy, she asked us what book we were writing. We told her about this book and said, "It's to help people find the root of their problems instead of dealing with the symptoms."

"I need that book," she stated quickly.

She then told of the year of marriage counseling she and her husband had been through. "And we're not one bit better today than when we started," she said.

"What seems to be your problem?" Fred asked.

"John and I just can't stand each other. We're both committed Christians and we know God brought us together. I'm angry at John all the time and keep nagging him to stand up to people. He's so laid back, he lets everyone push him around, including me. Why can't he be a real man?"

Here we had a Powerful Choleric woman with a Peaceful Phlegmatic husband. As we questioned her about her childhood, she couldn't remember anything before she was six. She had an alcoholic father and an angry mother. If we had to make a guess, we could assume that the combination of an alcoholic father and a loss of memory were symptoms of some kind of early childhood abuse. Her father was basically a passive man who became violent when drinking. The mother controlled the family while constantly degrading the father.

At sixteen Peggy went out with her friends and downed a six-pack of beer. They told her she was funny when she was drunk and so she continued to drink for their approval. This drinking led her to a pattern of behavior in which she would do anything if it made her friends pay attention. She was obviously desperate for love and sick of her dysfunctional home, so she ran away at seventeen and began a series of affairs with teens and older men.

In her early twenties she began to smoke pot and get involved in group sex. Before she was thirty she had been through two abortions and she hated what she had become. At that point a friend took her to hear a Christian speaker who challenged her to "try God for a week." She decided it couldn't hurt and she asked the Lord Jesus into her heart. The man she lived with was not about to put up with a religious woman, so she moved out by herself.

For the first time in her life she was without a lover, she had quit drinking, and she was alone. She began to attend church, got involved in the singles group and met John, a recently divorced dentist. He let her know he had no intention of ever marrying again because his divorce proceedings had been a two-year nightmare in which he had ended the fighting by letting his wife have everything except the clothes on his back.

Peggy was appalled to find this elegantly dressed man living in an unfurnished apartment and serving cheese and crackers for dinner. She felt so sorry for him and, as is typical of the adult child of an alcoholic, she tried to make everything right. She took control of his life and his office and put a big Band-aid over his problems. He was so glad to have someone who cared that much. John was a new Christian and they both studied and prayed together until they knew it was God's will that they marry.

This should have been happy-ever-after time for them both, but Peggy soon found that John's office staff controlled him, that his first wife created expenses for his children that cost him all he earned, and that he was deeply in debt. The more she pushed him to take control of his life, the more he clung to her and expressed fear that she might leave him. She got increasingly angry and he felt rejected.

In marriage counseling they received some behavioral suggestions, but their emotions didn't change. They prayed about each other, but no godly love healed their rift.

As we talked with Peggy, she had no idea that any of her problems came from her past. She was working so hard to be a devoted Christian wife, but she couldn't stand her weak husband. When we reviewed her past with her, she could suddenly see the connection. Although her husband was not an alcoholic, he had the same placid personality as her father and she was treating him as her mother had lashed out against her father. She couldn't believe she was repeating this pattern.

Then Fred met with John and found a kind, sweet man who had been "done in" by everyone in life. When he was two his mother had a boyfriend who didn't like children; her response was to get rid of John. He lived in a series of foster homes and whenever he misbehaved, they moved him on. Imagine the rejection felt by this little boy as he lived in fear that if he didn't keep quiet and do what people said, those he loved would turn against him and he would have to start all over again. Because he was a bright boy, he received good grades and did everything he could to please his teachers. He was a model of perfect behavior and he ultimately received a scholarship to college.

As could be expected, he married a strong Choleric woman who took control of his life. To avoid problems and keep peace, he allowed her to handle all the finances; by the time she sued for divorce, she had their two homes in her name. For two years she tormented him in court procedures until finally he gave up, gave in, and gave over. Lonely and without a director of life, John married Peggy, another strong and angry woman. Peggy had cried out to us, "He's been beaten down by everyone. Why does he sit there and take it?"

Why does he? In any kind of victimization we repeat our childhood emotional reactions unconsciously. We don't say to ourselves, "Because my mother was angry at my passive father I will be angry at my husband." We just react that way. We don't say, "Because I was repeatedly rejected as a child, I will always fear rejection and let people push me around." We just react that way.

Peggy and John could go to marriage counseling for years and perhaps learn to modify the extremes in their behavior, but they wouldn't come to a healthy resolution of their problems without getting down to the source.

Peggy has started attending ACA (Adult Children of Alcoholics) and has put together a support group for women who have grown up in alcoholic homes. She is journalizing her feelings about her parents and is prayerfully working to uncover the blanked-out memories of her childhood. John now understands that Peggy's anger was not caused by him and that he was the innocent recipient of her repressed emotions. For the first time in his life John now sees that his pattern of rejection started before he was two years old and that his extreme desire to please and his fear of being abandoned caused him to become the sitting target for every controlling companion who came along.

At our suggestion Peggy and John went away for a quiet weekend where they could each share their life's feelings with each other without fear of judgment or rejection. Their marriage may not have an overnight healing, but they at least understand where their problems have come from and they are working on freeing their minds from the memories that bind.

What If No Victory?

If you have conscientiously followed all the steps that have been recommended herein and you still don't feel you have made any progress, do not despair. God has promised you perfect peace, and He will do what He has promised. The resolution of painful memories is not an easy, overnight process. It takes time and perseverance, and it can be emotionally draining. But we can assure you that if you stay with the process, with the assistance of a knowledgeable counselor and with a compassionate friend at your side, God will give you victory.

One area you may want to look at carefully is your faith. Do you really believe Jesus can make you emotionally well? Has your faith grown to the point that you know deep within your soul that you do "Trust in the Lord with all thine heart; and lean not onto thine own understanding" (Proverbs 3:4)? As you do your daily Scripture study, notice how many times the Lord Jesus gave a blessing to the healed person by showing how his faith had been an integral part of his own healing or cleansing. In Matthew 9:20-22, He said to the woman who came to Him diseased with an issue of blood, "Daughter . . . thy faith has made thee whole." She knew within herself, "If I but touch his garment, I shall be whole." She came to Him, she was a part of her own healing, her faith made her whole.

The lady from Canaan in Matthew 15:22-28 came to Him complaining of her daughter. In healing both the mother and her daughter, the Lord said, "O woman, great is thy faith: be it unto thee even as thou wilt."

In healing the servant of the Centurion (Matthew 8:5-13) the Lord said, "I have not found so great faith, no, not in Israel."

The reverse is shown in Mark 6:4-6 where He could do no mighty work in Nazareth "because of their unbelief."

Therefore, if there is no victory or progress in your healing, examine your faith. "Examine yourselves, whether ye be in the faith, prove your own selves" (2 Corinthians 13:5).

Why Me?

It is almost the universal question that a person who has been victimized by sexual abuse asks. *Why me, God? Why was I the one who was attacked? Where were You, God, that You didn't protect me? I was only a child, an innocent victim. I couldn't protect myself. Where were You, God?*

It is a fair question that you ask, and one for which there is no simple answer. There is an answer, but it involves understanding how God works.

God *was* there. He *is* there. He *will always* be there. He does not always, however, prevent hurtful experiences from coming to us, even as children. But He did not *plan* your horrible experience. God created man with the power to choose between right and wrong. When man chooses wrong, there are inevitably innocent victims who suffer from the other person's sin. You were an innocent victim of another person's wrongful choice. Your hurt is real, and it is valid, but it does not diminish the love God has always had — and does have — for you. While we don't fully understand why He allows the innocent to suffer, we know without a doubt that He loves the innocent and will help them recover and become even stronger as a result of trusting Him.

We lost our two sons who were born without normal brains. Why? We wanted those two beautiful boys, one who died at two, and the other who died at nineteen, the same size he was at the age of one — a living vegetable for eighteen years. *Why me, God? Where were You?* Those losses were as devastating to us as your loss of your childhood has been to you.

It was through these experiences that a short time later the Lord was able to reach down, get our attention and call us to Himself. As a friend recently shared, our sons gave their lives that we might find life. We believe that is true. We are able now to honestly say, "Praise God! Thank You, Lord Jesus. Thank You for our two sons." We can see now how God has used this all in our lives. If some portion of this book brings you a blessing, can we then not praise God for the hurts we have faced? Without that sequence of events we might never have learned the truths of God that made this writing possible.

It all fits into what He has planned for all of us. His ultimate objective is simply that we, by our lives, should bring honor and glory to Him. That is not an unreasonable expectation when we think of the cost He paid for us. Can you agree with the psalmist that "It is *good* for me *that I have been afflicted*; that I might learn thy statutes" (Psalm 119:71)? Can you say that it was good for you as well? Has it drawn you closer to Him? Has it given you a deeper thirst for His word?

God also promises He will replace your tears with joy (Psalm 126:5). Romans 8:28 does promise " . . . that all things work together for good to them that love God, to them who are the called according to His purpose." As one

who is called by God, for God, He will bring comfort out of
your pain, beauty out of the ashes. It may be difficult for
you to see that now or to even imagine such a possibility.
Wait, be patient . . . for God will have His way. He will
fulfill His promises.

The story of Joseph in Genesis (chapters 37-47) power-
fully illustrates this truth. He was sold as a slave by his
jealous brothers to the Ishmaelites, ended up in Egypt,
spent two years in prison on a false charge, and later became second-in-command to the pharaoh of all Egypt. Here
he was used by God to preserve his family during the
famine. Not only did Joseph have the spirit of forgiveness,
but he was also a man of God, and could see that what his
brothers intended for evil, God meant for good. In Genesis
45:12 he said to his brothers after identifying himself to
them:

> Now therefore be not grieved, nor angry with yourselves, that
> ye sold me hither; for God did send me before you to preserve life.

God had a purpose in all the abuse that befell Joseph.
It was evil, unkind and unfair, but ultimately it worked
together for good, and all Joseph's family was preserved.
You, too, will see one day the good that will come out of it
all.

Can you identify with the story of the blind man in
John 9:1-3?

> And as Jesus passed by, he saw a man which was blind from
> his birth.
> And his disciples asked him, saying, "Master, who did sin, this
> man, or his parents, that he was born blind?"
> Jesus answered, "Neither hath this man sinned, nor his
> parents; but that the works of God should be made manifest in
> him."

Did we sin that our sons were born with defective
brains? Did you sin as a child that you were abused? Surely not, but that the works of God should be made manifest
in us. God will use all our experiences to His honor and
glory. And we will feel uplifted and valued!

Lifelong Pursuit

The love relationship that you will be establishing with the Lord will continue to bless you, as you serve Him for the rest of your life. It is even possible that the Lord will allow you to have enough residual concern, perhaps just a touch of hurt, to keep you clinging to Him forever. That is really His desire: He wants you to be completely dependent on Him. Rather than feeling defeated, or disappointed that there seem to be some areas that you think are not fully cleansed or healed, rejoice that the Lord has permitted you to bear some "thorn in the flesh" to keep you attached to Him.

We humans too often come eagerly unto our Lord when we are hurting, and then subtly find ourselves not having time for Him when the hurt is healed. That is the history of the Israelites. They cried out to the Lord when they were oppressed. He heard their voice and healed their hearts. When they felt well again, they found no time for Him, until once more they were hurting and called out to Him. Time and again God answered their prayers and the cycle repeated itself. We are all apt to be no different. When our lives are going well, it is easy for days to become encumbered with so many "important activities" that we no longer have time for the Lord. Rejoice if the Lord is keeping you on a string. Be thankful that He cares enough about you to keep you close to Himself.

No victory is won without a battle!

Walking hand in hand with your faith, the fundamental factor in winning is total commitment to Jesus. When asked by the wealthy young ruler what he must do to succeed, Jesus said to him, "One thing you still lack, sell all that you possess . . . and come, follow me" (Luke 18:22, NASB). So *sell out to Jesus*. He must be pre-eminent, foremost in your heart. Release all that is important to you, let go emotionally, and follow Him. We do not have to literally sell our household goods to obey this injunction. But we must make Him, not our possessions, the treasure in our hearts.

Then you will be able to say with Paul, "I am determined to know nothing among you, save Jesus Christ, and him crucified" (1 Corinthians 2:2).

5

YOUR READING PROGRAM

We have integrated a specially selected list of books into a ten week plan that will help you in healing the pains of your past. Please do not consider this reading program optional—you will find the process invaluable. At the end of your ten weeks, one of the benefits is that you will feel good about yourself for having read ten merit-worthy and helpful books. That will be a significant accomplishment. In order to read this many books, you will have to be disciplined. All but one of the books should be available in most Christian bookstores, or all can be ordered from our office as a package at a discount.

The purpose of your reading is three-fold. The first is to teach you as much as possible about the whole area of the emotional effects of childhood sexual abuse. The more you learn, the better you will be equipped to understand and deal with your own feelings. If you are a mother or father, you will be alert to the symptoms in children, especially your own and others close to you, and you will be able to report to the proper authorities according to the laws of your state. Proper and prompt treatment and understanding of a child who has been abused will spare the emotional dysfunction of later years.

The second purpose is to prepare you to be a comforter to others. As you have been comforted by the God of all comfort, you will surely be used to comfort others with the comfort with which you have been comforted. Everyone's abuse is different, the circumstances of the abuse vary greatly, and possibly even more important, the reactions to

273

abuse vary tremendously. Some people have severe emotional effects from the less violent forms, while others — victims of more physically painful abuse — may show fewer effects. To comfort another based only on your experiences would be helpful, but to comfort with the additional benefit of broad knowledge will be far more effective.

The third important value is that there is a desperate need for persons who have broad knowledge and skills to be leaders in bringing awareness, information, expertise and help to the vast hurting world of the sexually abused. Professionals are, to a large degree, behind the times in understanding the nature, depth, and extent of the problems. Those who are up to date cannot possibly begin to counsel and guide the huge number of persons seeking help. It is only in the most recent years that there has been even a semblance of an awakening. The floodgates have not yet opened wide, they have only been cracked slightly ajar. Where will these hurting people go?

We, the Christian community, must be alert, able, and prepared as the avalanche of awareness spreads. The Lord needs us all in this division of His army. He may call you as a battalion leader! A few years ago we could never possibly have conceived the plans He had for us, or how much of our time would be spent in the office, on the phone, at conferences, in airplanes, virtually everywhere we go — helping hurting persons identify the source of the symptoms they are experiencing. With each one the depth of our own understanding grows in an ever-increasing crescendo. You are desperately needed as well, for the fields are white unto harvest.

The books highlighted below are just the beginning of your self-education program.

1. *Hope for Hurting Women,* originally titled *Lives on the Mend,* is Florence's inspiring and uplifting collection of stories of fifteen women who have overcome severe pain or trauma in their lives through their faith in the Lord Jesus. Just one of them is Jan Frank's story. It is fast, powerful reading, and will reinforce your hope and faith that He will

see you, too, through to restoration.

2. *A Door of Hope* by Jan Frank. Not just Jan's personal experiences, though they are carefully woven through the tapestry of the book, but a work soundly founded on biblical truth that guides the victim through ten steps of recovery. Jan writes with the heart of one who has been there, supported by specialized training and the experience of working with many victims as a counselor and as a support group leader.

3. *God's Crippled Children* by Lana Bateman. Using her personal story of emotional pain, Lana helps set readers free by using healing prayer. Lana's ministry, Philippian Ministries, works with people by praying through the pain in their lives to reach a place of wholeness. Prayer directors are available throughout most of the United States.

4. *Personality Plus* by Florence Littauer. This book will give you revealing insight into the four basic personalities, and help you understand your God-given strengths and weaknesses, as well as those of each of your family. You will see yourself as Florence describes our own experiences, which gives the book so much life and humor.

5. *Your Personality Tree*. Florence's second book on the four personalities presents important issues not included in her first work. It will be particularly helpful in freeing you to remove the mask you may have been wearing as a result of parenting, childhood experiences, rejection, or even marriage. She shows clearly that God never created the Sanguine-Melancholy or the Choleric-Phlegmatic combination which so many people find in themselves. This revealing study also shows you how the personality traits of your parents, grandparents and forebears may have affected who you are today.

6. *From Rejection to Acceptance* by Barbara Taylor. Barbara grew up thinking she didn't measure up despite her "fine Christian home." Barbara was a victim of childhood rejection until eventually, as an adult, she was able to understand and then experience her heavenly Father's complete acceptance of her. Since virtually all vic-

tims of sexual abuse also have these same feelings, this book is an important step in your road to victory over rejection.

7. *It Takes So Little to Be Above Average* by Florence Littauer. An upbeat change of pace in your reading program. It is a positive book that will motivate you to be the best you can be, and do the best you can with each day's activities. It will give you specific and practical ideas that you will be able to put into immediate practice.

8. *Child Sexual Abuse: A Hope for Healing* by Maxine Hancock and Karen Burton Mains. A tool of liberation that will bring personal comfort, encourage the healing process to begin, and encourage your faltering belief system.

9. *Pain and Pretending* by Rich Buhler. The popular radio talk show host compassionately reaches into the heart of the victim. His own experiences, based on conversations with many listeners from all over the country, are told in language to which you will readily identify. No simple panaceas are offered, but you will find tender shepherding down the sometimes painful path to freedom and wholeness.

10. *What You Can Say When You Don't Know What to Say* by Lauren Briggs. Many well-intentioned people end up saying or doing the wrong thing because they do not understand the needs of the other person. If you are going to be a comforter, you will want to know how. Lauren shares from both her experiences as a comforter and from the hurts in her own life how to say the things that will help your hurting friend. An excellent resource you will refer to again and again.

NOTE

While we suggest one book per week for ten weeks, we recognize that some of these books may warrant a slower approach due to the emotional nature of their content. If you find you must "take a break" from a topic that troubles you, feel free to slow down a bit and read at a comfortable pace. The important thing is that you try to read a portion each day to gain the insight and encouragement each book offers.

P A R T   V

APPLICATION

The Ten Week Plan

THE WEEKLY
PROGRESS CHARTS

As you move forward toward the healing of painful memories, it is likely that you will encounter a roller coaster ride of emotions. Don't be afraid of your emotions, and don't try to suppress them. It is important that you work closely with your counselor and support person to release those pent-up feelings and learn from them. Often you will feel that you are taking two steps forward for every one step backward, and on some days it may feel more like two steps backward for each step forward. But God will help you grow through the experience, and you will gradually see light at the end of the long tunnel as you gain the strength to deal with the painful memories.

We encourage you to supplement this in-person help with the reading, prayer and activities recommended in the previous chapter. While we have suggested an intensive ten-week program, we recognize that it may be desirable to take a slower pace, to assimilate the reading material into your life and to handle with your counselor any emotions or flashbacks that may arise.

On the following ten pages are identical charts to help you record your progress and maintain your daily self-discipline. If you miss a day or two, you will see it quickly and easily. You should not feel bound to your charts or feel guilty if you miss a day now and then.

Each day, simply record your progress. In the column marked:

Oswald Chambers, if you read the daily selection, just place an X or checkmark in the appropriate space;

Scriptures Read Today, write in the chapters or passages you studied;

Written Prayer, indicate the number of minutes you spent in written prayer. Surely the number of minutes will have no effect on the efficacy of your prayers, or your spirituality, but it will be an interesting record for you.

Book of the Week, simply record the pages you have read, to chart your progress in the recommended book. For example: Sunday: 1-44, Monday: 45-78, etc;

Silver Box Project, describe briefly, just for your own information, what you did and for whom.

At the end of ten weeks you will likely enjoy these efforts so much and be so blessed you will want to continue forever!

Week

#1

Weekly Progress Chart

For Week
Ending _____

	Oswald Chambers	Scriptures Read Today	Written Prayer (Minutes)	*Hope for Hurting Women* Pages Read	"Silver Box Project" Describe
Sunday					
Monday					
Tuesday					
Wednes- day					
Thursday					
Friday					
Saturday					

My Evaluation: _____

_____

_____

Week

#2

For Week
Ending _____

Weekly Progress Chart

	Oswald Chambers	Scriptures Read Today	Written Prayer (Minutes)	*A Door of Hope* Pages Read	"Silver Box Project" Describe
Sunday					
Monday					
Tuesday					
Wednesday					
Thursday					
Friday					
Saturday					

My Evaluation: _____

_____

_____

Week

#3

For Week
Ending _____

Weekly Progress Chart

	Oswald Chambers	Scriptures Read Today	Written Prayer (Minutes)	*Understanding Your Past* Pages Read	"Silver Box Project" Describe
Sunday					
Monday					
Tuesday					
Wednes-day					
Thursday					
Friday					
Saturday					

My Evaluation: _____

_____

_____

Week

#4

For Week

Ending _____

Weekly Progress Chart

	Oswald Chambers	Scriptures Read Today	Written Prayer (Minutes)	*Personality Plus* Pages Read	"Silver Box Project" Describe
Sunday					
Monday					
Tuesday					
Wednes-day					
Thursday					
Friday					
Saturday					

My Evaluation: _____

_____

_____

Week

#5

Weekly Progress Chart

For Week

Ending _____

	Oswald Chambers	Scriptures Read Today	Written Prayer (Minutes)	Your Personality Tree Pages Read	"Silver Box Project" Describe
Sunday					
Monday					
Tuesday					
Wednes-day					
Thursday					
Friday					
Saturday					

My Evaluation: _____

_____

_____

Week

#6

For Week

Ending _____

Weekly Progress Chart

	Oswald Chambers	Scriptures Read Today	Written Prayer (Minutes)	*From Rejection to Acceptance* Pages Read	"Silver Box Project" Describe
Sunday					
Monday					
Tuesday					
Wednes-day					
Thursday					
Friday					
Saturday					

My Evaluation: _____

_____

_____

Week

#7

For Week Ending _____

Weekly Progress Chart

	Oswald Chambers	Scriptures Read Today	Written Prayer (Minutes)	It Takes So Little... Pages Read	"Silver Box Project" Describe
Sunday					
Monday					
Tuesday					
Wednes-day					
Thursday					
Friday					
Saturday					

My Evaluation: _____

_____

_____

Week

#8

For Week
Ending _____

Weekly Progress Chart

	Oswald Chambers	Scriptures Read Today	Written Prayer (Minutes)	Child Sexual Abuse Pages Read	"Silver Box Project" Describe
Sunday					
Monday					
Tuesday					
Wednes-day					
Thursday					
Friday					
Saturday					

My Evaluation: _____

_____

_____

Week #9

Weekly Progress Chart

	Oswald Chambers	Scriptures Read Today	Written Prayer (Minutes)	*Pain and Pretending* Pages Read	"Silver Box Project" Describe
Sunday					
Monday					
Tuesday					
Wednes-day					
Thursday					
Friday					
Saturday					

My Evaluation: _____

_____

_____

Week

#10

For Week

Ending _____

Weekly Progress Chart

	Oswald Chambers	Scriptures Read Today	Written Prayer (Minutes)	*What You Can Say...* Pages Read	"Silver Box Project" Describe
Sunday					
Monday					
Tuesday					
Wednes-day					
Thursday					
Friday					
Saturday					

My Evaluation: _____

_____

_____

PART VI

SUPPLEMENTATION

Additional Information,
Resources and Order Form

Appendix A

Assurance of Salvation

Jesus Christ extends a personal invitation to all of us, "Come unto me, all ye that labour and are heavy laden, and I will give you rest" (Matthew 11:28, KJV).

Christ presents God's plan of salvation very simply in John 3:16, "For God so loved the world, that he gave his only begotten Son, that whosoever believeth in him should not perish, but have everlasting life."

If you believe that Jesus is the Christ, the Son of God, stop right now and invite Him to come into your heart as the Lord of your life. Tell Him how heavy-laden you feel and how tired you are of carrying your burdens all by yourself. Confess your sins to Him and ask Him to cleanse you and become your Lord and Savior. Then thank Him for coming into your life and for giving you eternal salvation.

Now, before you read any further, take time to write in your journal or in the flyleaf of your Bible, "On __(date)__ I invited Jesus Christ to come into my life as my personal Lord and Savior. He, in turn, has forgiven me of all my sin and cleansed me from all unrighteousness."

Whenever doubts come into your mind as to whether you are really a Christian, quickly open your journal or your Bible and read out loud this profession of faith that you have made today. Then quote Hebrews 13:5: "I will never leave thee, nor forsake thee." Read also John 10:27-29: "My sheep hear my voice, and I know them, and they follow me: And I give unto them eternal life; and they shall never perish, neither shall any man pluck them out of my hand. My Father, which gave them to me, is greater than all; and no man is able to pluck them out of my Father's hand."

What Do I Do When I Sin?

Even though you are now a Christian, one of God's precious children for eternity, there will be times when you know you have done something wrong; you have sinned, and you will sense you are not in proper communication with God. First John 1:9 states, "If we confess our sins, he is faithful and just to forgive us our sins, and to cleanse us from all unrighteousness."

The moment the Holy Spirit makes you aware of sin in your life, stop right then, confess it to God, and ask Him to forgive you and cleanse you. Then ask the Holy Spirit to continue to fill you with His power so that you might continue to walk as one of God's obedient children.

Appendix B

Terms Defined

AGORAPHOBIA—literally fear of the market place; practically fear of the outside world.

ANOREXIA NERVOSA—a psychophysiologic condition characterized by severe and prolonged inability or refusal to eat.

BULIMIA—An insatiable appetite and excessive food intake followed by forced vomiting. This process is often referred to as gorge and purge.

COMPULSION—An irresistible impulse or drive to perform some irrational or uncontrollable act.

EMOTIONAL DEPRIVATION—the failure of parenting to provide a child's right to be loved unconditionally.

FORMS OF SEXUAL ABUSE—as described herein:

1. Suppression—of all normal sexual inquiry, expression and feelings.

2. Exploitation—inappropriate exposure of victim's or perpetrator's body for sexually satisfying purposes.

3. Molestation—sexually oriented touching or fondling of victim by perpetrator, by victim of perpetrator, or both.

4. Penetration—oral, vaginal, or anal insertion by penile, digital, or gadgetal means.

HOMOSEXUAL—a person who prefers same-sex physical relationships resulting from childhood abuse, or early seduction by a same-sex figure.

INCEST—any form of sexual abuse taking place within the family structure, or by anyone perceived by the victim to be part of the "family."

MEMORY GAP—any portion of childhood of which you can remember little or almost nothing.

MENTAL FLASHES—instantaneous images that recur in our

295

mind relating to some experience in our deep and distant past.

MULTIPLE PERSONALITY—a person who has a number of names for herself and lives at different times in those various names, each of which may have radically different characteristics, or tones of voice.

OBSESSION—a continuing preoccupation with disturbing or unreasonable feelings or a mental fixation that rules the emotions.

RAPE—forced sexual intercourse, involving oral, anal or vaginal penetration.

Appendix C

Resources

A Betrayal of Innocence: What You Should Know About Child Sexual Abuse, David Peters, Word Books.

A Door of Hope: Recognizing and Resolving the Pains of the Past, Jan Frank, Here's Life Publishers.

Another Chance: Hope and Health for the Alcoholic Family, Sharon Wedgscheider, Science and Behavior Books.

Answers to Your Questions About Homosexuality, Bristol Books.

"Are You the Victim of Your Wife's Past?" (tape) Don Frank.

Betrayal of Innocence: Incest and Its Devastation, Susan Forward and Craig Buck, Penguin.

Blow Away the Black Clouds, Florence Littauer, Harvest House.

Childhood Sexual Abuse, Maxine Hancock and Karen Mains, Harold Shaw.

Codependent No More, Melody Beattie, Harper/Hazelden.

Counseling the Homosexual, Michael R. Saia, Bethany House Publishers.

Effective Biblical Counseling, Lawrence J. Crabb, Jr., Zondervan.

Freeing Your Mind From Memories That Bind, Fred and Florence Littauer, Here's Life Publishers.

From Rejection to Acceptance, Barbara Taylor, Broadman Press.

God's Crippled Children, Lana Bateman, available through CLASS Book Service.

Healing for Damaged Emotions, David A. Seamands, Victor.

Healing of Memories, David A. Seamands, Victor.

Healing Victims of Sexual Abuse, Paula Sandford, Victory House.

Hope for Hurting Women, Florence Littauer, Word Books.

Intended for Pleasure, Ed Wheat, Fleming H. Revell.

It Takes So Little to be Above Average, Florence Littauer, Harvest House Publishers.

It Will Never Happen to Me, Claudia Black, Children of Alcoholics.

"Little Silver Boxes With Bows on Top," (tape) Florence Littauer.

My Utmost for His Highest, Oswald Chambers, Dodd, Mead & Company.

None of These Diseases, Samuel I. McMillan, Fleming H. Revell.

Pain and Pretending, Rich Buhler, Thomas Nelson.

Personality Plus, Florence Littauer, Fleming H. Revell.

Please Don't Hurt Me, Grant Martin, Victor.

PMS — What It Is and What You Can Do About It, Joe S. McIlhaney, Jr., M.D., and Sharon M. Sneed, Ph.D., Baker Book House.

Raising the Curtain on Raising Children, Florence Littauer, Word Books.

Reflections on the Psalms, C. S. Lewis, Harcourt, Brace, Jovanovich.

Self-Affirmation, Guy Greenfield, Baker Book House.

Surviving Separation and Divorce, Sharon Marshall, Baker Book House.

Taking Control: New Hope for Substance Abusers and Their Families, Frank Minirth, Paul Meier, et. al., Baker Book House.

The Broken Image: Healing of the Homosexuality Crisis, Leanne Payne, Crossway Books.

The Rights and Wrongs of Anger, H. Norman Wright, Harvest House.

Understanding Your Past: The Key to Your Future, Dr. Cecil Osborne, Yokefellows Press.

What You Can Say When You Don't Know What to Say, Lauren Briggs, Harvest House Publishers.

Will I Cry Tomorrow? Susan Stanford, Fleming H. Revell.

Your Inner Child of the Past, W. Hugh Missildine, M.D., Pocket Books.

Your Personality Tree, Florence Littauer, Word Books.

Marilyn Murray is now a nationally recognized authority on childhood trauma. She is currently conducting theory and training seminars for mental health professionals. For infomation concerning these seminars, contact (415) 344-3755.

Appendix D

150 Possible Adult Symptoms of Childhood Sexual Interference

Abortion
Absence of grief at death
Abused father
Abused mother
Abusive opposite-sex
Affairs during marriage
Age forty trauma
Agoraphobia
Alcoholism—parents
Alcoholism—self
Allergy hypersensitivity
Amenorrhea/late menses
Anger
Anorexia
Anxiety
Asthma
Bad dreams
Bad rooms/houses
BiPolar disease
Body has no value
Childhood depression
Childhood fear—something
    under bed
Childhood masturbation
Childhood teeth grinding
Childhood view of adult body
    (gross, disgusting)
Childlike emotions
Childlike voice
Choking/gagging
Claustrophobia
Compulsions
Constriction of normal bodily

functions
Crying
Demon presence
Denial of sexual abuse
Depression
Downcast looks
Dreams of snakes
Dreams of spiders
Early childhood sexual drive
Early puberty
Emotional reaction to questions
Emotionally unstable spouse
Environmental disease
Excessive control by father in teens
Family secrets
Fear
Fear of being alone
Fear of finding truth
Fear of losing weight
Fear of rape
Fear of trusting God
Feeling dirty
Flashbacks, especially sexual
Fits of rage
Generational revisitation of abuse
Guilt
Hate men
Hatred
Hiding face in hair
Homosexuality
"I'm sorry" syndrome
Inability to call God "Father"
Inability to forgive

Inhibition to liquid medicine
Insecurity
Insomnia
Intense fear of child being abused
Interracial marriage
Jealousy
Known molestation
Lack of resistance to sexual attack
Late bedwetting
"Little mother" syndrome
Low self-worth
Lying/half-truths
Manic depressive
Marital sexual dysfunction
Marrying to escape
Masturbation
Memory gap
Mental flashes
Migraines
Missionary, social work
Molested others
Mood swings
Multiple clothing layers
Multiple divorces/marriages
Multiple personalities
Need light on to sleep
Negative thought patterns
No feelings
Obsessions
Obsessive-compulsive disorder
Out of touch with God
Overreactions
Overweight
Painful eyes
Parent adoration
Parental preoccupation with sex
Phantoms in your life
Physical reaction to questions
PMS (PMD)
Poor opposite-sex relationships
Pornography at home
Post partum depression
Premature physical aging

Preoccupation with sex
Preoccupation with personal hygiene
Pulling out/cutting hair
Reactive anger to hearing Scripture
Refusal to nurse baby
Rejection
Repugnance to oral sex
Repugnance to touching by opposite sex
Resentment
Self-deception
Self-destructive patterns
Self-hatred
Self-protection
Self-punishment
Sexual relieving of depression
Smells/odors reaction
"Something blocking me"
Split on personality profile
Stress
Struggle for holiness
Suicidal feelings
Teenage promiscuity
Teenage runaway
Tension
Threatened as child
TMJ
Traumatic reaction to abuse on film, TV
Trembling
Troubling memory fragments
Uncontrollable crying as adult
Uncomfortable with nudity in marriage
Undiagnosed pains
Unexplained childhood vomiting
Unmet emotional needs
Unusual physical problems
Urge to molest
Use of drugs
Vaginismus
Workaholic

Appendix E

Notes

PART I

Chapter 3

1. Maxine Hancock and Karen Burton Mains, *Child Sexual Abuse: A Hope for Healing* (Wheaton, IL: Harold Shaw Publishers, 1987), pp. 12-14.

2. Susan Forward and Craig Buck, *Betrayal of Innocence* (New York: Penguin Books, 1979).

Chapter 4

1. William Shakespeare, *King Richard III,* Act I, Scene 3.

Chapter 8

1. Oswald Chambers, *My Utmost for His Highest* (New York: Dodd, Mead & Company, 1963), p. 183.

PART II

1. C. S. Lewis, *Reflections on the Psalms* (Eugene, OR: Harvest House Publishers/HBJ Books, 1958), p. 23.

PART III

1. Oswald Chambers, *Oswald Chambers: The Best From All His Books,* Harry Verploegh, ed. (Nashville: Oliver-Nelson Publishers, 1987), p. 170.

2. Cecil Osborne, *Understanding Your Past: The Key to Your Future* (Yokefellows Press), p. 35.

3. Barbara Taylor, *From Rejection to Acceptance* (Nashville: Broadman Press, n.d.).

4. C. S. Lewis, *Reflections on the Psalms* (Eugene, OR: Harvest House/HBJ Books, 1958), pp. 25-26.

5. Ed Magnuson, "David Burke's Deadly Revenge," *Time* (December 21, 1987), p. 30.

6. Joe McIlhaney and Sharon M. Sneed, *PMS: What It Is and What You Can Do About It* (Grand Rapids, MI: Baker Book House, 1988).

7. "Truth: The reality lying at the basis of an appearance," W. E. Vine, *Expository Dictionary of New Testament Words,* (Old Tappan, NJ: Fleming H. Revell Company, 1940).

8. John 14:6.

9. Bruce Bower, "The Orderly Disorder," *The Los Angeles Times* (August 15, 1988).

10. Cecil Osborne, *Understanding Your Past: The Key to Your Future* (Yokefellows Press).

11. Osborne, p. 80.

12. Oswald Chambers, *My Utmost for His Highest* (New York: Dodd, Mead & Company, 1963), p. 261.

13. David Peters, *A Betrayal of Innocence* (Waco, TX: Word Publishers, 1986), p. 40.

14. Peters, p. 41.

15. William Shakespeare, *Hamlet,* Act III, Scene 2.

16. Peters, pp. 50-51.

PART IV
Chapter 2

1. Norman Cousins, *Anatomy of an Illness* (New York: Norton Publishers, 1979).

Chapter 3

1. Doris Boydston, "How to Walk Free," (Mental Health Unit, Palmdale General Hospital, Palmdale, California).

NOTE

If you are reading another person's copy of this book and the Recommended Resources Order Form (page 303) has already been used, you may order materials or obtain another copy of the order form by writing us at

CLASS
1645 S. Rancho Santa Fe Road, Suite 102
San Marcos, CA 92069

RECOMMENDED RESOURCE ORDER FORM

Number Ordered		$	Total
____	1. *Hope for Hurting Women*, Florence Littauer (originally published as *Lives on the Mend*)	9.00	____
____	2. *A Door of Hope*, Jan Frank	9.00	____
____	3. *God's Crippled Children*, Lana Bateman	9.00	____
____	4. *Personality Plus*, Florence Littauer	9.00	____
____	5. *Your Personality Tree*, Florence Littauer	9.00	____
____	6. *From Rejection to Acceptance*, Barbara Taylor	11.00	____
____	7. *It Takes So Little to be Above Average*, Florence Littauer	8.00	____
____	8. *Child Sexual Abuse*, Hancock and Mains	8.00	____
____	9. *Pain and Pretending*, Rich Buhler	15.00	____
____	10. *What You Can Say When You Don't Know What to Say*, Lauren Briggs	7.00	____
____	11. "Little Silver Boxes with Bows on Top," (tape) Florence Littauer	6.00	____
____	12. "Are You the Victim of Your Wife's Past?" (tape) Don Frank	6.00	____
____	13. *The Passion of Christ*	.50	____
____	14. Complete Package at Discount (# 1 - 13) (Only available when set ordered at one time. Total cost if ordered individually is $106.50.)	75.00	____

Shipping & Handling (Please add $1.00 per book.) ____

SUB TOTAL ____

California residents please add 7.75% sales tax ____

TOTAL AMOUNT ENCLOSED (Check or Money Order) ____

CHARGE: Mastercard/Visa # _____

Name on Card _____ Expiration Date ____

Make Checks Payable and Mail To: CLASS BOOK SERVICE
1645 So. Rancho Santa Fe, Suite 102
San Marcos, CA 92069
(619) 471-0233

"Payment Plan" may be made by sending three checks, each for one-third of total amount, one payable currently and the other two dated a month and two months later. International Orders: Please send checks in U. S. funds only and add $3.00 per book for shipping by air.